GRATEFUL TO BE ALIVE

MY ROAD TO RECOVERY FROM ADDICTION

D.K. SANZ

GRATEFUL TO BE ALIVE

MY ROAD TO RECOVERY
FROM ADDICTION

D. K. SANZ

GRATEFUL TO BE ALIVE

CONTENTS

TRIGGER WARNING

This book discusses a specific person's experiences with drug overdose, HIV/AIDS, and mental health issues as a result of violence, abuse, and sexual assault. If necessary, please engage in self-care.

AUTHOR'S NOTE

To protect the privacy of individuals, all names, except for my own, have been changed. Most identifying details, except for my own, have also been changed.

Dedicated to everyone.

ACKNOWLEDGMENTS

First and foremost, I want to express my deep and sincere gratitude to "David" for his invaluable input and support as my alpha reader.

I am exceedingly grateful to "Jace" for his patience, guidance, and support. Thank you for your words of wisdom. I treasure all that you've shared with me.

Praise and thanks to K.H. Koehler for her endless talents in editing, formatting, and cover design.

Thank you to my beta readers, Denise, Nitin, and Kody.

Thank you, Jason, for your insight and support.

And a special thank you to everyone who has encouraged me. Your support never goes unnoticed and is appreciated more than you can imagine.

INTRODUCTION

When people think of addiction, they usually associate it with substance abuse, but, as we know, addiction manifests itself in many ways. Obsession is the hallmark of addiction. Just as we can be obsessed with alcohol and drugs, we can be obsessed with people and feelings, and, as addicts, we are prone to find one obsession after another. Placing people on pedestals is one of the often-overlooked infatuations manifested by addiction, and I did this relentlessly throughout my life.

Even after twenty-seven years of sobriety, when people tell me they have no regrets about their life decisions, I'm sure I misunderstand what they mean by that. Perhaps I'm taking it too literally, but I can't imagine not having at least some regrets. Most of us have caused pain for others (and ourselves), even if we never meant to, and the one thing I regret more than anything is the people I've hurt in my oblivion and ignorance.

My experiences seem absurd to the kind of people I've befriended after my self-sabotaging years. They've led far more sheltered lives, where their parents took them to museums and ballet performances, and it surprised them that I hung out on street corners with friends and in parks.

Anyway, what matters is what's real.

My story is about addiction and recovery (from many things), and I am one of the fortunate ones who lived to tell how it went for me.

I never wanted to tell this story—at least not this way. Sure, I was forthcoming in sharing bits and pieces of it with certain groups and individuals, but, for the most part, I aimed to spare my loved ones. Now that I have been given the green light by those who mean the most to me, and after what I've witnessed over the past few years, I'm going ahead with my uncensored confessions. Down the rabbit hole we go to unearth the dark tales about lies that save and destroy us, paying the piper when the master is ego, and the challenges accepted at the end of the forbidden road.

In sharing this journey with you, I will include the humor and joy along with all of the tragic madness. The aim is not to gain sympathy but to shed some light on how certain things develop and how we overcome those challenges even when the odds are against us.

Understanding is critical in the world we live in today.

Some people actually think there's *too much* empathy in the world and that we as a species may have to be a little more vicious and cruel to survive, like in the olden days. Maybe even with a bit of medieval torture thrown in for good measure. Those people are wrong, and I'm pleased as punch that both time and history have taught us more about humanity. It's part of our evolution as a species.

One thing I've heard and can relate to as a poet and writer is, "Don't waste your pain." Life is beautiful and tragic, happy, sad, and everything in between, and, as a poet, I'm here for all of it. The pain is often long gone by the time we relay things in poetry and books, but we can still empathize with people struggling to navigate whatever we've already sorted out.

Recovery, for me, has been an ongoing journey toward authenticity, removing the veils layer by layer and discarding the masks. I was told in recovery that we are only as sick as our secrets. Of course, we are allowed to have secrets. But suppose our hidden truth has us living a double life or creating a barrier between us and the world? We tend to compartmentalize aspects of our lives as part of the deception. In that case, it either limits or restricts our healing and impedes our goal of authenticity.

We evolve as we become aware of our patterns and vulnerabilities—and we seek *answers*. Raw honesty combined with accountability helps everyone, especially those of us who've gotten caught in a cycle of self-loathing and self-sabotage. We need truth, spiritual courage, and to remain teachable.

Our job is to keep resolving things internally so we continue evolving as humans, deepening our understanding, empathy, and compassion. Suffering can be beautiful when we constantly grow, but not if we're emotionally stuck in the same place without learning from what we've endured.

Think of this for a moment: When depicted as fire-breathing monsters, mythical dragons are harmful and dangerous—perhaps diabolical. And, like dragons, some people constantly and painfully attempt to incinerate others with their scathing flames. Even those of us who aren't so malevolent can wear a dragon's facade to guard and protect ourselves in the darkest of times, but we must relinquish it before it destroys us.

The continuous goal is healing—not simply individual healing but collective healing. We each have our gifts and tools for contributing to the greater good, and it turns out that it's one massive, collaborative effort, during which time we remain connected as part of a larger entity.

It amazes me, still, the shocking things we can survive, especially when we never lose hope or give up on laughter and love. The weight, venom, mire, and bondage of our obsessions create roadblocks and wreak havoc until we take that yellow brick road back to sanity. If you've seen the movie, *Wizard of Oz,* you know what I'm talking about. The wizard at the end of the road is a fraud, but you always had the shoes, right?

So, my friend, I write this book from the heart. All I ask is that when the story gets a little too dark and ugly, please try to hang in there with me.

Thanks for reading!

PART I
MY STORY

RECKLESS ADVENTURE

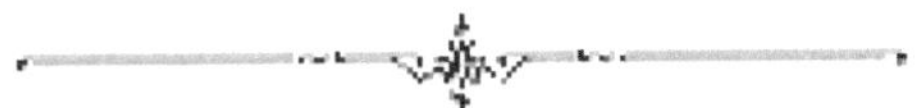

My dad loved Woodside for its convenience and often raved about the supermarkets and train stations being only six blocks away. He was right that, in many ways, Woodside was an ideal place to live. He just never imagined it to have a seedy, drug-infested underbelly, where narcotics were readily available to children.

Older friends gave me drugs from the time I was eleven. They were kids, too, so I never blamed them. Besides, I rarely hesitated or refused. Excessively curious and recklessly adventurous as I was, I fully embraced it.

We hung out in doorways of bleak factory buildings that seemed abandoned for how rare it was to spot anyone entering or leaving. It was relatively quiet in those places with an occasional beep of a car horn, kids huddled together chatting, or a shout to someone on the other side of the road. We sat on the concrete steps outside the factory door or on the nearby curb, singing pop and rock songs.

That was Woodside, Queens, New York, where I was born and raised—the western end of Queens and the southern part of New York State. Manhattan was just across the river.

At the tender age of twelve, I became part of the crowd at 69th Street Park. These kids, too, were several years older than me, and I liked them because they didn't bully me about my ethnicity or for any other reason. The kids on *my* block were one hundred percent Italian, and most families in the outlying neighborhood were Irish, Italian, or both. My sisters and I, although half Italian, were called "spics." One kid spat at us and told us to go back to Cuba.

Sixty-ninth Street Park was the same park where my sisters and I had played in the sandbox, and where we had run through the sprinklers. Those of us hanging out there now bummed cigarettes from one another. We drank beer and wine and smoked pot or hash. Like the kids we still were, we also climbed the monkey bars and swung on the swings. When we heard the Mr. Softee truck jingle, we ran to get ice cream.

When it was the high-pitched New York police sirens we heard, we climbed fences and bailed—or wished we had. Cops rushed into the park before some of us made it to the gate with flashlights beaming brightly in the dark.

"Up against the wall, guys," a booming male voice would growl through a megaphone. "Girls can leave."

The boys got frisked while facing the wall on the basketball court.

Unlike me, most of these kids lived in "The Mets," a federally subsidized housing complex right across the street from the park. Many of them had come from broken homes, and a few of the guys ended up in youth houses—most often for stealing cars. I used to wish I lived in that low-income complex. They had archways and courtyards and the tenants, including my friends, talked back and forth from their windows.

Home for me was several blocks away. I had a nine o'clock curfew (yes, at twelve), and I dreaded trekking up this one steep hill in pitch blackness. If I heard the whoosh of a car, and if the driver slowed and leaned in my direction, trying to catch a glimpse of me, I'd run the rest of the way. Often, one of the guys in our crowd walked me home or offered to, but since I didn't reward anyone for that with a kiss or beyond, it didn't happen often.

During that trek, I had to cross Roosevelt Avenue, another of our frequent haunts. It lurked below the frame of our elevated train system that we called "The El." Beneath the trestle were restaurants, coffee shops, and stores from one end of the thoroughfare to the other. In daylight, people were everywhere, some with baby strollers and prancing children. Drivers double-parked in the always-filled parking spaces, and you had to shout above the rolling and rumbling of oncoming trains.

In earlier childhood days, my sisters and I accompanied my mother to the bank and bakery there and even the corner coffee store, where a bespectacled, gray-haired man would grind coffee for my mom as she waited. I was fascinated by the big, industrial-sized grinding machines and loved the aroma of freshly ground coffee.

The Deluxe movie theatre on Roosevelt Avenue was once a place where we enjoyed Saturday matinees and double features as kids, including *Pinocchio*, which I begged my mom to see over and over again. I loved *Pinocchio* almost as much as I loved *The Wizard of Oz*. I must have been five the first time I saw it, and the beauty of this elaborate tale about munchkins and witches and yellow brick roads drew me in at once. I was spellbound by its magic.

Seven years later, the Deluxe was where I watched adventure films with a bunch of kids from the park while high.

Our crowd hung out at Klee's, too, the ice cream parlor on that same avenue. Klee's had bold red swivel stools at the counter, but we sat in the cushioned booths, feeding quarters into the mini jukeboxes. We ordered sandwiches, egg creams, and sodas.

Sometimes, we got high on rooftops under grey skies or skies of crystal blue, sitting on the asphalt. Or we'd crawl under a fence and trek down a grassy hill to the railroad tracks, the dead leaves crunching under our feet. The rattling trains and their urgently blaring horns didn't faze us.

On one cloudy afternoon, a bunch of us partied in one of the Mets building apartments. Music was blasting. Among my favorite bands then, and to this day, were the soul music vocalists and dancers known as The Temptations. Their *Puzzle People* album was sacred to me—every song, including their excellent rendition of "Little Green Apples." My other favorite band was Santana, which I also still love. Their Latin-infused rock combined salsa, blues, and African rhythms. I've watched their Woodstock performance of "Soul Sacrifice" on video more times than I can count.

I was absorbed by listening to Santana *that* day and then Traffic's song called "Empty Pages" from their album *John Barleycorn Must Die*. Before we knew it, a kid peering out of the living room window shouted, "The MPs are here! The MPs are here! They're coming into the building!"

"Get rid of your stash!" someone yelled. "Flush it!"

The guy who lived there, his eyes signaling urgency, shouted, "Out the fucking window now!"

As people leaped out the second-floor window, one after the other, another girl and I scrambled into the tiny bathroom and locked the door. We held hands in the dark, shaking and holding our breaths, trying to be perfectly silent. The MPs pounded on the door, and then we heard them come in, stomping all around the place. From the crack under the bathroom doorway, we saw they'd switched on the light, and, soon enough, they spotted the open window and decided whoever had been there was gone. They took off in pursuit of a soldier who was AWOL from the U. S. Army. That soldier was in custody by the end of the night.

It was the guy who'd been living there with his grandmother!

I mean, who the hell thought it was a good idea to throw a party with drugs in the apartment of an AWOL soldier? And he didn't think they'd come looking for him at his own apartment? In retrospect, it is mind-boggling.

That was one of *many* uncomfortable moments I had while being part of that crowd, but most of my uneasiness stemmed from my social awkwardness as well as my being plagued by disturbing realizations.

Although I've never sought an official diagnosis, I took professional tests over the years that indicated I am high-functioning autistic. Some might even call it "borderline autistic." My mere existence was an affront to some people, including certain relatives, and, of course, it led to bullying and ostracization. Hundreds of years ago, their reaction would have been attributed to clinical ignorance and/or superstition of the times. Unfortunately, despite our society having a better understanding of these issues today, that kind of ignorance and superstition hasn't entirely vanished.

Bullying and ostracization are forms of narcissistic abuse. Granted, people don't necessarily realize it when they contribute to the erosion of a child's self-worth, but kids pay attention to how people treat them, and they get the message loud and clear. I wish I could say it didn't distort our self-perception and make us more sensitive and insecure, but it does.

Having said that, I wouldn't trade my brain for anything.

I'll admit that the bullying made me vigilantly defensive, and I became a bully myself for a while. The phase didn't last, but I still hate that I went that route for any amount of time.

Meanwhile, I craved nonstop euphoria. Reality for me fluctuated between oblivion and distress. Boys told me I was cute and paid me compliments, but I wondered if they were making fun of me.

They didn't know me when I was a preschooler with pronounced strabismus (lazy eye). The kids who *did* know me then continued to make fun of it even after I'd had two corrective surgeries. It didn't matter that it was far less noticeable. It was as if they'd never unsee it—how my left eye was once entirely off to the side.

"It happened because you got scared," my grandmother once said.

I never got any further explanation.

THE FAM

We were in Havana, Cuba, my mother's birthplace. I was three years old and my sister Bridget, walking beside us, was four. My younger sister, Melissa, was there as well, but in my mother's womb.

Oddly enough, I remember a lot about this trip. We'd visited beautiful Varadero Beach, and then we were at some marketplace. Bridget and I held my mother's hand as we padded along.

My mom had described Fidel Castro to me when I asked her what he looked like, so every time a man with a beard passed by, I tugged at her skirt, asking, "Mommy, is that Castro?"

"Shush," she'd say, trying not to laugh. "People can hear you. And he's not going to be walking around here."

I lost interest in that when I noticed there were baby chickens for sale wherever I looked. "I want a baby chicken!"

"Those are *pollitos*," my mother said. She laughed, taking my hand. "Come on."

When we returned to my aunt's house, she told my aunt with much amusement how I had loved the *pollitos*, and my aunt motioned for us to follow her.

She took us to the yard, which, to my surprise and delight, was full of baby chickens! A low wall surrounded their concrete pen, which took up half of the yard. My uncle gave Bridget and me a handful of corn to feed them, and we were eager to oblige. They let us pick up the chickens, but whenever I got one in my hands, Bridget would grab it away from me.

"That one is mine," she'd say.

I swooped up another. "This one's mine!"

"No, it isn't!" This time, she tried to get it away from me, and I held it firmly away.

My mother was yelling in Spanish. She couldn't get my attention fast enough, so she rushed toward me and opened my hand.

"You killed it!" Bridget was screaming.

She was right. I had crushed the little bird. Tears streamed down my face faster than I could breathe.

"She didn't mean to," my mother said. "It was an accident." She handed the poor dead bird to my aunt and led me inside, where she washed my hands in the bathroom sink.

"I was trying to save him, Mommy."

She dried my hands and my tears. "Don't worry about it."

Despite the altercations between my sister and me, Bridget was my idol almost from the moment I knew her. Without realizing it, I'd placed her on a pedestal, and for over a decade, I followed her around, sensing I had to protect her. Somehow, I didn't need space to carve out my own life away from the family. Bridget did. I didn't understand that because she appeared to have as much fun as I did when we were together—away from her friends. I'd convinced myself that I was as essential to her wellbeing as she was to mine.

The problem is that once we place someone on a pedestal, they're almost elevated to the status of a god and, in many ways, not permitted to be human. We can't really see them for who they are because we define what they are to us—whatever we want them to be. They can't possibly live up to the image we created of them or meet all of our expectations.

Nevertheless, by second grade, Bridget and I got roped into learning the accordion and playing simple Scottish folk songs. My parents didn't believe us when we told them that the music teacher sat there picking his nose through the entire lesson and then flicked his boogers clear across the room. They thought we just didn't want to go for our music lessons. (But he really did!)

When it was time to practice at home, I whined that it was a "punishment." My poor parents were spending money to teach us something nice, and I made them feel bad. So, the accordion and lessons went bye-bye.

Home, by the way, was a redbrick, two-family center hall with a steep concrete stoop ideal for sitting or playing ball and a black gated porch large enough for our dark green wooden bench where three people sat comfortably. We were known for our pumpkin orange front door with its gleaming brass eagle door knocker. Yeah, it was a bizarre, sort of conspicuous-looking house, but it barely fazed anyone. My grandparents lived downstairs from us.

We had plenty of places to play and hide in that huge house, but we preferred to be in the yard or out front skating, riding bikes, or playing ball, hopscotch, and jump rope. We sold Kool-Aid in front of the house, but my mother hated that because she was afraid people would think we were poor.

Two doors down from us was a family with four boys who threw the best "spook house" events in their basement. Two of the boys were teenagers who formed a rock and roll band and jammed, deafeningly loud, in that same basement. We were fans mainly because we knew them, and we watched enthusiastically during their one television appearance. Their house was next door to a TV repair shop, and then there was a beer and soda shop next to that.

Otherwise, ours was a boring block. All you saw was concrete and asphalt and something merely resembling a tree. For that reason, since the age of nine, I went alone on wandering quests to parts of the neighborhood that had silver maples, pin oaks, London plane trees, and gorgeous flowerbeds sprucing up the lawns. I searched for apartment buildings that struck me as gothic or medieval—any ominous, overpowering structure that made me think of a castle or a crypt. There was one I found that had a magnificent courtyard, and I was in awe of it.

During these peaceful wanderings, I listened to songbirds and hawk cries. It was beautiful, with musky and floral scents permeating the air, and I'd often stop and watch little butterflies flutter past me.

When I found a special place, I'd sit there and enjoy the peace, admiring and appreciating it all. I called these "my secret places," and I was always eager to share them with Melissa because I loved her so dearly.

Once we got there, she'd sit beside me, glancing around.

"Isn't it beautiful?" I'd ask.

"It's nice," she'd say.

"But I'm only sharing it with you," I'd tell her. "You have to promise to keep it a secret."

"Okay, I promise," she'd reply. "Thank you for sharing your secret."

A year or two later Bridget often took me to Klee's ice cream parlor on Roosevelt Avenue—that is whenever she scrounged up enough money. We'd order caramel nut sundaes, our favorite, with chopped walnuts, whipped cream, and a cherry on top. It was delicious to the last melted bit, as we swished it through a straw.

By the time we were eleven and twelve, Bridget and I often babysat. Single moms hired us, and they'd return home after midnight with lecherous drunks who would visibly salivate as they offered to drive us home. We always declined. One lady had a gigantic cat that hid on us, and when he finally came out, he dashed across the room so fast that you'd swear it was a cheetah. We laughed and laughed. Later, we hectically explained to people that he ate an umbrella and two shoes, but I'm pretty sure that wasn't true.

Melissa was the sister I listened to music with as we sang in the basement or leafed through teen idol magazines. We made scrapbooks of our idols, but our admiration for them was as innocent as it could be.

One grey, windy day, Missy helped me hand out flyers for a local candidate running for office. The wind blew our papers all over the streets and in every direction. Frantically, we ran after them, attempting to catch as many as possible, and then finally dropped to the ground, laughing. We held onto our stomachs because we were laughing so hard.

No matter what was happening, I loved being with my sisters.

And not that it should matter much, but we did inherit some good family genes. My mother's dark curly hair and dark eyes were as gorgeous as she was, and my father was this impossibly handsome northern Italian with hazel eyes and sculpted cheekbones. My older sister, Bridget, inherited my mom's dark hair and eyes, and Melissa has light hair and our dad's hazel gem-like eyes. I'm a brunette who'd turned blonde for years and years. My eyes are brown with flecks of gold and can appear anywhere from light and honey-colored to medium brown and maybe even a brown hazel. My mom, sisters, and I have always worn our hair long, or, at least, past shoulder length.

Yes, I was the middle child, and, as a middle child, I'd never felt entitled to anything. I was just happy to have a place at the table. At the same time, I'd never back down from an argument with my father when it came to injustice toward anyone, myself included.

One of those times, he roared and suddenly charged at me—all six feet of him—and smacked my head against the wall so hard that my blood formed an eerie crimson pool in the sink shortly afterward. I heard nothing but the clanging of utensils at the dining room table, a couple of gasps, and one shriek of agony from my mom. My sisters wore expressions of horror. A harrowing energy of crisis and panic ensued, and my dad whisked me off to the emergency room. At that time, I was still twelve.

He drove us to the hospital in his blue-green Oldsmobile '88 (model not year). I was nauseated the whole time, with alternating waves of dizziness and tingling throughout my body. The pain was distressing and excruciating, but none of it was physical. Unbearable guilt tortured me, and I whimpered, offering sorrowful apologies for creating circumstances that led to another's violent haste.

As much as I adored my father, I believe that marked the end of *his* pedestal stance in my eyes, but I still had Bridget up there. She seemed a tad confused when I sang "To Sir with Love" to her. It was a gushing tribute to a cherished mentor, so I'd be in tears by the end. My immense pride in her was accompanied by a strange sense that I had to hang on to her. It always seemed she was slipping away.

But, truthfully, so was I.

HIGH SCHOOL

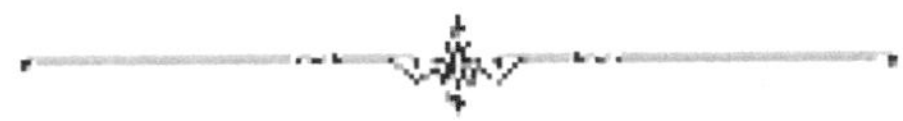

When it was time to apply to high schools, I was aware of the need to steer myself in the proper direction and avoid pressure from curious boys. For those reasons, I chose Our Lady of Perpetual Help in Manhattan (OLPH), an all-girls Catholic school. Manhattan was "the city" to us, even though Queens was also a part of New York City, so I would take the train there every morning. The stop I'd be getting off at was 59th Street—right in front of Bloomingdale's. I couldn't wait!

I'm not sure why I thought continuing with Catholic school would make any difference. Grade school, for me, had been Blessed Virgin Mary Help of Christians School (Saint Mary's), where the mood was grave and often silent except for church bells and the nuns' stern, authoritative voices. I get chills remembering that ancient church and school.

My first classroom was in the school basement. There, I had my crayons furiously yanked away when I colored a second longer after Sister Mary told the class to stop. In that same basement, a kid at the desk in front of me was too terrified to ask if he could use the bathroom. He peed his pants, making a huge puddle on the floor that almost reached my shoes. Then, during the winter, when girls wore stockings under their socks for added warmth, Sister Mary forced them to go behind a partition in the back and remove them.

In fifth grade, one nun thought I'd deliberately forgotten my school shoes because I wanted to keep my stylish boots on. It wasn't true, but I had to remain in stocking feet the whole day, including for assembly in the auditorium. Still, that wasn't as bad as what happened to the two eighth-grade boys who'd been caught throwing snowballs at recess. Sister Cecilia dunked their faces in the snow over and over again.

None of that dampened my excitement about attending Our Lady of Perpetual Help, however. In school, I was the class clown and a typical teen, passing notes back and forth with friends. Once, a friend and I laughed so much that our English teacher asked, "What'd you two take?" We were straight, so it made us laugh more. Even *he* was laughing, so I guess it was contagious. Another teacher asked me to contribute some of my poems to the school newspaper and encouraged me to become our paper's editor. That made me quite happy.

In freshman year, though, the usual train I took was delayed one day, so I'd switched to the Number 7 train that would leave me at the 61st Street stop instead of 65th Place. The busy side of the platform was too crowded, so I exited onto the opposite platform, where it was relatively quiet. As I reached the platform's middle, a man standing there turned to face me and asked where the B train went.

"I don't know," I said. "I've never taken that train."

"Do you know what a knife is?" he hissed.

Petrified, I nodded, fully aware that he and I were the only ones on that platform.

"Am I going to have to use it?" His tone was menacing.

"Why?" I was shaking. "I really have no idea where this train goes. If I did, I'd tell you, but I have to go home. My mother is waiting for me."

He searched my eyes and then stepped aside to let me pass.

For all my "innocence," however, nothing seemed to quell my burgeoning love for drugs. Kids like me seemed to believe we were invincible. Most of us had an ingrained belief that we were somehow divinely protected. Conveniently, we didn't notice that any divine protection only went so far. People died all of the time of overdoses, and the truth of that stared us in the face consistently.

There was a time while flying high on amphetamines when I knelt before the casket of a fifteen-year-old acquaintance who jumped off her roof after doing acid (LSD). Amid whimpers, tears, moans, and fragrant floral arrangements half masking the funeral parlor smell, the sight of her young ashen face made me feel like I was suffocating. But the guilt and discouragement were fleeting as I comprehended the heaviness of what had happened. Down deep, there was sadness and pain, I am sure of it, but nothing changed. I lived in denial and fear—fear of everything but that chemically-induced ecstasy.

Speed was next, then mescaline, LSD, and finally cocaine. Those drugs made me believe I could do anything—like if I auditioned for a movie role or a rock band, I'd get the job. Everything and everyone around me seemed more beautiful—including me, and I wanted to feel that way always.

"You can't do it every day," a friend told me about LSD. "It won't work if you do."

It didn't matter what anyone said. I'd lost count of how many times I did it, and not even the occasional bad trip gave me pause. I'd learned how to talk people out of bad trips, to calm and soothe them. We'd stroll along the dark streets as I kept them talking, answering my questions. That was, somehow, my specialty, so people "flipping out" were sent right over to me. Once, after a tab of Orange Sunshine, everything around me was tinted orange for two days, or so I imagined. I wasn't sure the world would ever look right again.

During the winter I was fourteen, my friends helped me navigate three feet of snow while wasted on Quaaludes and, not long after that, I drunkenly defended a friend against the park bully. For months afterward, the bully threatened to kill me, but, obviously, that didn't happen.

My friends and I drank screwdrivers or rum and Coke and took the train to Fifth Avenue in Manhattan for the St. Patrick's Day parade. There were plenty of Irish pubs in the neighborhood, including one right next door to us, where we knew most of the patrons by name and the changing owners. I couldn't go to *that* one while underage, but I managed to slither into TJs on Woodside Avenue near 69th Street—about five blocks away.

To my surprise, the guy who'd lived next door to me all of my life was sitting at the bar, watching a ballgame. He was a decade or so older than me, and his mom once gave me his old collection of *Superman* comic books because she knew I was a fan of the show. He told the bartender not to serve me and that whatever "proof" I showed him was fake because I couldn't have been more than fourteen years old. As a result, my friends and I found another bar in Elmhurst, where they accepted our phony proof.

We also hung out at Forest Park in Woodhaven, Queens, especially during the summer. Rock bands played there under a large white dome we either called "the Dome" or

"the Bandshell." Despite organized rows of benches facing the stage, most of us preferred to wander around the park, high or stoned. The acres and acres of woods were incredible—an endless canopy of red, black, and white oaks, witch hazel shrubs, and wildflowers.

And then there were all of the forest birds. Wherever you roamed, you'd hear them along with music from the bandshell. Lovers chose their spots in the woods or on the golf course. Meanwhile, drug dealers made a killing in the parking lot, which emptied quickly when the cops arrived.

At the time, I'd just gotten over thinking anything beyond kissing was disgusting. At fifteen, I was a dutiful virgin.

Then it happened.

My friend Shelley and I were dancing and running around barefoot on the early evening sand at Rockaway Beach. We were like enraptured little fairies, singing along with the radio, carefree and laughing. People like being attractive at the beach, and we were no exception in our floral halter tops and shorts. We were delighted that guys kept watching us—even the two on the boardwalk who eventually came over to talk to us. They were easily twice our age, but we saw no harm in chatting. It was a public place.

We were still overly trusting, however, and alarmingly naïve. I wasn't attracted to either of these guys, but Shelley liked one of them, and older guys with cars impressed her. So, when they asked us to go to Great Adventure the following day, I likely would have said no, but Shelley jumped at the chance. She nudged me, and I acquiesced.

It never occurred to me that these guys would drug us and whisk us away to an apartment they shared. The idea, to me, was unfathomable. But they did.

The next thing I knew, Shelley and the one she'd liked were gone. The other guy was sitting next to me on the sofa. When I got up, he sat me back down. He ran his fingers through my hair, telling me I needed to relax. I tried to stand again, but I was lightheaded and stumbled. He caught me and tried to kiss me, but I didn't want to kiss him. I didn't want to be there. The room spun, and I fell back on the sofa with only a blurred impression of my surroundings. His voice sounded like it was a distance away, and I couldn't see his face. It felt like a dream when he lifted me into his arms and carried me to one of the bedrooms. Inside the room, I was slipping in and out of consciousness.

Once, when I came to, he was lying over me. I told him I felt sick, so he took me to the bathroom and waited outside the door. I tried vomiting over the toilet but couldn't. So, he brought me to the kitchen for a drink of water. That was when the other guy strolled in naked, making me even sicker.

"I want to go home," I said.

The guy who'd partnered with me held out his hand. "Come back inside."

He brought me to a different bedroom, a smaller one. After a while, the other guy strolled in, closed the door, and fiddled with the lock.

Now they were both in there with me. They had me trapped in that room for hours, and whatever they were doing, the pain was excruciating. I never knew I could scream like that or cry so hard. But it was as if the person lying there screaming and crying was not me, and I was somewhere nearby. It was the same when I fought them. I fought so hard, and, again, it was as if I had separated from my body and someone else was fighting for me. Other times, it appeared I had surrendered. At the same time, the terror, chaos, and confusion continued to swirl violently in the inner recesses of my mind.

I kept asking for Shelley and trying to get up. Each time, they would push me back down. How do you explain what it's like to be held down by two men, knowing it could get a lot worse? And that it had been so much worse for many other victims of rape?

"Shelley!" I was screaming her name.

I thought they had killed her.

Well, they *could have* killed us. The drug alone could have killed us.

But our rapists drove us home that night, and they continued to call me for months while I kept refusing to speak to them.

The idea of reporting it to anyone scared the hell out of me, so I didn't. Part of me thought it was my fault, or that people would say that it was.

TRANSITION

The Atlantic Ocean seemed as vast as the aching within me, and it represented the same somber foreboding. One might see it as a leviathan that could quickly devour you. Another might view it as a source of comfort and life and forever be in awe of its power and seemingly infinite depths.

I saw the monster. And, in those moments, it looked as foreign to me as everything else that was once familiar.

I was on the sandy shores of Rockaway Beach, somewhere around 108th Street, sitting cross-legged on my beach blanket, playing with a stick in the sand. Aggressive seagulls descended effortlessly from the clear blue sky—ravenous and predatory like some humans I knew. The calls of piping plovers and other shorebirds seemed ominous, too.

The warmth of the sun felt good though as I took in the ocean's briny aroma mingled with the fragrances of cocoa butter, coconut oil, and the glorious traces of jasmine. The ocean breeze provided a hypnotic tranquility—so much so that, as the salty waves thrashed against the shore, I'd managed to believe that somehow, someday, it would all be okay. The music on my radio soothed me then, pretty much the way it always did, and I listened to the laughter of yesterday.

My mom had brought us here as kids and, afterward, we'd head to Rockaway's Playland. Once we were old enough to go to the beach without her, we sat with friends against the rear window of the bus with our towels in hand and radios blasting. We ate Marino Italian ices on the beach, along with fries, potato chips, and potato knishes with mustard.

I was sixteen now, and when men approached my blanket, I immediately told them, "I'm leaving in two minutes."

By this time, I didn't want to meet any more people.

I had difficulty accepting what had happened to Shelley and me. On top of everything else I grappled with, it was ingrained in me that my virginity and sexual innocence were sacred. From behind a podium, priests said mere thoughts about sex were a sin. The subject was taboo—anything to do with sex evoked shame. Priests repeatedly emphasized that "sin" had already tarnished us and that we were unworthy. Anything to do with premarital sex would bring more shame. And as long as my denial persisted, I would continue to self-destruct with my distorted judgment and perception.

I can safely say that the rape nearly destroyed me—full stop. I was in some level of shock for the next twenty years and somewhat stuck in a teenage mindset. The visual of one of my perpetrators suddenly strutting around naked never left me, nor did the waves of panic that had set in when they locked me in that room.

In retrospect, I had this ridiculous faith in people that I very much wanted to hang on to. It made me appear naïve, but it was mostly stubbornness. I didn't want to believe people were cruel and deceptive even after witnessing it time and time again. Quite often, I was determined to fix what was wrong.

As a little girl—and then as a not-so-little girl—I'd wanted approval and friendship with people I'd have to defend to others—others who saw through them when I didn't. In truth, it was *How can I get this antagonizing person to finally be okay with my presence in the world and treat me kindly?* It was never going to happen. My thoughts were, *I love them. How could anyone not love them?* Maybe the real question I wanted to ask was, "How can they not love *me?*"

Those experiences left me reluctant to reach out and trust friendships. Even though I continued to do it, my faith was shaken a little more with every rude awakening.

It didn't help that, no matter what park or bar my friends and I visited, what street we crossed or what train we took, it wasn't unusual to run into someone who'd turned into a burnt-out junkie or who would tell us that so and so had died.

Strange as it may sound, most people never saw me as a substance abuser or considered me a heavy drinker. It was relative. I appeared fine, spoke coherently, never got arrested or had a blackout, and never missed school. I was able to work when the time came. And, whether lying on my bed or scribbling on a napkin in some bar, I continued to write poetry while my friends at the table chatted amongst themselves.

And I had this "never heroin" rule.

One of the female heroin addicts I was well acquainted with managed to steal my checkbook while she was at the house. She tried writing checks in my name, but I busted her before she could do any damage. My impression was that the heroin addicts I knew were bound to begin stealing, dealing, turning tricks, and venturing all the way to Harlem to score. Streets frequented by dope dealers at night were bound to be dangerous and, sometimes, instead of getting their fix, they got knifed and ripped off. As far as I could tell, they were all more likely to die or land in jail, but I conveniently ignored the fact that I nearly died myself *without* ever using heroin. There was, after all, the night my friends revived me in a hallway. I was unconscious after a Phencyclidine (PCP) overdose. That happened not long after the rape, and I was still fifteen.

Back on the home front, when it came to my sister Melissa, I wanted for her what I couldn't hold on to for myself—innocence. At home, I'd sometimes draw silly pictures of Charlie Brown for her. It was the one character I knew how to do, and it made her laugh to see I'd included the little tongue poking out of the corner of his mouth as he scribbled away with his pen.

There *is* such a thing as a functional addict.

By senior year, I got a part-time after-school job as a secretary for a lighting fixture distributor company. It was on East 61st Street between First and Second Avenue in Manhattan—right around the corner from my school.

The first floor was a showroom with lighting fixtures and a reception area. Most of the offices were on the second floor. The manager put me wherever they needed me—on the switchboard of the reception desk, in the typist pool, or in an office and on the phone dealing with vendors and contractors. It was a busy place, with phones constantly ringing, and, for the most part, it was fun and I loved it.

It's interesting how I could go from that to doing a tab of acid for our senior class trip to Rye Playland in Rye, New York. That amusement park was a colorful art deco wonderland with bumper cars, a carousel, and a small beach. My friends were shocked that I rode the Dragon Coaster while tripping on acid because it was a 128-foot drop into the dragon's mouth. They figured it would be terrifying for me, but the wooden rollercoaster's rickety-rackety rambling and sputtering was a thrill. Even when it reached the peak and then the rapid descent, it was fantastic.

A former high school classmate that I'd reconnected with recently told me I'd given *her* acid, too, on that day, all those years ago. I felt guilty and sad because I don't even remember that.

COMPTON

At 625 Madison Avenue, situated between 58th and 59th Street, Compton Advertising occupied four floors of a 204-foot, seventeen-story high-rise that covered the entire block. I got a full-time job there right after high school graduation.

This area of Manhattan, the midtown plaza district near Central Park South, was (and still is) one of my favorites. But if anyone was going to notice a famous person strolling along Fifth Avenue, it was the person next to me—a testament to how oblivious I was. It's not that I wasn't star-struck. It was only that I was preoccupied with thoughts or conversations. Even if I had noticed, I wouldn't have imposed. When they spoke to me, I responded. Otherwise, an acknowledging smile sufficed.

Nevertheless, my favorite floor at the ad agency was the sixth. It housed the creative division, primarily the art and copy departments. It was also where actors waited to audition for commercials or dropped off head sheets. While the other floors were drab, ordinary offices, the sixth floor had bright orange carpeting. The logo on the glass doors matched the orange color scheme, as did the seating in the waiting area. The other secretaries and I rotated the manning of that reception desk, which was a little hectic but fun.

I'd decided by then that writing was my calling in life. It was automatic and nearly equal to breathing for me. With my college plans on hold, I studied writing whenever and however possible. My father paid for a lengthy correspondence course that included a series of books on writing. I'd read each one cover to cover. Subscribing to the industry magazines was a must, too, along with purchasing yearly up-to-date versions *of Writer's Market.*

The head of the copy department at Compton knew I'd been writing a book and had read a few pages. It was about a kid who'd made it as a rock star but ultimately gave in to his demons. I was also putting together a collection of my poetry. For whatever reason, my writing impressed him, and he wanted me to become a junior copywriter. He said he'd help me put together a portfolio. My dad thought it was a terrific idea and encouraged me to do it.

It was easy to get comfortable at Compton. This department head treated me like a friend, and with the younger friends I made there, we became a family.

My first buddies were a couple of Black men who listened to the same music I did—Motown soul music and the rhythm and blues they played on New York's 107.5 WBLS radio station. They were good to me from the day I started to the day I left. Another friend was an older woman in her late twenties. She had a doctor who'd prescribed amphetamines and barbiturates as long as you gave him a good story. He didn't care if it was true or not.

"Say you're a dancer or an actress," she told me. "Or, basically, just make up reasons why you need to stay awake and can't."The first time I went to him, I was still only seventeen, and he prescribed the pills to me without hesitation.

Meanwhile, there was a vendor at Compton who, from time to time, swaggered around the creative floor. Leo Salvini had brown hair in a short, crisp cut and hazel eyes. At five-foot-seven, he wasn't imposing but had a good build. Female coworkers considered him easily attractive—handsome and harmless.

I was seventeen when he asked me out, and he'd asked many times before I said yes.

He arrived in a Dodge Colt, eager to take me to this "great club in Brooklyn" where he lived.

"I've never been to Brooklyn," I confessed.

"You're kidding!" He grinned. "Oh, you'll love it."

Along the drive, he suddenly began to hold on to his head with one hand. I asked if he was okay.

"Yeah," he said. "I've been getting headaches. It gets worse and then unbearable if I don't take something for it. You don't happen to have any aspirin, do you?"

I didn't.

"I have some at home," he said. "I'll swing by there, take the aspirin, and we'll go."

He lived in a four-story brownstone.

"This isn't the best neighborhood for a girl to wait in a car by herself," he told me with a nudge. "Come with me."

Once upstairs, he vanished to another room while I sat on the blue sectional in his living room. He entered and exited a couple of times and, ultimately, placed a tray on the coffee table with a bottle of wine and two goblets.

He poured wine into both goblets as he spoke. "Took the aspirin."

I didn't drink anything, and when he sat on the sofa, I moved to sit on the rug.

Leo laughed. "Are you trying to get farther away from me?"

"No," I replied. "I'm fine here."

"You're a tease!" he roared. Before I could respond, he lurched toward me and spun my head around, kissing me forcefully. In alarm, I pulled away, and he responded by grabbing me by my hair. "Oh, you're not getting out of this," he hissed in his now grating voice. He was like a beast let out of the cage—positively consumed with anger.

But I was angry, too. "I see your headache's gone," I snapped. "Or did you ever really have a headache?"

I fought the way I had while being raped two years before—kicking, punching, pulling his hair, and pushing him off—except, unlike the first time, I was fully conscious, not impaired in any way, and that helped tremendously. At the same time, I had a shivery realization about the darkness outside his window. Not only did I have no clue where I was, but I also didn't have money—two things I noted to be rectified in the future. And, as a result of my fear, I negotiated.

"It's not you. I feel sick. It came on suddenly," I lied. "I really want to do this with you, but I want it to be perfect when it happens." His ego let him believe that, so I talked him into taking me home, afraid that at any moment, he'd suddenly turn on me.

About a week later, he approached me again at the office as if nothing untoward had happened. "Hey, beautiful. I've been missing you."

Since I gave him a cold stare in response and stormed off, he stopped bothering me. But, again, I felt responsible, so I didn't tell a soul, and I regret that.

It was around this time that BDD (Body Dysmorphic Disorder) began to rear its head.

This excerpt from my fiction novel *Shattering Truths* was a description of my personal experience:

I touched up my makeup, but it wasn't enough. My hair was all wrong. I brushed it this way and that, but no matter where I parted it or what I did, the face looking back at me was repulsive. I hated it. I hated her. I had no idea who she was.

My heart pounded, and I brushed my hair until my head hurt. Then everything blurred. I couldn't see that horrid face anymore. I set the brush down and tried closing my eyes then opening them again. I had to turn away from the mirror and not look at it for a few minutes. It seemed to have beguiled or bewitched me. When I faced it again, my image was no longer blurred or particularly unattractive. It was okay, albeit rather plain, and I was able to fix that with a few minor adjustments.

Alas, I saw what I wanted to see—the beauty I figured they wanted. I was good enough to walk out the door, my heart still pounding.

In my experience, BDD, like other obsessions, impairs your judgment and distorts your perception, so there's an ongoing conflict between hating and loving yourself. You convince yourself you are beautiful sometimes, and, at other times, you're sure you are hideous. Almost everywhere you turn, you come face to face with twisted, seemingly demonic mirrors that show no mercy.

I believe, too, that I showed *myself* no mercy—no mercy at all.

KRISTINA

Kristina was five-foot-eight and shapely with dark brown hair and brown eyes. She was attractive, and although we didn't look alike, it was hard for people to think about one of us without the other. On occasion, they'd call me Kristina and her Diane. (As a reminder, I'm not using her real name here. Everyone in this book has a fictitious name except me.)

Ironically, however, *unlike* me, Kristina was a strait-laced girl. She didn't smoke, drink, or abuse drugs. She was completely devoted to her fiancé, her family, her friends, and her dog. And she was loyal to a fault.

Kristina was part of our girl squad at Compton. There were four of us, but Kristina was the one I truly connected with because she and I loved being silly and irreverent. We made each other laugh. If the four of us didn't eat lunch together in the cafeteria, we ate at a nearby Burger King and then strolled around the neighborhood. Once, we sneaked into the lobby of the Plaza Hotel.

Kristina left Compton at some point, but we continued to meet for lunch. That didn't change until a tragic event occurred. Details in the following two paragraphs are what I've pieced together from all I had learned.

Kristina went dancing at a club in the Bronx with a friend. Upon their return, they talked in the car for a while. Of course, it was pitch-dark by then and eerily quiet when, quite suddenly, a man crept out of the shadows and aimed a .44 revolver at point-blank range. He didn't know Kristina or her friend, but they became his target.

One of several shots he fired hit Kristina in the head. In an instant, she slumped over and collapsed onto the pavement. And just like that, she was dead. Her friend survived a bullet wound to the leg.

The day after it happened, a mutual acquaintance called me at work to break the news.

Before I could put the phone down, all eyes were on me—the eyes of shocked and curious coworkers gauging my reaction. Speculation ensued within earshot.

"Maybe it was a mob hit. Her family's Italian."

"What was she doing out at one o'clock in the morning?"

It infuriated me that Kristina's integrity was in question because she was the victim. I was stunned into silence. I had chills. But despite the crushing pain, I didn't cry until later, when the distress made me wonder again about the divine protection we so naïvely expected.

Why Kristina? I asked myself. *Why anyone? But why Kristina?*

Eventually, we'd learn that The Son of Sam, aka David Berkowitz, executed her. He was the serial killer who'd terrorized New York City for over a year before getting caught and sentenced to 365 years in prison, but, at the time, this was merely the beginning of his reign of terror. His initial victims were young brunettes sitting in parked cars with a friend or boyfriend, so many of us dyed our hair blonde. At the time, people were always talking or thinking about him. We huddled over newspapers with others glimpsing over our shoulders, eager for updates.

The killer's identity was still a mystery when I attended Kristina's wake, so there was collective fear—*intense* fear. Throughout that balmy summer evening, I kept peering over my shoulder, shuddering at the notion that the monster who did this to Kristina was roaming around free somewhere.

Lying in her casket, she looked so young. She was just a kid like me—eighteen years old. I'll never forget her.

HAVEN

I visited incarcerated friends—one in the Manhattan Detention Center and the other imprisoned in North Caldwell, New Jersey. Both of them were heroin addicts who did time for robbery. The North Caldwell prison complex, surrounded by woods, had the expected grim façade. My companion and I heard crashing noises as we got closer, along with whistles and shouting from the prisoners at the windows of the men's section. That facility is now abandoned, but I don't think I'll ever forget it. I was eighteen, and I didn't want to end up in a place like that.

It was one of the many reasons my home now became a haven to me. I'd awaken at 5:00 a. M.—my favorite time because it's quiet and dark, and I couldn't wait to write. It didn't matter if it was pouring rain or blinding sun outside. Just beyond my tiny window, adorned with white lace curtains, the night sky lurked over the concrete steps and pathway from my grandmother's kitchen door to the yard. It was eerie in its stillness, but the beautiful moon loomed above in all of its glorious phases.

My twin bed was draped in a white chenille bedspread. A vanity tray adorned with perfume bottles sat on the mirrored wood bureau covered in lace. The matching armoire displayed my pink floral musical jewelry box with its dancing ballerina. There was a stereo with speakers. Posters of rock stars lined the walls, and somewhere, a four-foot, inflated orange tiger stood guard. (Someone had won it for me at the circus.) Most important to me, however, were my old-fashioned wood desk and six-foot-tall bookcases. The bookcases showcased various gems of classic literature, along with many other fascinating subjects.

My daily dusting of the furniture was well-known. While I polished with Pledge one Saturday morning, my godfather passed by the room. "You don't have to do that every day," he said, amused.

But I cherished my room and everything in it, and, more often than not, I closed the door to shut the world out. I didn't want to see anyone connected to reality. I didn't want to hear stomping feet, whizzing appliances, jingling keys or voices, my father growling, or my mother muttering to herself. I didn't want to smell the magnificent aroma of food cooking. Those were sights and sounds I usually treasured, but all of them ceased to exist during those coveted moments when I was writing.

Melissa sometimes knocked on my bedroom door or came in if it was open, wanting to talk to me. Although I loved seeing her and always wanted to speak to her, I couldn't surrender my full attention.

"I guess I'm bothering you," she'd say.

The guilt plagued me, and the hurt in her eyes broke my heart. I'd say, "No, no, no. you're not bothering me!"

I understand now that I couldn't filter out distractions and focus the way others could—not in the same way I'd scribble a few lines of poetry while sitting in a bar. Once I managed to get locked in, I couldn't risk prolonged distraction.

But Melissa was precious to me. I'd often ask her to read stuff I'd written, and she'd do her best to oblige. Poor girl. I'd sit right by her the whole time as she read silently. Whenever she laughed, I'd say, "What? What? What's funny?"

Ironically, though, I was paranoid when no one was home—easily distracted by noise—and often unnerved. I'd quickly rise to investigate if I heard something—anything, really. If the phone rang, my hand jumped to my heart. An underlying fear of violence persisted as if I had to somehow co-exist with it, and I did, but this constant terror sometimes invaded my peace.

I wrote until dinner was ready and arrived in time to remove the large centerpiece of hand-painted faux fruit in a ceramic bowl so I could set the table. Then one of my sisters or I collected plates and utensils for the place settings.

Weekday dinners included a meat dish with French fries, oil and vinegar salad, and Italian bread—except Friday. On Fridays, we had fish, or my mother made spaghetti or pizza. If there wasn't time to make the pizza herself, we ordered one.

During our dinners, the wine flowed. My dad did the honors and offered everyone a glass, but I declined, as did my sisters. I'm not sure why we refused it. Maybe it became a habit from when we were kids. He'd offer us whiskey shots, and we'd scowl in disgust after one sip.

Additionally, abandoning the fictional world for the real world, framed by my mom's French Provincial décor, was never a smooth transition for me. I likened it to keeping a tenacious grip on your glorious glimpse of the afterlife while in a coma and making a vacillating attempt to return to your loved ones. I'd think, *okay, the voices you hear now are real. Quick, snap out of it. Get back to the mundane.* I didn't switch it off immediately. For the first five or ten minutes, I was a zombie.

Before long, though Bridget, Melissa, and I would relay funny things that had happened during our day.

My dad, in response, gave us a sarcastic, "Pass the feather."

But my mom giggled with us.

When *he* told funny stories, however, my father killed himself with laughter, ending with, "Oh, boy, I'm telling you!"

A hilarious family, we were.

That was one side of it anyway. My dad and many extended family members on both sides were quite comfortable with their bigoted opinions. It was as if they had no clue they were saying or doing anything wrong in expressing those opinions.

All I know is that ever since the age of twelve, I'd gotten physically ill listening to some of them spew their hatred for other races or ethnicities. Sometimes, it made me feel as if the walls were closing in, and I almost couldn't breathe. It broke my heart a thousand times over while also causing deep anguish and despair.

SWEET MEMORIES

One Saturday afternoon, my grandmother called me from the bottom of the stairwell. My first response was an eyeroll. I was alone upstairs, intent on putting in nine full hours of writing. Nonetheless, I emerged and appeared on the landing. "What?"

"That's Diane," my grandmother said to a woman who was with her. "The one who writes—and she sings! Beautiful, she sings! I hear her from the window."

Her acknowledgment moved me to the point of tears. It was also good to see a spark of light, and a bit of joy, in her tiny brown eyes beyond the lenses of her black-framed glasses. She kept her dark, silver-streaked hair to collarbone level and wore a pink, sleeveless dress.

It was true; I did often sing along with whatever I played on my stereo, experimenting a great deal with my voice. It surprised me when I was able to reach the highest notes. I loved singing.

"Aw, well, good luck, honey. God bless you," the woman with her said. She beamed at me, her brown eyes wide and engaging.

"Thank you." I smiled at her.

After my grandmother ushered her out, she returned to the stairwell. "Come down," she said. "I'll make you something to eat."

My hands rested on the banister. "Oh, Grandma, no, thank you, I—"

"Whattsamatta? You work, work, work, write, write, write. You never stop," she argued. "Come."

Even the heavenly aroma of her deep-frying zeppoles didn't tempt me. "I can't." Releasing the banister, I crouched on bended knees. "Look, I ate breakfast. By the time I'm finished working, dinner will be ready, and I'll eat enough for two people, I promise. I'll be okay, Grandma. Please don't worry. The longer I'm away from my work, the harder it is to get back to it. It's nothing more than that." It was futile to explain to her how a full stomach stifled my creativity.

"I hope so, Dolly," she said. "God bless."

On another day, I returned home to find her seated on the dark green porch bench, smiling and waving at me. Beside her was a shoebox with a hole in its center. I kissed her and spent the next ten minutes peeking through the hole she'd made in the cardboard box. Inside, a tiny sparrow peered up at me, flapping its wings.

"It's a little bitty thing," she said. "Cry, cry, cry. He can't fly. May be hurt."

"Where'd you find him?" I asked.

She pressed her hand to her mouth and chuckled. "Right here on the steps." She wanted me to go to the backyard along with her and the bird.

Since we were kids, she'd summoned us to the yard to show us the tomatoes she'd grown. She'd marvel, admiring them with one hand across her cheek. "How beautiful!"

We would assure her that, yes, indeed, they were beautiful.

The yard had a grape arbor that formed a canopy over half of it, creating a shady spot. The other end housed a tall fig tree that thrived in the sun. Both sides had tables with accompanying benches and chairs, and, for a few summers, we had a kiddie pool near the fig tree. Birds were happy to visit—sparrows, robins, blackbirds, blue jays, mourning doves, and blood-red cardinals.

My grandmother's garden was half in the shade and half in the sun. She planted herbs, vegetables, and purple morning glories. The ledge around it was another place to sit and relax. We sat on that ledge now, under the grape arbor, with the shoebox between us. As we talked, the bird chirped and scraped the bottom of the box with its teeny feet. Soon enough, familiar footsteps pounded hard on the concrete.

"Your father," my grandmother said. He came from her kitchen door, taking the stairs to the end of the pathway, where he pivoted into the yard.

"Hello there!" He looked at me, smiling.

We told him about the bird, and it amused him. In his wide grin, I saw the curious boy raised in the mountains of Campochiaro, Italy. I pictured the photo I'd seen of him propped up on a cushioned footstool with his thick blond curls. He'd told us stories of his boyhood—how he'd climbed trees to reach the bird nests and cup the baby birds in his palms. He'd built houses for them, fed and cared for them.

"I used to have a pony," he'd told us once, grinning. "I'd ride him standing and waving my hat. Mama would be making the sign of the cross over by the house, yelling at me to sit." He laughed. "Then, I used to build big sleds, big enough to carry the kids in the town. We'd go down the mountains—the kids in the back and me in front, hanging off the side."

I was in awe of his Italian-accented tales, and I loved when he was in this kind of mood.

"But nobody ever got to drive my sled," he went on, shaking his finger. "And when we got down the mountain, I made them drag the sled to the top again." He winked. "I'd hike back alone."

I swear, when that man was happy, he was so sweet.

As for the bird, my grandmother kept it warm and safe in the shoebox, fed and healed it, and, soon, it was able to fly and return to its nest. I was happy for that bird and wished I could fly, too—simply flee at will.

BONE OF CONTENTION

While I never lost sight of how blessed I was to find any amount of time to write, I desperately wanted more. If I had more, I imagined I'd achieve fame and fortune in less than a year. So delusional I was!

There was much I had to learn and, in truth, the learning never stops. But I did it: I quit my job at Compton and, before leaving, equipped myself with several months' supply of amphetamines. For a few months afterward, I popped amphetamines every morning and wrote until I heard my father arrive home from work.

"What'd you do all day?" he asked when I greeted him.

"It's Saturday," I reminded him. "I've been writing."

"All day?" There was that glassy, incredulous stare. "You're nineteen years old, and you spend the whole day cooped up here doing nothing! Today was beautiful outside!"

Surely, it struck him as odd that his daughter isolated herself at such a young age. Of course, he had no idea what had happened to me out there when I *wasn't* isolating.

"What the hell do you write that it takes the whole goddamn day?" he bellowed.

"Do you want to see?" My body tensed as I guessed what he'd say. I'd asked him before.

"Not now."

One night, while he complained about me writing the whole day, my mom stared at him with disdain. "But why don't you mind your own goddamn business? She's not bothering anybody. She's good. I never had any problems with her."

"I'm not saying she's not good," he replied. "I want her to live a happy life."

My eyes focused on the one painting hanging on the eggshell-colored walls—dogwood trees, in full bloom, forming an arch above a mountain stream, the waters roaring in their divine prepotency over the stone boulders embedded in the soil. It depicted something fierce joining forces with something gentle, and I saw my mother as the gentle force subduing my father's roar.

"Okay, you say you want us to have everything, right?" My heart was beating so rapidly that my hands were shaking. "Writing, to me, is everything. Why should that bother you? As for me not having a job, I've had one since I was sixteen years old. I'm taking a short break. What's the big deal?"

"You could have made better use of your education," he barked. "Made a secure future. Instead, you'll be hopping around in dead-end jobs for the rest of your life. I told you before. You should have gone for journalism."

Some may say writing is writing, but, as far as I was concerned, he might as well have suggested that I randomly become a molecular biologist.

"Uh, no. It's not me," I argued. "And copywriting is not me. I have no desire or interest in doing those things and would have no motivation or energy for that. How do you put your heart and soul into something you have no interest or energy for? Besides, I'm not going to use my God-given talent to sell a box of Tide!"

As absurd as that statement was, it made sense to me at the time. Writing was so much a part of me that I'd have done it even if I didn't love and crave it as much as I did.

"No kidding!" Any trace of warmth in my father's eyes vanished in that moment. "You're too good for that? You type letters. You put stuff away in the drawer. You answer the phone. You could've been a nurse, a doctor, or a lawyer. I couldn't afford the education to be any of those things! You want to be a writer? Yeah, sure. Hey. I wish you luck."

With my dad, "I wish you luck" meant go fuck yourself. "You're going to end up a bum on a park bench," he said. "Or, you'll be living in a ramshackle shithole without a pot to piss in."

My stomach churned, and the lump in my throat blocked any food from passing. I'd lost my appetite anyway. The room sparkled like coveted jewels with its fancy chandelier and china cabinet collection of eye-catching relics and statues, but it wasn't warm to me. It was cold and bland with unremitting overhead lights that intensified the wall-to-wall pain and humiliation.

My sisters were too stunned to say anything, and I stormed away from the table. I sat in my room crying, shaking, and hating myself. I hated that I was such a disappointment to him.

My father hadn't always been unhappy with my dream. When I was eight, someone asked me what I wanted to be when I grew up, and I said, "I'm already what I want to be—I am a writer."In response to that, he bought me a journal.

I had to bear my father's situation in mind, too. He'd come from a long line of skilled laborers. Both he and my mother had been limited in terms of language and education when they first came to this country. They took jobs they could manage while learning the language. My mother became an assembly-line worker at the Bulova Watch factory. My father was a butcher—ultimately the meat manager at Grand Union in Astoria, near Ditmars Boulevard. He fought in the Korean War as a sergeant. After that, providing for his family became his priority. We always had a complete meal on the table and many wonderful celebrations.

His dream for the next generation was to produce a doctor or a lawyer, at most. One of his children achieving any respectable level of success in the arts was a pipe dream. I didn't see that he was terrified for me and, in his misguided way, trying to prevent me from doing what *he* had to do. I couldn't process any of it then because what I kept hearing was that he had no confidence in me and didn't believe in me. The message got imprinted in my brain: *You won't succeed. You can't do it. You're not good enough.*

It's an important truth because, throughout life, I've encountered otherwise brilliant individuals who have trouble motivating themselves enough to change their lives or gravitate toward what they want most. They tell themselves they don't deserve love or money or anything good—like *I* did. And they fear success as much as they fear failure—like *I* do.

Admittedly, my father and I, quite often, misunderstood what the other said. There was a generation gap compounded by somewhat of a language barrier. And because he was drinking when these conversations took place, he got loud, angry, and often insulted me. He had his demons; I had mine. It didn't help that I was just as stubborn as he was.

Perhaps I was waiting for him to reinforce the notion that I could write and, at the same time, pursue my goal and find a promising career—not limited to the ones he suggested. Between college and working, I imagined I'd figure out what to do if I needed to fall back on some other career.

That night, after I'd left the table without finishing my dinner, he summoned me back. "Okay, okay, I'm sorry," he said. "Come and eat."

I sat with the sensibility of a helpless four-year-old while he refilled my plate and poured soda into my glass. He disarmed me, too, with his innocent little boy grin.

"My dreams are my future," I explained to him and my mother, seated across the table. "Those dead-end jobs are perfect for pursuing my dreams. I don't have to work long hours, and I have plenty of time and energy to make a go of my writing career. Hey, I might be rich someday!"

His laughter was intended to mock me. "I got news for you. There's no way to become rich without being dishonest."

My mom gave me a wink. "When she gets rich, she's going to buy me a house in Brazil. Diane and I, we're partners."

"Yeah, sure," my dad quipped. "Ha! You'll be behind her in line at the soup kitchen."

"Don't pay attention," my mother advised. "You do your thing and don't worry about it."

My father flipped a switch again. "Goddamn it, but why don't you keep your mouth shut? You don't know what you're talking about, and you have to put in your two cents!"

My mother bounded from the table and dashed into the bathroom, slamming the door shut.

I rushed after her and knocked at the bathroom door, hearing sniffles in response.

"Mom?" I knocked again.

"I'm okay," she said in a soft voice.

Returning to the table, I tried a different angle. "Daddy, I understand you want what's best for me, but I'll never make it if I don't try. Success comes to those willing to take risks. Failure hurts, I'm sure, but letting the opportunity pass would destroy me."

"I talked to people about this, Diane," he said gently. "It's not so easy. A lot of people want to become writers."

My mother returned then, wiping her tears.

"Where'd you disappear to?" he asked her. "Your food's getting cold."

She waved him off.

He played innocent. "All I said was—"

"I heard what you said." She sipped her wine without meeting his gaze. "You are the expert. You know everything, and I know nothing."

They continued to bicker until he apologized.

My limbs felt heavy as I rose to clear the table, taking things to the kitchen. I began washing dishes, and the water from the faucet soothed me as it drowned out the noise from the dining room.

"Watch out! You're getting water on the floor. I told you—wash low." My mother was standing behind me.

Soon, she took over, and I slinked away. It wasn't long before my father passed out on the couch.

I have to say that no matter what happened between my father and me, I clung to the belief that he loved me. He was a brave, modest man, generous with his assistance and advice, and solid as a rock—always. As a child, I worried obsessively about him when it was near the time for him to come home from work. I was afraid that something would happen to him, and he might not make it home to us. I guess you can say my love for him was as out of proportion as my fear of him.

YEAH, BYE

Much of what I'd been writing was crap. Strung out on amphetamines, it became increasingly difficult to relate to anyone or to do my best work. I'd hit bottom. Soon, I ran out of pills and the money to buy them. There may have been a way to get another prescription, but I opted to quit cold turkey. It was clear to me that I had to get back to work and school and regain control of my life.

Going on interviews left me depressed. I got lost under gray, drizzling skies along the waterfront in the industrial complex of Long Island City and never got to *that* interview. During the interviews I'd made it to, I barely remembered what to say, let alone how to say it.

Personal agency recruiters passed along the degrading feedback they'd gotten about me from potential employers. "You sent me a centerfold," one woman complained.

Someone should have told her that merely having big boobs you never asked for didn't make you a centerfold. What I'd worn was modest and appropriate.

Another employer relayed that I talked too low, never smiled, played with my hair, and avoided eye contact. My attempt to loosen up in the next interview resulted in the assessment that I rambled on and on like a runaway train. The interviewer asked what I loved to do, and I talked about my writing. Of course, they always asked about the three-month gap in my employment history, which didn't help.

It was humiliating and frustrating, but as you learn, you adjust, right? You get used to the process. And you get better at it. So, one sunny day in May, I made my first good impression at a chemical company somewhere in the Times Square area. They occupied a small suite that was colorless and bland with blaring fluorescent lights overhead.

"They offered me the job," I told my father at dinner.

He asked one question after another—what kind of business it was, what the job entailed, what they'd pay me. He asked more questions than I'd asked the recruiter at the interview.

"Did you call and tell 'em you're going to accept?"

"Not yet," I said. "I'm not sure I'd like this job."

"I got news for you," he sneered. "Nobody likes a job. A job is your bread and butter, and you do it whether you like it or not. Heh! Who was going to support my kids if I stayed home because I didn't like my job? When you kids were small, I put in twelve hours a day. Why? Because I liked it? You got to be kidding me! I wanted you kids to have the things I never had for myself."

My heart broke for him. "I know, Daddy. And don't worry. I'm going to call and accept it."

"I don't understand why you had to leave the other job," he lamented. "It was a big company with good benefits, and the boss, he seemed fair. You said yourself, he was nice."

"He was."

"And the other guy was in a position to help you get ahead."

"You're right. I should've stayed there."

A few weeks into the chemical company job, the previous secretary was still training me, but my mind kept checking out. It was so boring. I couldn't focus. Meanwhile, flirty salesmen breezed in and out, and while they were harmless enough, my boss was another story. Whenever he summoned me to "go over" something in his office, he made inappropriate comments.

The man had to be at least twenty years older than me. He was six feet tall and heavyset, his brown hair short and curly. His beady little brown eyes clashed with his cherubic face.

"You've been distant lately," he said one day. "Let's talk about it. Are you happy here?"

Feeling like I was walking on broken glass, I came clean. "I am uncomfortable."

"Oh?" He feigned surprise. "If it's the workload, we can discuss what might make it easier. If it's a person, on the other hand, tell me who it is, and I'll talk to him."

I was afraid to incur his wrath, but I had to be honest. "It's you."

"*Me?*"He pointed to himself. "*I'm* making you uncomfortable?"

"Yes."

The following day, he fired me.

"You're a nice kid," he said. "I can appreciate that this isn't the most exciting job for a

young person. You deserve a break. So, here's what I'm going to do for you. A friend of mine is looking for a secretary. I think it's the perfect job for you. It's more interesting—more fun. If you want, I'll send you over with a recommendation. The only thing I ask is that you sign a letter saying the workload here is too heavy for you, and you wish to resign."

"Of course!" The whole thing bothered me, but at this point, I wanted out.

So, he gave me the guy's phone number for the interview and advised me to, "Wear high heels—it makes a better impression."

I figured I had nothing to lose by going on the interview, and I wore the heels. All the trudging back and forth I had to do just to find this place left me limping. When I got there, some guy came out and took my application, but I never heard from him again. Of course, it was a set-up—retaliation from my ex-boss for having the nerve to say he made me uncomfortable.

After that, Melissa and I escaped to Fort Lauderdale with a couple of friends. It was exactly what I needed—especially those umbrella drinks we enjoyed by the pool.

When we returned, I landed another job with a public relations firm in Manhattan's midtown east section. The elevator was slightly larger than a linen closet, with tarnished silver floor buttons, and, usually, no one stepped in while I ascended or descended.

The president of the firm was in his forties, easily six-three, with medium-length brown hair, round glasses, and a walrus mustache. He worked there with his partner, whom he lived with—an attractive woman about five-ten with curly brown hair and big brown eyes. It would be them and me, no one else. What could possibly go wrong?

He had a large corner office with a massive desk. His partner's office was small, and the secretary's desk was right outside it, near the entry door. There was a conference room and a library where books, papers, and boxes covered every shelf, table, chair, and practically the entire floor. I doubted they could find anything in that mess.

To my delight, there were no bright fluorescent overhead lights. Instead, they left the rooms dark, flipping the switches on when they entered and off when they left. The offices and secretarial desk had charming, old-fashioned lamps.

"I got the job," I excitedly told my father, rattling off the details.

We were all sitting around the table, digging into our slices of apple crumb cake.

"Where is it going to lead—you working in this little place with these two whatever the hell they are?" he asked.

I had no idea, but they said they traveled often, and I was free to write my book there when I ran out of work to do.

It was creepy, though. When I got off the elevator each morning and made my way to the opposite end of the floor to the office, I'd peer over my shoulder because, more than once, someone started following me. The door to the suite was always locked, and most days, I let myself in with the keys they gave me because they either weren't in or just weren't in yet. As a result, I left the suite only to go to the ladies' room down the hall or to grab lunch from a nearby deli, which I brought back to eat at my desk.

Throughout the day, there were knocks on the door. It was either the mailman or the messenger guy. Other than that, the silence was chilling.

It was even creepier when the boss *was* there.

"You're an unusual but interesting young lady," he said to me one day when he and I were alone. He parked his ass on top of my desk and said he wanted to learn more about me and my writing. If his partner had been in her office, it might have been no big deal, but I doubted he would've done it if she was. And when I say the situation was unfortunate, it truly was because, for the most part, he was intelligent, interesting, and kind.

"Let me ask you something," he said before long. "If I were to make a pass at you, would it affect our business relationship?"

No matter the consequences, I had to get it out there immediately. "Yes."

"Oh, really how?" he asked.

"It would end it," I said.

Someone was at the door, so he answered it, returning with a bunch of pens in fancy cases, which he showed me. "The guy's selling these."

I admitted they were nice. Well, I love pens, but when he bought one of them for me, I hesitated to take it.

"Go on," he urged. "It's a small token of my appreciation."

"No. No, thank you."

He shrugged and slinked back to his office.

I suspected I wouldn't be long for this job. When his partner returned to the office, she sensed something was amiss. There was a sudden awkwardness. My boundaries were firmer, his demeanor more sheepish. They were prepared to go to Dallas for a conference, and she assigned me the impossible task of cleaning that mess of a library and organizing it during the week they'd be away. It came across as a punishment she'd doled out in anger.

I didn't know where to begin. The dust in there was toxic. There were no gloves anywhere and no cleaning supplies unless they were somewhere in the rubble. Every time I ventured into that room, I was repulsed and walked out. Melissa came by one day to help me and was equally disgusted. We tried for a while, then surrendered and headed out to lunch.

Of course, the woman was livid when she returned since I hadn't cleaned up the room. In a furious state, she kept piling things on my desk for typing. I imagine she'd written those in an equally furious state, making her words on the page impossible to decipher. She also called the personnel agency that had sent me to complain while I sat outside her office.

I couldn't blame her. Nor could I make any of it better by staying there. In fact, things were more likely to get a lot worse, so I resigned. You'd think she would've been thrilled about that, but it angered her even more. The two-week notice wasn't going to work out either since she was so hurt and pissed.

The lecherous guy came shuffling out as I gathered my things. From the pathetic look on his face, it was obvious he knew there was nothing he could say or do, and I didn't wait to find out if he would try. It was time to fly again—off to my next adventure.

PUBLISHING

In a matter of weeks, I was hired as an assistant in the book manufacturing department of a large publishing company. There, I got to observe both ends of the industry I'd chosen.

Even as I worked on the nineteenth floor, hopeful writers breezed in, clutching their manuscripts, asking me to read their work and help them get published. I'm sure they asked anyone they bumped into, having no clue how to go about accomplishing it, having done no studying or research. Still, I was sympathetic because I understood the magnitude of a dream and the earnestness in pursuing it. Manhattan was full of young hopefuls. With minimal effort on my part, I was inclined to run into them, and there was an immediate bond.

I loved that—and everything about Manhattan. I loved Broadway—the theaters with the lighted marquees and billboards. I loved the slew of yellow cabs and wall-to-wall pedestrians. This city was becoming part of me, seeping into my veins, and I fed off the energy it inspired.

By this point, I'd allowed the publication of one of my poems in an anthology, but they didn't pay me for it. *Writer's Digest* published one of my letters in response to an article, as did *Creem*, a popular rock and roll magazine. At the time, I thought it was a big deal. It really wasn't. I bought a press kit and a tape recorder because a well-connected friend got me an opportunity to do interviews with musicians for a rock music publication. Somewhere along the line, however, I chickened out.

Meanwhile, some shyster wanted $20,000 to help me publish my book. He had no qualms about ripping off some kid.

My father said, "Tell him, 'You get paid when *I* do. Twenty percent.'"

When I did that, the scam artist went from praising me to no end to unleashing his irrepressible wrath upon me. Lesson learned.

The next agent I queried agreed to read my book. He'd had a number of books published himself and was well-known in the industry at that time. "The talent is there," he said, "but this book has a long way to go." He gave me advice, and that was that.

My problem was that just like those authors who'd wandered into the publishing firm I was working for, I was so damned impatient. I wanted what I wanted the second I wanted it.

Like the TV for my bedroom that I kept bugging my father about. "If a big one is too expensive, I can get a tiny one," I said.

"The tiny ones are expensive, too," he replied.

"No, they're not." Of course, I hadn't checked into it.

"How much are they?" he asked.

I hesitated. "They can't be more than twenty dollars."

"Twenty dollars!" His eyes widened spectacularly. "I'll take six!"

The entire family laughed at that, including me.

With that same kind of impatience, I kept lightening my hair until I was blonder than blonde. I wanted to be glamorous, so I wore more makeup than I needed and began shopping at Saks Fifth Avenue and Bloomingdales for work outfits. Their price tags were steep, but I lived at home and had no bills to pay. My dad would say, "You got champagne taste and a beer pocket."

He was right in that fancy, exotic things genuinely appealed to me, but while I loved champagne, caviar, and French cuisine, including escargot, I also found joy in the simplest things.

At work, I was shy about participating when everyone in the department went to lunch to celebrate birthdays, anniversaries, pregnancies, and engagements. They talked nonstop and with giddiness about marriage and babies and other safe, traditional topics, whereas I was more interested in writing and reading, now fascinated by Buddhism, Hinduism, and the supernatural world. When I began to go along to the luncheons, I was always afraid I'd say or do something wrong. I wished I was as outgoing as the others—more comfortable in my own skin.

In every other sense, the luncheons were great. A frequent choice was Ramayana on 52nd Street, a wonderful Indonesian restaurant that closed many years ago. Sometimes it was the trendy Italian place of the moment. We'd gone to Windows on the World at the top of the World Trade Center and to the Rainbow Room in Rockefeller Plaza.

Co-workers complimented my outfits, and at least *part* of me believed them. A bigger part of me didn't. My BDD was at an all-time high, and I maintain that it tied in with the narcissistic abuse I'd experienced.

There were many narcissistic abusers in my life. Some were related to me, and some were not. I met the first one when I was a child, but I continued to get entangled with them throughout life, both male and female. Most of the stories are not worth retelling because it's what I've learned that matters.

But those experiences seem to explain why I set an impossible standard for myself that didn't apply to others. I'd make every effort to look perfect, and even after that, I made several trips to the restroom during dates and other social events to check myself in the mirror.

I became addicted to getting attention, praise, and validation. Of course, it's natural for all of us to enjoy attention and praise, but there's a difference between wanting it and being helplessly addicted to it—as in letting it become another drug. The "fix" wears off, and then you desperately crave more.

You'd think it was about men, but it wasn't. I had to prove something to myself. My people-pleasing response was born out of trauma; I never liked to disappoint.

At the same time, I didn't understand why women competed with me. While part of me came to believe I was no longer the awkward kid whose looks others could mock, another part of me was still much in doubt about that. And the weird part is how long it takes to alter the latter perception, and how much work it entails.

Narcissistic abuse does that to you, and, as you likely know, those that inflict it can be parents, lovers, siblings, friends, aunts, uncles, grandparents, cousins, co-workers, employers, teachers, etc. Many of us are unwittingly drawn to narcissists because of their familiarity. We have long-term contact with some of these people, which can amount to significant damage.

Abusers intentionally or unintentionally break our wings so that when we don't fly, they can say they knew we never would or that we might have succeeded if only we'd listened to them.

DEFINITELY BENIGN

Diagnosed with bilateral breast tumors, I was hospitalized for nearly a week. I was twenty years old. Two much older women shared a room with me at Lenox Hill Hospital on Manhattan's Upper East Side.

The women acted surprised that I remained calm and in good spirits. "How do you manage to have so much courage?" one asked.

"Well, the doctor says they're probably benign," I replied.

No doubt, I was also holding on to the notion that I was divinely protected. I never cried or took it seriously. The staff was surprisingly responsive—so magnanimous and approving. They took good care of me, and I felt safe. It was also a nice break from the world.

My mother had reassured me that it was nothing and that everything would be fine. There was concern and compassion in my father's eyes when he visited me that first time, and it made for some awkward but friendly conversation.

My grandmother sat on my hospital bed and held my hand in hers. "You're a brave girl. God bless you." Her eyes were flooded with tears. "You're a wonderful, wonderful girl."

She had remembered the kind of earrings I loved—gold at the time and preferably hearts that were small, dainty, pretty, and hung just below the earlobe. She'd brought me a pair like that then. They were from Italy, and I wore and cherished them for years.

Sweet Melissa, who was sixteen or seventeen then, came straight from her job to visit me. She got caught in a downpour but still stopped to buy flowers! She was beside herself, handing me the wet flowers with her hair soaked, and it was clear to me how worried she was. Whenever I remember that incident, I just want to hug her again.

Bridget was away at the time, but she'd called the hospital when she found out— furious that no one told her sooner. My parents hadn't wanted to upset her.

"Not wanting to bother or upset me is bullshit," she said then. "If the whole family is worrying, I should be worrying with them."

A little note about Bridget—she is sharp as a tack, and she always noticed even the tiniest nuance of dysfunction in our family.

Months after my hospital stay, she and I were seated on the bed in my room, and she suddenly asked, "Why do you do that?"

"What?" I had no idea what she meant.

"Whenever I pick something up from your dresser and then put it back, you move it from where I put it to where you had it."

I didn't realize it, so I laughed.

"Why do you do it?" she demanded.

"I don't know," I said. "Probably for the same reason you keep picking up stuff on my dresser. Why do *you* do it?"

"No reason," she said, "but I think you moved it back because I didn't put it in the exact same place it was before. Even if it's just a quarter of an inch away from where it was."

"You don't have a reason," I said, "so, maybe *I* don't have a reason."

Was it obsessive-compulsive behavior? Or was it just my neurodivergent brain? For all I know, it's *normal* to discourage someone from continuing to mess around with your stuff. I'm no expert, but it does make sense to me that after what many of us have experienced in life, we want, at least, the *illusion* of control.

HOTHEADS

I had a few boyfriends over the next several years. They were dangerous men—all of them a good five years older than I was, and they were on a much faster track. They lived in worlds I hadn't experienced and, sometimes, it was almost the equivalent of being at the movies with popcorn or curling up with a book for some crazy adventure. It was as if I saw myself as an actor who couldn't *really* be in danger. There was this notion I had, too, that it was my job to explore—to pass through every forbidden door.

Let me just say that, despite our well-meaning intentions, we often find ourselves in unhealthy or unholy alliances in the aftermath of trauma. Denial is one of our coping mechanisms, and we live in survival mode, often oblivious to what we're doing and why.

Rather than go into detail about all of these guys, I'll give a brief summary.

One had a two-inch scar on his face from a knife fight. He and I snorted a lot of coke together, and we did speed, acid, and PCP. He smoked a lot of weed because he was always dealing it, so I did that with him, too. We were together for years before he became physically abusive and I left.

The next boyfriend was another hothead, but for some crazy reason, I accepted his engagement ring when he asked me to marry him.

It's strange. I'd gotten a number of proposals over the years and always attributed it to the fact that I didn't want to get married. That seemed to make men feel safe from any pressure. It amused me because I wasn't exactly the girl next door, the one your mother would love, etc., and, as much as I enjoyed being with my then fiancé, I found it impossible to balance my writing with any draining relationship drama. Rather than cling to people when there were relationship problems, I preferred they leave, and I'd hold the door wide open.

I was so anxious to get rid of my then fiancé one night that I loaned him my car. An hour later, the police called. They thought he'd stolen the car. When they'd pulled him over for speeding, he sped away! They chased him, and he resisted arrest when they finally caught him.

That was when I ended things.

We were in his apartment.

"It's over," I told him. "I can't do this."

In response, he threw his television clear across the room. His face was red with anger, and he protested. He laid a hand on me only to hold onto my arm before I yanked it away.

After that, I was in a relationship with an artist/musician who had a dark side when he got drunk. He and I drank a lot when we were together. In fact, we were rarely sober, and, within a couple of months, he became abusive—throwing me up against the wall, pushing me, and pinning me down. As much as I still wanted him, I didn't stick around for any more. Once was enough.

He kept calling, apologizing, and begging me for another chance, but he scared me too much, and I wouldn't risk it.

MELISSA AND ME

Missy was one of my favorite people to hang out with when I wasn't writing. We started a tradition of holiday shopping on Steinway Street in Astoria. The strip had more than two miles of stores, and it was always brightly decorated for Christmas shopping. Year-round, we combed the boutiques for the latest fashions, stopping for lunch at a pizza parlor or buying hot dogs and shish kebabs from street vendors. We'd found our favorite hair salon on Steinway Street—one we patronized for years called *She Goes to Your Head.* Yep.

She and I spent a couple of winter weekends at a dude ranch in the hamlet of Wallkill, New York. Riding a horse over rolling hills and through a sparkling stream was as exhilarating as it was beautiful. We were surrounded by a forest with bald eagles in midflight.

We often vacationed together. We watched the sunrise on Virginia Beach and sat in on a recording session with a rock band in L. A. Our California trip had begun in San Francisco, but before we made it to Disneyland in Anaheim, Melissa and I had a fight. We were waiting for the bus to Knotts Berry Farm.

I remember saying, "You resent me for something. What is it?"

To which she exhaustedly yelled, "I don't resent you!"

We stood ten feet apart, refusing to talk to each other. Frustrated, I went into a deli for a soda. After I paid, I asked the woman behind the counter for a straw, but the way we New Yorkers pronounce it, it rhymes with "law." They didn't understand. My accent does have influences from both of my parents, and cabdrivers often took me for a foreigner, but this was a bit much. They were calling people over to help figure out what I wanted. It was humiliating—me being from America and all.

Melissa came in then to see what was taking so long.

Finally, someone said, "Oh, I know what she wants. A straw!" And she pronounced it *"straaa."*

Melissa busted out in laughter and hugged my side as we hurried out the door. That's how we made up that day.

Despite the many fits of laughter, however, there was one time at an

Oktoberfest near Forest Park when we weren't so happy. A brass band played. People strolled around in colorful Bavarian costumes. A Ferris wheel lit up the night sky, and the aroma of roasted chicken, sausages, and dumplings wafted from the tents to the open air. Despite that and the beer wagons, games, rides, and soft pretzels, my mood switched from gleeful exuberance to sudden and out-of-the-blue sadness. It started with tears and then full-on crying. Seeing me cry, Melissa cried, too.

She and I would hit clubs in midtown and uptown Manhattan. We'd check out the hotspots for artists, hopefuls, and celebrity musicians. We'd been to Studio 54. We went to Trax and CBGB several times.

Trax was so inconspicuous that you'd walk past it more than once before spotting it. CBGB, for those who have never heard of it, was a little club under a flop house in the East Village near Bleeker Street. It was situated in between a cheap hotel and a record shop café. Inside the club, it was darker than the average bar and had an ever-present smoke-filled haze. The bands that performed there played original hardcore punk music, no covers, and they were deafeningly loud.

It was the excitement of the music and the freedom I craved, and of course, the drinking made it even more fun.

Melissa and I saw Broadway shows as well. We attended auto shows and concerts—so many concerts. We'd ride the subway home at two in the morning.

Regrettably, I flipped out at a Rod Stewart concert at Madison Square Garden after doing a hit of THC—another hallucinogenic type drug. Plus, Missy and I were drinking tequila. The arena was packed, with the dark red curtains drawn, and some guys onstage were performing a sound check. I heard clanging and pop sounds, along with the static of a mike and gruff, male voices.

All of a sudden, I decided I wasn't secure in my balcony seat. "I'm going to fall," I whispered to Melissa.

"No, you're not," she said. "How would you fall? You're not going to fall."

I muttered it again once or twice. "I'm going to fall."

It wasn't obvious to anyone else, but I continued to panic, believing I'd either fall out of the seat or jump from there, and I'd be dead when I hit the stage. The visual horrified me, and I was sure I would completely lose my mind, if not my life.

By the time Rod Stewart and his band took the stage, I'd begun to calm down, but the moments in between seemed like hours. I took it as a symbolic warning, and I was pretty much done with street drugs after that.

What I didn't know was, the madness had merely begun.

NICE GUY

At work, I usually went about my business with practiced poise. Now and again, when someone challenged me by being self-serving and ridiculously petty, I became a spitfire dragon, getting my point across in no uncertain terms.

While media news outlets were still covering the Son of Sam serial killer who'd murdered Kristina, one of my supervisors began discussing it with some other employees who'd gathered around my desk. For story purposes, we'll call him Hank.

Hank said, "I can understand how this guy got to the point of wanting to kill women. Sometimes, you say hello to a woman, you're just being nice, and they don't even smile or say hello back. I thought women were flattered by a man's attention and praise, but I'm telling ya—nice guys can't win."

I was livid. "As if that gives someone the right to go on a killing spree and gun down as many women as possible!"

For all I knew, that wasn't even the motive or *sole* motive in the Son of Sam murders, but Hank seemed pretty certain that it was. He talked about men like himself being out of options because beautiful girls weren't interested in him. Yeah, out of options based on *his* standards of attractiveness. Did he ever consider the women who didn't meet those standards? I wondered.

I realized, too, that Hank saw himself as a nice guy even while saying what he said.

He was not a nice guy. There's a considerable difference between genuinely lovely people (which I'd describe more as *kind*) and people who act nice to further a hidden agenda. In the latter case, the "niceness" comes with expectations, and if the recipient of such benevolence isn't receptive, this person becomes, to put it mildly, not so nice. They continue in their attempts to impress, seduce, manipulate, and control until they reach the point where they have no choice but to accept that it's not going to happen. Then they demonize you. At worst, they rape or kill you.

Hank and I argued for a while. He didn't change his position even when I told him that my friend was one of the Son of Sam's victims.

"I mean, when you come to work, don't you want to look good?" he blathered on. "Would you rather someone say you don't or you do?"

"Yes, you want to look good," I said. "You may want to be pretty, too, even sexy. It doesn't necessarily mean you're dangling a line to bait someone."

It's hard to explain it to the "Hanks" of the world, but I sometimes wore a blazer to go out at lunchtime when it was ninety degrees so the catcalling would be less humiliating. People are often of the mindset that busty women are a good target, and that we expect their extravagant approval.

No one is saying women don't enjoy attention, including compliments, or that they don't want anybody flirting with them. Catcalling, however, is usually more than one guy—often a group of guys shouting at you. Their goal, for the most part, is not to get to know you. Their bold and degrading "compliments" are more about power and control, possibly even anger.

Hank said, "How are men supposed to tell the difference between women who want that and women who don't?" He said he thought the way a woman dressed was the signal.

Well, when women don't want that, we try not to make eye contact. We don't respond. We quicken our pace. We may attempt a response or an awkward smile, but everything about our body language is saying, *please leave me alone.* Some men refuse to acknowledge your reaction, or your discomfort amuses them. They don't seem to care if you are humiliated or scared.

I'd been groped in the street twice. One guy followed me for blocks, taunting me, and told me if I didn't like it, I shouldn't wear a tank top. There were witnesses to what happened. They did nothing. It wasn't the only time a guy followed me around the streets, talking to me about sex. And then there were the train incidents.

When these things happen to a woman, it shakes her to her core, so attention from strangers may scare her. It is unfortunate because there are so many genuinely good men, but you don't know who to trust after a while.

"Plenty of guys, regardless of what's on their minds, have figured out how to admire a woman without disrespecting or degrading her," I told Hank that day.

As for flirting, it works when genuinely interested people take their cues from each other—when there's no dehumanizing of the other person and no blatant disrespect. Making someone blush is one thing; making them cringe or fear for their safety is quite another. Whatever two consenting adults enjoy is their business.

It didn't matter what I said to Hank. He didn't get it. The fact that I was even trying to reason with someone who'd defended my friend's executioner defies all logic.

Of course, a woman's anger or protest makes someone with Hank's perspective uncomfortable—maybe even as uncomfortable as many of us are when we go out alone, especially at night or while wearing weather-appropriate clothes.

That's why advocating awareness is a good thing. A message to Hank: If you're not a culprit, you don't have to get defensive on behalf of the culprits. You can listen, without shame or guilt, to the heartache and grief of women everywhere. You have to want to understand and do your part in fixing it. You want to be able to, at least, empathize—put yourself in that person's place. It means dealing with your own issues and your denial. The important thing is that we support each other, so we can happily coexist. That's the answer, as far as I'm concerned—empathy and mutual respect. It's not a contest if we're all on the same side.

PARTY

It happened at a small ad agency where I'd worked for six months after leaving the publishing firm. There were less than twenty employees, and I was an executive secretary to the president and the two vice presidents.

My birthday came along while I was still new, and someone led me into a conference room full of people who yelled, "Surprise!"

It was primarily men. The receptionist handed me a knife to cut the cake—a cake I'd barely caught a glimpse of, but the knife glistened. I didn't reach out to take it. Alarmed, I glanced from face to face. The room, while holding at least ten people, felt entirely too small. Everyone stood too close to me. The nearest man smoked a cigar, so the room had a cedar smell and puffy clouds. His wide grin appeared deceptively sinister like in one of those dreams when you figure out who the bad guy is, and he suddenly realizes you suspect him.

My response was purely emotional—this suffocating fearfulness of being confined in a small space with men I didn't know. Waves of trepidation became so unbearably intense that, without hesitation, I dashed right out the door.

It was near the end of the day, so I retrieved my shoulder bag from my desk drawer and quickly left the building. No one came after me. Undoubtedly, they were shocked and disappointed, and I thought, *If I even dare to return, I'll probably get fired.*

With that in mind, I scurried along the streets of Manhattan with downcast eyes, loathing myself. As a native New Yorker, I'd quickly learned to swerve, duck, slip, and slide through leisurely mobs of people. Three nights a week I had classes at CCNY after work, but not *that* night.

My mother was home when I arrived, and I told her what had happened.

"That was nice of them," she said. "You could have had a piece of cake. They went to all that trouble…"

"Mom, that's just it. I *couldn't* have a piece of cake." My frustration was obvious. "I couldn't even *stand* there. It was unbearable."

"Yeah, but you should have said thank you and—"

"Well, I understand I was wrong to leave, but—" I sat at the kitchen table and started to cry. "Am I crazy?"

She moved in and hugged me, holding me close to her bosom. "You're not crazy, no."

"You are the one who always believed in me," I lamented. "I can't imagine how you could have loved me all this time. Even when I was little. I was such an ugly freak!"

"Ah, come on," she replied. "You were not ugly—ever. You were a beautiful girl, so cute and sweet—such a doll. And you still are. When you were small, there was something about you—you were very lovable. You would come to me and give me a hug. I felt that love from my little girl. You were always reaching out to hug or hugging your dolls. So, don't say that, please. I am not good with words the way you are, but you mean the world to me and to everyone you love. I love you, always."

I hugged her tight. "What would you have done if you were me?" It was a silly question to ask. She wasn't me, and I already knew what normal people would've done.

She backed away and appeared to study me. Her smile was kind. "I would have cut the cake and had a ball. Listen, they'll forget about it. Go there and do your thing. What's done is done. Next time, you'll do better."

At dinner that night, I complained about the job. "My boss asks me to make coffee when I'm in the middle of a rush job. Meanwhile, the men are standing around doing nothing but talking."

My dad was appalled. "You mean to say, if there were no women in this world, nobody would drink coffee? You should've told him to make it himself. If that happens again, here's what you do—make mud. Or put ten lumps of sugar in the cup and say, 'Here you are.' That'll fix him." He winked.

"Don't tell her that," my mother implored. "She'll lose her job."

He waved it off with disgust. "Why? She doesn't go there to be no goddamn housewife! You heard her say they got guys standing around there doing nothing, and they bother her when she's working. She doesn't even drink coffee there!"

He was yelling now. "She drinks coffee only here in the morning when I make it for her! Besides, from what she says, he's some goofy ball, that guy."

"It's *goofball*, Dad," Bridget corrected him.

"Yeah, what the heck's a goofy ball?" That was Melissa.

We laughed ourselves to tears, including my mother, whose shoulders shook a little when she laughed.

"And I'm gonna tell *you* the same thing, goofball, when you sit on your ass and keep bugging me," my mother said to him.

Now he laughed, too.

Much to my relief, my grand return to work was uneventful. After hanging my coat, I peeked into the conference room. It was empty. Did I half expect the whole scene with the cake and the knife to have paused and waited for my return? I was so self-absorbed. People went about their business as if it never happened. There were greetings, but nobody asked where I'd gone or why. I suppose I was glad about that. The boss plopped work on my desk—a rush job.

So, I hadn't shattered the earth—or even put a dent in it, really.

VOGUE

A client at the ad agency wanted to use me as the model in a print ad for pajamas.

I overheard the conversation, and one of my bosses said, "I don't know. She might resent my asking, not wanting to be looked at that way."

Another time, Frank "Frankie" Basso, the agency's casting director, shimmied over to me. "We're doing a four-color print ad for a new client," he said. "We'll have a model in a leotard and tights wearing a top hat. She'll be standing between two male models, arm-in-arm, kicking her leg in the air. Want to do it?"

"Do what?" I played dumb.

"Be the model."

"Why?" I asked him.

"Why not?"

"The guys who work here? I don't want to parade in front of them in a leotard and tights." I took a moment to process that. "You know, at one time, I would have thought I could do that kind of stuff, but now? I just want to be appreciated for my mind."

He laughed. Frankie was a cute, pudgy guy in his early forties with dark balding hair and a mustache. He was always endearing when he displayed his amusement.

"What's so funny?" I demanded.

His dark eyes twinkled with merriment. "What do you think your image is? A serious-looking plain Jane? That's not your image."

"Okay, but why do people assume every woman wants to be a model? Many of us do have other goals and aspirations. Not that modeling is a bad thing if that's what someone wants to do; it's just crazy when people keep telling you that you should."

"I'm sure it's used as a pickup line," he said, laughing.

My eyes widened. "Ya think?"

"Yeah, but I'm in the business. I'm a happily married man not looking to hit on you, and I'm asking as a professional. I'll give you the same fee we'd pay any model. That's $500 an hour."

"No."

He bit his lower lip and stared, but then he shook his head and smiled. "You're crazy." Someone called him then, which typically happened in the middle of conversations with him. As usual, he took off to respond.

Frankie didn't realize that I didn't relate to being beautiful and never would. It was odd, too, that he never mentioned my lazy eye. My mom said it was only noticeable when I was tired and not wearing eye make-up, but, even then, not that much. Besides, there were some famous models and actors who had the same thing. They never bothered with corrective surgery, and I'd never deny that they were still beautiful, but I didn't think the same was true for me. I was the awkward, insecure kid hiding behind fashion and makeup, still vulnerable and naïve.

Frankie was a good guy, though. He had a heart of gold, and he was funny. Everyone loved him. *I* loved him.

He gave me a rare opportunity to be on the other side of things by assigning me to work with the art director. The art director taught me how to hire photographers for an ad, and I helped him plan an upcoming shoot. Meanwhile, Frankie trained me to assist him in hiring models, to pore over headshot sheets, contact certain ones, and tell them to bring in their portfolios, at which time I'd have them do that dreaded spin around to show off their assets.

The first and only time I went on a shoot, I rode with Frankie, the photographer, and two models. The woman, a beauty with long red hair and sparkling blue eyes, was terrified and feeling insecure. The male model was tall, handsome, blond, friendly, and quite sure of himself. Frankie told me to talk to the young woman, to keep her calm, and to help her with whatever she needed. I did, and she seemed to relax.

Unfortunately, the client didn't like how the pictures turned out. He decided they wanted the guy but a different female model and a reshoot. The gorgeous redhead cried when she found out at our offices, and I remember hugging her. The good news is she went on to act in primetime television shows and did pretty well for herself. And I saw the male model in a 7 Up commercial.

SESSIONS WITH STAVROS

The notion that I was in serious need of therapy first dawned on me when I was just sixteen. Something was wrong with me, or rather, a lot was wrong with me, and now that I'd reached the age of twenty, I couldn't put it off any longer.

Dr. Stavros Diakos was a highly recommended West Village psychiatrist. Whatever insurance I had didn't cover therapy, so I paid out of pocket for two sessions a month.

I was nervous while I sat, for the first time, in the waiting room of his first-floor office—twiddling my thumbs as I observed the lush palm in a brass urn and the framed contemporary prints. The lighting was soft, the music of Beethoven soothing, but none of it helped. I couldn't bring myself to take one of the magazines organized on a rack and read it.

For some reason, I pictured Dr. Diakos as a white-haired sage like Obi-Wan Kenobi. I half expected him to drift out the door of his office in a long robe or cloak.

I heard muffled voices behind the single closed door, and then the voices grew louder. They were saying their goodbyes. The first to emerge was a thickset man with glasses who glanced in my direction. Dr. Diakos followed—a clean-shaven, smartly dressed man in a collared shirt and tie with dress trousers. He was maybe five-eight and fairly attractive with his brown hair in a businessman's cut.

Before the other patient reached the exit door, Dr. Diakos's big, brown eyes were upon me. "Diane?" He spoke with a Greek accent and was both gracious and disarming when I stood to shake his hand. "I am Stavros. It's a pleasure to meet you. Come on in."

Filled with trepidation, I followed him. Inside the office, he filled a small paper cup from a water cooler. "Would you care for some?"

"No, thank you." I sank into the comfortable high-back armchair facing his desk.

He drank quickly from the cup and then tossed it into a wastebasket before taking his seat.

The office was neat and organized, with numerous framed degrees, nature-inspired wall art, and several well-nourished plants.

Stavros gazed undeviatingly into my eyes. "So, Diane, how are you today?" He had a pleasant face. His wide smile was warm and reached his eyes.

"I'm okay."

"Good!" He relaxed into his chair. "What brings you here?"

He steepled his fingers while I talked at length about my life and family, and, when I was done, he drew many startling conclusions.

"It seems everyone in your family wanted the attention of the patriarch and to have more of it than the others. Your mom went about it by putting firm boundaries on your relationships with him as if he was a predator, and you were baiting him as his prey. Bridget went about getting his attention by taking the direct route of getting into trouble and always getting caught. She also manipulates with divide-and-conquer strategies, pitting one against the other. Melissa pleases your father. She is his little angel, so to speak. You were at a loss to compete with all of that. So, you devised a brilliant scheme of your own, one you are not even aware of. You set out to make yourself special, seductive in every conceivable way—not just to your father but to all."

I shook my head. "But I'm not usually trying to seduce anyone, especially not—"

"Seduction is not only physical, Diane," he said quickly. "At home, you became, more or less, the helpless child. What parent can resist being needed, especially by older teen children and young adult children who begin to come and go with barely a nod in their direction? Your sisters were age-appropriately independent, but you continued to need them. You created the perfect balance of, 'I need you, and I am always here for you,' and 'Now, I don't need you.' You turn hot and cold, give them a taste, and then take it away. Now, they crave it.

"Your doing this was not intentional, but it was a mastermind, genius plan, and you can hold the family together as easily as you can tear it apart. This is why you've become the most difficult to resist and, perhaps, the most resented."

"I'm confused," I said.

"Okay," he continued. "We will explore that more in future sessions. The seduction, however, has progressed beyond your family to the world. It has become prevalent in your voice, in the way you move, dress, stand, sit, talk, use your eyes, lips, and, perhaps, other attributes. I noticed this immediately about you. You may not be aware of it, but it is all designed to seduce, and seduction is always your power, your weapon. In this way, you can collect and conquer, perhaps trap others in your web. Everything you exude, Diane, has been created and designed by you to make you unique and to ensure that you will stand out and be noticed."

I was stunned throughout this revelation—and a bit skeptical. He came across to me as having the ready answers before deeply examining the questions. It was odd how, at the same time, there was a twisted sense of validation, relief, and shame. It made me feel more naked, more vulnerable. I resented it, and it saddened me. I wasn't quite sure about the other stuff, but it was true that I wanted men to find me attractive and to want me, although the feeling wasn't usually mutual. Wasn't that true for all women? It was probably true for men as well.

"Tell me what you are thinking in response to this, Diane," he said. "Do you feel this is accurate? Inaccurate? Unfair?"

"I told you: What you see now is not who I've been most of my life. I was a prude and really innocent for the longest time."

Stavros nodded. "A lot has happened in the past few years; I am certain. Perhaps it has made you angrier, more determined, more rebellious. You have felt defeated, discouraged, and disillusioned, which has intensified that need to be special." He seemed amused, adding, "You have brought out the complete arsenal of ammunition." He paused then, studying me. "What we are going to do here is take away that need to be special. We will get beneath all that and find out who the real Diane is."

That scared the hell out of me. Of course, I understand now that my desperation to be special was a quest to prove myself worthy and good enough for the world. I had an inferiority complex flipped inside out and, thus, a superiority complex—two sides of the same coin. Although unaware at the time, I lived in bondage to my ego and the rewards reaped from my behavior, so I didn't want anything to change.

It's clear to me now where he was heading with his observations.

Reading and participating in narcissistic abuse recovery groups over the years has taught me that there's a difference between people with full-blown narcissistic personality disorder and those who get "fleas" from narcissistic abuse—the latter having acquired the narcissistic abuser's strategies and behaviors to cope and survive. There's a spectrum, I believe, with varying degrees of impact. Some narcissistic abuse survivors don't seem to exhibit any of the behavior they were subjected to, while others appear to have inherited every trace of it.

Personally, I believe I topped out somewhere in the midrange of that spectrum, and what I'd ultimately learn about this subject was essential to my recovery.

I've found that narcissistic abusers and many of their victims tend to become ashamed of who they are. As a result, they manufacture an image of who they want to be. That's where the obsession with one's self-image develops—and whatever the narcissist stands for becomes part of that façade. It becomes necessary for them to buy into and sell their superiority because, in the narcissist's conscious or subconscious mind, there is no in-between when it comes to superiority and inferiority. Equal isn't an option, and they don't want anyone to see them as inferior. Damage control becomes a survival strategy and an automatic response to any threat to the ideology that comforts and, quite frankly, saves them.

The continuous derailment in my life had so much to do with this perspective. Motivated by insecurity, fear, and habit, I was oblivious to what caused me to act the way I did. I never saw the trains coming. And sometimes I *was* that train coming. So, I've had to work hard to unlearn the narcissistic behavior acquired from my experiences, and I will continue to do that for the rest of my life.

I should point out, too, that while Stavros seemed to have gotten the impression that my mother's firm boundaries when it came to my father were due to jealousy and a sense of competitiveness, I ultimately came to realize that my mother was protecting us.

There were many indications that whatever my mother experienced in her childhood had led her to a hypervigilant distrust of men when it came to her daughters, and I'm not even sure she was fully aware of it. My mother loved and trusted my father more than any other man, but she never wholly relaxed her concerns about him. She clearly tried to steer us away from provoking his anger. And I think she harbored subconscious thoughts that men were a certain way by nature, and you didn't want to create situations that were even remotely tempting for them.

Nevertheless, I share this and other sessions with Stavros in this book primarily because he was the first to effectively plant the seeds of my recovery.

CONTINUED SESSIONS

"How do you define that by way of category?" I asked Stavros once. "I mean, what am I suffering from in medical terms?"

"Ah!" Once again, I had amused him. "You would very much like me to give you a category. That way, you can attach another label to yourself to set yourself apart from others. A category in those terms would acknowledge you as different and somehow special. But I do not think of you in that way, with a label attached. I see you, Diane, as a woman and an individual. My purpose is to get beneath the labels you have designed for yourself."

Again, with the "getting beneath that." I hated any mention of the task. But these sessions with the charismatic sage were jaw dropping.

When I was more relaxed with him, I told him how I'd often asked several people for their opinions on things when I wasn't sure what to do.

"You find it necessary to take a poll," he concluded. "Do you not have faith in your assessments or judgment?"

I responded with a shrug.

"Have you been contradicted a lot in the past? How often would you say your perception was accurate and someone insisted you were wrong? Somehow, maybe, your reality was reconstructed or denied to the point where you don't trust yourself."

The issue of body dysmorphia arose, as well. No surprise was evident on Stavros's face when I described those experiences to him, the time spent on improving my looks, and how I'd see only the ugly or beautiful face in the mirror.

"The seduction thing has become exhausting for you," he said. "You look into a mirror, and you cannot see anything but perfection or something of a horror. Okay, that is the same as when you describe yourself as having been the ugly duckling as a child, whereas, in adulthood, you have emerged as the beautiful swan. But neither extreme exists. There is no perfection, and you could not have been so terrible a vision as a child. Both are fantasies."

It was a gut punch, necessitating a deep swallow before asking the next question. "Do you mean that if I appear beautiful in the mirror, it isn't real?"

"Well, there is no denying that you are an attractive woman with a good figure, a very pretty girl," he said. "I am sure when men tell you that you are beautiful, you appear that way to them and others. But the image of perfection is not real. The perception of yourself as a grotesque child and the pathetic face staring back at you in the mirror, it is a fantasy. Why you have those fantasies has something to do with the need you have to be special, to be different, and to be the best."

I supposed I had the impression that by becoming physically irresistible, I'd get people to protect and care about me, but it was still mind-blowing.

"It is part of the quest for perfection," he explained, "and it leads to an attack of anxiety for you. Deep down, you realize, this quest is a futile one. It also is another thing that sets you apart from others and makes you different from them. It isolates you, and you constantly devise ways to achieve that aloneness. You are a writer. What could be more isolating than that?"

"That's my destiny," I protested.

"Ah, yes, but it is your choice just the same. You would not have it any other way. You had opportunities to be a model or, perhaps, a singer. You are not comfortable in those roles that will put you out there on a stage with others and, also, in a much more brutal light, exposing you to reality itself."

It amazed me how someone with such an appealing old-world charm managed to piss me off half the time. He truly impressed me.

Stavros was the first person I confided in about having children.

"I'm not sure I could ever have a child," I said. "It's an ambiguous stance I take because I actually fantasize about what I will name my children. I imagine those little eyes peering up at me in total innocence, depending on me to teach them everything they need to know to survive, trusting me to make it a good life, and having a bewildered expression when something bad happens. God, I would die if he or she weren't happy! That would be so heartbreaking and painful. I couldn't bear the thought of that precious child going through a lot of what I experienced."

He appeared sympathetic. "You feel that way, Diane, because you have not dealt with your own pain. You have crystallized it and will project it onto the person you care the most about at any given time. That means you must deal with it. You have to deal with it, so you can teach your little ones to deal with it, too."

Those words made me cry.

At the time, seeing Stavros and going to school after work meant getting home as late as nine p.m. on some nights. A familiar feeling of panic and anxiety would take control as I emerged from the subway station. I'd rush down two flights of stairs, cross another platform, trudge up a hill, go two more blocks straight, and then cross the street on Woodside Avenue. I held mace in one hand and hid an emergency siren in the pocket of my coat near the other hand. I faced the traffic flow, looking ahead and to the sides, frequently peering over my shoulders. The avenue was quiet at this time—the side streets a dark and silent graveyard. Quite often, startled by the rustling of leaves, I decided to run.

When I talked about it with Stavros, he was, as usual, quick with observations.

"The darkness flashes on and off in your subconscious as if it was a reminder of some wicked fate that awaits you, but I do not think it's indicative of any fear you have of being attacked. Tell me. What do you associate with your fear when you walk the streets at night? For example, do you envision being attacked? Does that come to mind, or is your preoccupation with the darkness itself?"

"I don't envision being attacked."

"Was there ever a time, Diane, when you were not afraid of darkness?"

I shrugged. "In the womb, I guess. But who knows?"

He laughed heartily. Suddenly, the lights flickered. He rose, but the lights steadied the moment he stood.

"Ghosts, maybe," he joked, laughing again.

I wasn't as amused.

"But you don't picture an attacker, someone attempting to grab your purse or pull you? Grab you? You don't picture anything in your mind when you are running?"

"Nope."

He paused before concluding, "So, you are running, and you do not know from what or whom."

"Wow." It took me a while to process that. Eventually, I let out a deep sigh and said, "I just want to stay home."

He grinned. "Not home, Diane, in a cage—maybe one with wires and bars where only you control who enters and who speaks to you or touches you. You want to be protected. Even at home, you want that, and this is not a criticism. It is an observation."

In retrospect, I'm not sure he understood why I'd developed such an intense obsession with feeling safe. But he did seem to grasp how powerful that need was, while I remained oblivious. I had yet to acknowledge that I consistently rejected reality—preferring fantasy, delusion, and a false sense of calm or any manufactured euphoria which, ironically, wasn't safe. I also hid from others, not because I didn't care. I just cared too much, and it hurt.

MIXED EMOTIONS

It was just me and my parents that night. My mom wore her apron over shorts and a sleeveless top. My dad, wearing a button-down, short-sleeved shirt, was already at the table, grinning and hungry. Steaks sizzled in the broiler, while an invigorating breeze fluttered in from the open windows. I wiped the plastic over the floral tablecloth. My dad popped the wine cork. Soon, the table was set, our food was the centerpiece, and the two of them clinked their wine-filled goblets with a customary, "Salute."

They seemed happy during the meal. It was the perfect time to ask them if I could move out on my own.

"No daughter of mine moves out of this house until she's married!" my father bellowed.

"Any woman who lives alone will never find a man," my mother chimed in. "A decent man doesn't want a woman like that. They know what goes on."

We had different ideas about what a decent man was.

I'm sure my expression was pained. "What are you talking about? You were not married when you first came here!" Did she have *amnesia* or something?

My father smiled with a surprising look of compassion in his eyes. "Her sister was like a mother to her. She supported her and took care of her. It was a whole different thing."

Well, my mom *had* been a bit lost and confused when she first came to America. That time we visited Havana, Cuban officials detained her at the airport because she was still a Cuban citizen. It took a while, but, finally, in her nervous frustration, she told them she was married to a U. S. citizen. My dad had to fly to Cuba from the States with the documentation to bring us all home. She was always fuzzy about her history as well. She knew only that her parents were from Spain and ended up in Cuba, where she was born.

"Right," she said now. "A man isn't going to buy the cow if the milk is free."

I shook my head. "Nobody says that anymore! And who says women living on their own are giving away anything? Besides, men go around giving out free stuff all they want. I don't have to go out and buy a cow, either."

With that came the rattling call of our cuckoo clock above the china cabinet. The yellow wooden bird popped out seven times.

My father's pleasant smile lingered. "Stay here," he said. "We want you here. You're no trouble. All I ever asked is that you make something of your life. We don't deprive you of anything, do we? You know, they say, 'The grass is always greener.'" He nodded. "Same as when you have a good job—right away, you want to quit."

A weighted feeling coursed through my body. "Uh, that wasn't a good job I had before this one."

He flashed a wide grin. "Heh! It's not a good job. And the one before that was not a good job. You change jobs like you change clothes."

"I plan to cook and everything," I said. "I want to learn."

"So, who the hell's stopping you? Your mother can show you how. Your grandmother can show you, too, if you want to learn."

"Grandma! When I ask her how she made something, she just tells me she 'banga the eggs' and that's it. Besides, everything I do here is wrong. If I wash the dishes, I'm holding the dishes too high. Mommy says I throw water all over the floor."

"You do," my mother replied with a smirk.

My father chuckled. "Heh, you take ten minutes to wash one dish."

My mother cackled before she stood and came around to give me a squeeze. "You're my little girl. You could stay forever for all I care."

"I don't say forever!" My father threw in. "She can take however much time she needs, but you can't expect her to stay here forever."

They tugged at my heartstrings. I didn't want to hurt them, and I didn't want to get married.

I mean, I was always a romantic soul—a poet at heart. I've always loved seeing devoted couples happily growing old together. As a little girl, I saw *Rodgers and Hammerstein's Cinderella* and fell madly in love with Prince Charming. Songs from that musical are still on my iPod, right along with soul, rock, pop, metal, Latin, bachata, and classical music. When Princess Diana married Prince Charles, I was glued to the television set. Yes, bring on the pageantry and the pomp and circumstance—I love it. Take me back in time to the Renaissance in romantic Rome, or to medieval times, or the fascinating Victorian era—royal palaces, minstrels, moats, hungry dragons, swordplay. Yes, it's all fantastic! Horse-pulled carriages, knights, and chivalry—even the whispery-soft and floaty gowns women used to wear with their long, meticulously curled hair.

What I loved, with all of these things was the *fantasy*. When it came to being the center of attention on a single day of nonstop pressure, my attitude became *You go ahead; I'll watch. Maybe I'll even cry tears of joy for you.* As for me, I had other plans.

Nevertheless, I knew I had to move out of there before I completely lost my mind.

APPREHENSIVE AND CONFUSED

My latest job was as an administrative assistant in the new technology department of another New York City publishing company. Wendy Carlson, a short, blonde woman with a pixie haircut and green eyes behind clear-framed glasses, sat at a nearby desk. She and I frequently ate lunch together, sometimes with a few other people. She invited me to dinner at her new apartment shortly after she'd moved in, admitting she still had a lot of unpacking to do.

"I don't want to impose," I said. "You're not settled yet."

She dismissed that with a wave of her hand. "Believe me, you wouldn't be imposing. I can certainly ignore the boxes if you can." She grinned. "I'll make us some fried cutlets, some veggies. We'll have wine or whatever. It'll be fun. If you're worried about traveling back, you can stay over for the night. No big deal."

"I'll let you get settled first," was my final response. And then I changed the subject.

When I talked about that in a session with Stavros, he appeared sympathetic. "Understand, Diane, when you attempt to give your heart in friendship, you come already very skeptical from experience. Part of you feels abandoned by friends of the past. You really do not trust anyone, whether you think you do or not. You do not trust even yourself."

I sighed, disappointed. "She seems nice. I'm just afraid of being wrong again. I haven't been a good judge of character. On the other hand, I don't want to miss an opportunity to have or be a good friend."

"I am sure that's true," he said, "but you also cannot accept she wants to have you for a friend and will want that more as you become closer. You feel unworthy of her friendship—of any friendship with another woman. The closer she gets, the more you fear she will discover you are not worthy. I believe you are progressing at your own pace, and it is with utmost care and consideration that you must be led onto the next step. Wendy, not knowing that, moved quickly, and I am not surprised that you, uh, blocked that. You were not ready."

He produced the pipe he sometimes smoked, lit it, and continued.

"When she suggests, for your peace of mind, that you would not be imposing, you don't take her at her word. It is a handy excuse that she isn't settled into her new place. She has reached out to you and is offering friendship. Let me put it this way. If I were to go to someone's home, Diane, and they asked me if I would care for something to drink, I will say, 'Yes, thank you.' If they ask would I like to have a Coke, and I want to have that, I would not glance into the refrigerator and say, 'Oh, I see you have only one. Keep it for yourself.'"

I laughed.

"The important thing here is to respond when someone reaches out to you. That is what keeps the steady flow of responding to one another, because everyone has, to some degree, the fear of rejection. If she asks you to come, why worry about inconveniencing her? She should not have offered that if she could not accommodate you. I am quite sure she would not have.

"Perhaps if you felt really it would be an imposition, you may have offered to help prepare the meal or something. If it was not convenient for you to spend the night, you had simply to say, 'Well, I cannot do that, but perhaps we can do it another time.' And you plan some alternative. If someone puts up a block, it discourages the person who extended the effort. They may not want to reach out the next time."

Oh, well.

Wendy and I had a tense but friendly relationship from then on. We were similarly enchanted by a man named Ian Taylor, an executive from our subsidiary office in London. Women swooned over Ian whenever he came for a temporary stay at our offices. He was handsome—five-nine with a nice build. He wore his light brown hair in a businessman's cut, donned elegant suits, and his accent was divine.

As a fan of nineteenth-century British literature, British rock bands, and possibly all things British at the time, I may have been considered an anglophile. I almost booked a writer's tour to visit London and the Swiss chalet in Rochester, Kent, where Dickens wrote many of his books. So, when my boss, Dr. Alden, asked me to deliver copies of memos and reports to Ian while he occupied one of the offices near my workstation, I jumped at the chance.

The sight of him alone caused a butterfly swarm to go wild with my furiously pounding heart. He looked up from his desk with pale blue eyes and prominent cheekbones, and I could barely speak. Though he was gracious and kind with his shy, slightly hesitant smile, it took me a while to relax in his presence. After that, I found what I thought was an ideal way to initiate further interaction. The protagonist in my novel at that time was a teenage boy from England, and I told Ian I'd love to consult with him.

He was returning to England the next day (it figures that would happen by the time I summoned the courage), but he gave me his address to write to him and ask any questions I wanted. Just like in the book, *84, Charing Cross Road*, we exchanged letter after letter. We shared a mutual love for many of the same authors, so, around Christmastime, he sent me a present—a tiny, adorable book about Charles Dickens, and he'd signed it *Love, Ian.*

Oh, I did love him; I was sure of that. I was over the moon, as they say, somewhere between infatuation and obsession. He was ten years older than me, but I found him incredibly sexy. Unfortunately, he was 3,000 miles away and a busy man who would ultimately rise in the ranks to Vice President. It seemed he'd never be more than a fantasy.

In the meantime, I met Blaise.

Blaise was tall, dark, and handsome, with slicked-back hair in a short, tidy style and a big, bright, and beautiful smile. More importantly, he struck me as humble and kind—an absolute sweetheart.

We certainly enjoyed each other's company—often visiting his sister and her husband. I was impressed by their heartwarming colonial home and endless backyard as well as the sheer coziness of their lives. We ate cheese and crackers, drank rum and Coke, and, every so often, enjoyed a roast beef dinner or something equally scrumptious. They had a golden retriever named Tansy, and, soon, a newborn baby boy. Tansy and the baby loved me, and that made me happy.

The first time Blaise came to *my* house, he noticed all of the books on the shelves in my room and said, "If I were you, I'd burn every single one of those occult books."

"Why?" I asked. "I read them already."

"They're evil books," he said, "and whether you read them or not, you're receiving subliminal messages."

"Do I act like I'm receiving subliminal messages?" I was always the curious one.

"No," he replied. "But if you're not going to burn them, at least, get rid of them—including that cat statue with the glowing green eyes."

I wanted to laugh at that, and I certainly didn't agree. At the same time, I figured, given what had happened in my life thus far, what did I have to lose? If it held any promise of keeping me solid, sane, and on the right path, I'd do it, sure. I'd get rid of them.

Blaise was encouraging and supportive when I submitted my manuscript to Random House, and he was easy to love in the limited way I knew how to love then. Without meaning or wanting to, I became as dependent on his company as he was on mine. Of course, by then, Ian and I were no longer exchanging letters.

I spoke to Stavros about it. "You said I was out to seduce the whole world, but all I want is Blaise."

"At the *moment*, Diane," he replied with a smirk.

"No!" I was unyielding in my conviction. "Okay, I saw this poem once. Actually, I don't remember if it was a card or a letter—probably a card. Anyway, it said something like, 'All I ever wanted was that one person to say, you are all I ever need or want. I would not cry if you walked away—I would die.'"

My eyes filled with tears. "I want to feel that way about someone. It's something I've never felt."

"And still don't," he said. "Perhaps a part of you, a very deep part, may long for this, but it is not currently a part of your agenda, Diane, for that is not what you seek. You are seeking not really to pierce the heart of that one true love, but rather to seduce the whole world, and this is what we have been learning here—the reasons behind that."

"There is that part of me who wants to be that special angel written about in songs—the one they saw crying in the rain," I said. "The one who inspires the greatest love and most undying loyalty. I think she'd be wearing a floaty white dress." I continued with a smile.

He knew I was somewhat exaggerating. "Oh, yes, and a fedora."

I went with it. "She'd be smart enough to carry a sun parasol."

"Yes, *Mary Poppins*," he said.

I laughed heartily at that.

His gaze was intense. "So, more simply put, you are conflicted."

I laughed again.

"You act amused, but you are angry," he said.

"No, I dealt with what happened to me, if that's what you mean."

"It really hasn't been that long, Diane. Perhaps you're still shell-shocked and often relive the fear and helplessness."

This session was probably my last with Stavros because he didn't think I should develop a serious relationship with Blaise. He knew it was not a good idea, and I didn't want to believe him. What he had discovered about me thus far overwhelmed me. I think, too, I wasn't quite ready for whatever else he might uncover about me.

Two months later, I did it. Out of the blue, I married Blaise at City Hall.

MARRIAGE AND MODELING

Blaise and I honeymooned in Barbados. It was fun, even though I should have realized that we'd be riding with English saddles when we opted to ride horses across a sugarcane plantation. I was used to the heavier, more comfortable western saddle. And although it was always about eighty-five degrees in Barbados, I never should have worn sneakers and shorts. The sun felt close enough to incinerate me, and the horse often lagged because I didn't kick hard enough with my sneakers.

When we returned, the footstool I'd used to mount the horse wasn't there, so in my clumsy dismount, I managed to kick the horse hard enough to get him running, with me hanging off the side and clinging for dear life to the saddle.

Ranch hands yelled, "Whoa!" Together, they raced to rescue me, and I'm not sure if I was more humiliated or more scared out of my wits.

When we returned from our honeymoon, Blaise and I moved straight into the basement of his brother's house in southwestern Queens. We made it cozy with a beige microfiber sleeper sofa, a dusty rose area rug, my bedroom stereo system and Sony TV, comfy quilts, and a kerosene heater.

We bought two dwarf parrots from a Jamaica Avenue pet shop. They were parrotlets from the South American Amazon rainforest—bright green little creatures with pale blue foreheads and yellow-green bellies. We named them Pip and Nicholas after characters in the Charles Dickens novels. I was crazy about them both but especially partial to Nicholas. Before we got him, someone had clipped his wings so badly that he couldn't fly.

We had a good-sized fish tank. Blaise bought Siamese fighting fish (my favorite), angelfish, guppies, and pink kissing gourami fish. He made a beautiful home for them with coral, rocks, and driftwood, and he knew how to manage them when problems arose.

He and I cooked basic meals at first. Then I tried making my mom's arroz con pollo, getting directions from her over the phone.

I'll try to rehash the conversation.

"Mom, how much garlic?"

"Yes."

"How much?"

"The whole thing."

"The whole thing? This entire thing?"

"Yeah."

I later learned "the whole thing" to her was one clove, not one bunch. Needless to say, I used way too much garlic.

The second time I made it, we had Blaise's sister and her family over as a thank-you for the many times she'd had us over for dinner. All I had to work with was a two-burner plug-in stove, and I was nervous, so I kept drinking tequila. After it was done, I got sick and made a beeline for the bathroom while Blaise served the meal. I couldn't puke, but I sat on the floor for a while, leaning against the wall, with my hand over my stomach.

I was totally drunk. The room spun. And when I joined the others, they raved about how delicious the meal was, eagerly opting for seconds. I couldn't believe it, but of course, I was thrilled.

During this time, Blaise supported my brief experiment with modeling. Yeah, even though it wasn't something I ever wanted to do, people continued to suggest it, so I caved.

The funny thing is that when you actually become the thing people say you should become—the model, the writer, or whatever—the comments shift from "You should do it," to "Why do you think you're *good enough* to do it? Who do you think you are?" It triggers your fears about shame and rejection because, at least for me, there was always that little person inside me who suspected I was deluding myself about everything.

When I showed up at nine a. M. on the first day of my portfolio shoot sans makeup, the photographer said, "Look at you! You're a natural beauty! Even your ears are perfect!"

But then I was made up to the point where I barely recognized myself in the mirror. "You look fabulous," she assured me. "And you *will* look like yourself in the photos. Trust me. Photography is tricky that way."

Model photographers adjust you constantly while they photograph you. "Okay, don't move," they say. "Stay exactly like that." Minutes seem like hours. Or maybe they constantly adjusted me because I didn't stay still. But there was no doubt that I was uncomfortable, insecure, and still such a puritan despite all of my rebelliousness.

Another model told me, "Clients and photographers do not like 'difficult.' You have to be 'on' all the time—cheerful. If they say you're going in a canoe for this shoot, you must show up on time, hop aboard, and be thrilled."

Well, I knew for sure that wasn't me.

My portfolio photographer met me at the U. N. Plaza when the proofs arrived, and we had lunch at a nearby coffee shop while trading photo slides. We held each one up to the light to examine it. While she marveled, I cringed. She arranged my photos in a nine-by-twelve portfolio case I had picked up at Sam Flax, but whenever I combed through the book, I failed to see the "beauty" she saw.

Of course, the beauty industry encourages this unattainable illusion of flawlessness, and back then, I embraced it. I mean there's not a thing wrong with wanting to be attractive, and modeling is great, but I'm sure most people agree that merely having a coveted look doesn't amount to much.

Beauty, after all, is so much more than that. It comes with wisdom, compassion, and generosity. It's a grin or a laugh, something in a person's eyes —a certain radiance that bursts from a person's heart because they are so full of laughter and love. It's about the things people say and do. It's about one's essence, signature style, and, yes, their endearing imperfections!

With men, that was always clear to me. It took me longer to understand that the same was true for women, including me.

A FINE MESS

D r. Alden was a chemist who'd also worked as a book editor. He was this intense little bespectacled scientist. When I received my first rejection slip (from Random House), I sat in the chair across from his desk and talked to him about it.

"I give them a book I spent years writing, and they send it back to me with one word—rejected. They didn't even give me any reason. I want to have some idea of where to go from here. I wish they'd told me why."

Dr. Alden leaned back and put his feet on his desk, the way he often did whenever he dictated assignments. He was curious, too, and loved to talk rather than work, so he'd take breaks to ask a million questions.

"Well, you're a writer, so write them a letter," he said. "It'll be a testament to your talent if you can persuade them to respond."

"You sure?" I asked.

"Why not?" He shrugged. "They're busy people. They're not going to send every author an explanation, but maybe if you ask—"

"What do I say?"

"Say exactly what you told me, but as politely as you can."

I took his suggestion and got a response.

"It's publishable. The problem is you root for this kid throughout the book, and in the end, he simply gives up. Consider reconstructing it and going with a conclusion that will be more satisfying to the reader. Have him live and succeed. If you decide to do that, we'll be happy to read it again."

Of course, I was thrilled about getting a response, and that they called my book publishable. At the same time, I was crushed by the recommendation to change my story.

"I would not have written this book if he survived," I lamented. "The whole point was that he didn't."

Stubborn as ever, I was.

Grateful for Dr. Alden's sage advice, however, I'd initiated a tradition of gifting him a bottle of my dad's homemade wine every Christmas. He was delighted.

I was also grateful to Dr. Alden because he'd discovered my knack for new technology. He sent me to seminars and workshops and made me a computer system administrator in addition to whatever clerical work I did for him. My duties pulled me every which way—teaching the support staff and department heads new programs, performing small group demonstrations, and general troubleshooting. And what I did wasn't exclusively for the New York office; I worked with the key people in our subsidiary offices overseas, including Ian Taylor. I wrote system documentation and attended meetings.

Introverted as I was, when I knew my stuff, and it was my niche, I was able to compartmentalize my insecurities. It was good to learn I could easily solve problems, and usually while wearing one of the new suits I'd bought along with a pair of high-heel pumps. With my new position and even newer business wardrobe, I felt professional, valuable, and useful. I loved my new role, and I soared with it.

Blaise's dad had something to say about that, and of course, Blaise relayed it to me. "A girl like that will never stay with you," he'd said. "She has big ambitions, big dreams, and she'll come to realize you'll be the one to hold her back."

He wasn't exaggerating about the big dreams. At one point, I made a tape of my singing and talked about putting a band together. Deep down, I probably knew it was a fantasy, but I clung to denial. I was way too shy to perform publicly. Modeling alone had been difficult for me. And to become a good enough singer to rise to fame would have taken a much more significant investment than I was willing to make.

Blaise assured me, however, that he'd never hold me back, and he didn't. Although, sometimes, he told me what to wear and not wear, or how to act and not act because he was old-fashioned and religious. I didn't acquiesce in that regard, but the extent to which I embraced his protection did scare me. Of course, at the time, I was in denial about the fact that I married him to get out of my parents' house. Still, I was determined to make our marriage work.

I forgot how the subject arose but, at some point, he flat-out stated, "If my wife ever left me, I'd take the kids, and she'd never see them again."

Well, I was the wife. We didn't have any kids yet, but that led me to the chilling realization that this thing with him wasn't going to end well.

"Thanks for the warning," I replied.

Then there was the matter of him allowing his sixteen-year-old brother to live with us against my wishes. Their parents had moved to Florida, and the boy didn't want to go. I loved the kid, but the first year of marriage is difficult enough to navigate.

Blaise responded to my objection by telling me his boss said to him, "'He's your brother. Your brother comes first.'"

The way *I* was raised, the person you marry comes first.

I do believe it was always Blaise's intention to do what he thought was the right thing. He had a good heart, but we often locked horns with our conflicting philosophies.

By then, he and I had moved to a three-room apartment in Howard Beach, but it was still a tight space to share with two guys. I insisted that if my brother-in-law was going to stay, he had to have a job. He got one at McDonald's, but then his boss chastised him for too much chatting instead of working, so he mouthed off to the boss in front of everyone and got fired. I told him to apologize and get his job back. Blaise suggested they let the air out of his boss's tires.

"Great," I quipped. "I have *two* kids." That wasn't going to fly with me.

Near the end of that first year, I had panic attacks. They stopped me dead in my tracks as if I couldn't take another step. In those moments, I believed I was a mere second away from losing my mind, and I felt like I couldn't breathe. I thought everything would suddenly go dark, and I'd simply be gone. My instinct was to call 911, but I just held onto the walls for a while, summoned my strength, and then mustered the courage to get on with my business.

I left our apartment after midnight once and wandered through the streets in pitch blackness. Strangely, I'd put aside my fear. It was a chilly night, but I didn't have a jacket or sweater. My heart pounded and I cried silent tears. It didn't matter to me that I was cold; the torment within me was so intense I could barely stand it. Except for the wind rustling through the trees, there was a peaceful quiet that began to calm me, and then there was the honking of a car horn.

Blaise stopped alongside me and urged me to get in the car. It didn't take long for me to oblige.

He finally agreed to take his brother to Florida, though I was certain it was too late. I didn't go with him. Then, as fate would have it, Ian Taylor was back in town.

Dr. Alden asked me to meet with Ian in the conference room and use the computer there to show him some of the things we were doing. It was supposed to take half an hour, but the session lasted a good two hours.

"I'd heard you'd gotten married," Ian said. "Congratulations!"

"Thanks," I replied.

"You don't seem happy about it."

"I don't?"

"No," he said. "When we went over the business stuff, you were cheerful and excited. When I asked about your marriage, that changed."

"Yeah, well…"

He appeared genuinely sympathetic. "I understand how difficult that is. My wife and I separated years ago. I was unhappy. You're too young to be this unhappy, and you've got good things going on with your new role here.

I'd hate for anything to spoil that for you."

When the conference was over, and I was back at my desk, he and I discussed having lunch together. And at lunch the next day, we revealed our attraction to each other.

"But my guilt would be threefold," he said. "One, you're married. Two, I'm ten years older than you. And three, I live in England. Where does that leave you? I don't want to hurt you."

"You won't," I said.

He quirked an eyebrow then. "We'll see."

We planned an evening rendezvous—dinner at an authentic English pub called David Copperfield's in midtown Manhattan. (That was *my* idea.) I remember having bangers and mash, while he ordered shepherd's pie. We had fun—eating, talking, laughing, and drinking. After leaving David Copperfield's, we bought a bottle of wine, moseyed over to the hotel he'd booked, and rode the elevator to his room.

Throughout the night, the room remained dimly lit by the bedside lamp. There were two full-size beds, one of which I sat on, drinking from the bottle of wine. Whenever he came close to me, whenever he touched me, I trembled visibly, tears clouding my eyes. Suddenly, I was like a scared little child. As hard as I tried, I couldn't get drunk enough to succumb, and he didn't push it.

After a while, we simply lay next to each other on the bed, and he held me in his arms while I cried. I didn't understand the deep, wrenching pain I felt, but I knew for sure that when Blaise returned from his trip, I'd ask him for a divorce.

Nothing could have prepared me for Blaise's reaction. I witnessed the full range of emotions—shock, anger, grief, and sadness. One minute he yelled. In another, he pleaded with me not to go. I was heartbroken for him, but I knew he'd find the right woman—someone who'd be perfect for him. I had to rip the Band-Aid off sooner rather than later.

MANHATTAN LIFE

Wendy Carlson, my co-worker, needed a roommate. Her apartment was in a prewar high-rise on 96th Street and Amsterdam Avenue—Manhattan's Upper West Side. Going to school and then working in Manhattan had been a thrill for me, but living there was my ultimate dream. Wendy was somehow convinced we'd get along great, so I agreed to move in with her.

Blaise, along with his brother and a couple of friends, helped me with the move. I'm not sure why Blaise decided to help—probably because he thought it was the right thing to do. His buddies, on the other hand, made wisecracks about me throughout the ordeal. To them, I was the spoiled brat leaving Blaise to move into this doorman building. They rode the elevator to the sixth floor several times with my boxes, sometimes menacingly tossing my stuff around.

"Stop!" Blaise told them on more than one occasion.

But I saw myself as I supposed his loved ones saw me—as some monster who should have left this guy alone.

Blaise thought the Manhattan apartment was great with its nine-foot ceilings, parquet floors, and thick walls. With the high-rise across from us blocking out the sun, it was a little dark, but, for me, it was perfect.

The sofa bed Blaise and I had shared was mine and came with me, along with the dusty rose area rug, my Sony TV, and my stereo. He let me take one of two beautiful amber glass lamps we'd bought together. He got custody of the birds and the fish, which was just as well since Wendy had two cats. My dad gave me the desk and bookcase from my old room and went shopping with me for new sheets, blankets, and pillows. He also helped to arrange the furnishings, positioning the desk and bookcase near the window for me and the television facing the sofa bed.

Wendy's room was the darkest, completely obscured from the sun, and the windows featured heavy drapes. It had several old-fashioned wall sconces that I loved.

"I'm going to make dinner," I announced that first night. "Chicken Cacciatore, white rice, salad, and Italian bread. Want to join me?"

Wendy's eyes widened. "One of your mom's recipes? You bet! I'll be there with bells on."

The kitchen wasn't blocked by the tall building, so it was the sunniest room in the apartment. Wendy had a rustic farmhouse table with four ladder-back chairs. The knickknacks she hung on the walls and placed on the counter added to the room's overall warmth.

"Smells heavenly," she said when dinner was well underway. "How many times has Blaise called today?"

"Several." I stirred my bubbling sauce. "He doesn't understand why we can't work out our issues. I do everything I can not to encourage him, and it's hard because he's so sweet. I don't want to play with his heart."

"There are two sides to this," Wendy said. "There always is. You were unhappy, and your happiness matters, too, darling."

Wendy loved the meal, and that delighted me.

As time passed, many of our chat fests involved sitting at that kitchen table—often while eating Ruffles with bacon horseradish dip. Half of the time, she'd be in her long, fuzzy green robe and slippers, and I'd be in my short terrycloth bathrobe.

For a while, I wasn't dating anyone, but Wendy had a few different guys who, at one time or another, stayed with her until morning. As an early riser, it made me nervous because the only bathroom was located right outside my room. Once or twice, I encountered a shirtless stranger in the kitchen, and it unnerved me. I responded to their wide, friendly grins and hellos by lowering my eyes and mumbling a hello back before hightailing it out of there.

There were no complaints, however, about the neighborhood. People were everywhere, even at night. Stores and streetlamps provided adequate illumination. Whatever we wanted was two blocks away—the drugstore, the supermarket, and the fresh bagel stores. We had a great Szechuan Chinese restaurant right on our corner. Wendy and I ate there sometimes. Others met me there for dinner.

Central Park was within walking distance and gorgeous any time of year. Wendy and I would roam around there or sit by the lake to enjoy the stunning view. With and without her, I strolled along Broadway some forty-plus blocks to 59th Street. I'd always loved Manhattan's architecture—the prewar buildings, brownstones, and all of the different styles.

Sometimes, there were street fairs. At one of those, I found a sepia portrait of Raul Julia as Shakespeare's Petruchio and Meryl Streep as Kate. It had the words *The Taming of the Shrew* in big blue letters on the lower right and "Free Shakespeare Delacorte Theater Central Park" in the upper left corner. Only a few colors were used—brown, white, blue, beige, and rose. The illustrator was Paul Davis, and he created it for Joseph Papp's New York Shakespeare Festival and Public Theater. I thought it was beautiful and the perfect addition to my new room, so I bought it.

I went to book reading events with co-workers and attended a lecture by renowned sci-fi author Isaac Asimov. We got to chat with Asimov afterward. To my delight, he was warm, friendly, and funny! It was an exciting time of my life.

Then, after a couple of months of me not getting involved with anyone, Wendy dragged me along to a local bar somewhere about 72nd Street. Despite the pleasant ambiance and red cushioned booths, I wasn't particularly comfortable, but Wendy had a crush on some guy she hoped would be there.

It was one of those things where we'd paired off with two guys to go to a party, and the one I was with got me alone and then refused to take no for an answer. I fought him off and left.

I took karate lessons for a couple of months after that, hoping to master the art of defending myself, but my inhibitions hindered my progress. In truth, I'd run out of patience with everyone and everything.

Even sweet Dr. Alden was being a tool. He got jealous of a top executive's idea for a new acquisition. The executive had copied him in an e-mail memo, along with many other people, explaining the idea and how it would benefit the company. Dr. Alden dictated a Reply to All for me to send, dismissing and criticizing the idea to no end.

"You can't send this," I told him.

He played dumb. "Why not?"

"Because you are ripping apart his ideas," I said, "and copying twelve people on it. It'll be seen as an attempt to humiliate him. It's so transparent and, honestly, it reflects badly on you, not him. Talk to him one on one, at least."

He disregarded my advice and sent it anyway. He got hell for it and nearly lost his job.

"You were right," he said.

That wasn't his only power struggle. He even initiated one with *me*. Although he'd initially encouraged me to take on new responsibilities in the firm, he thought nothing of interrupting my group demonstrations to ask me to make copies of things for him immediately. He could easily have asked someone else, waited for me to finish, or made them himself. I took that in stride, but when someone recommended me for a promotion, and he blocked it, that was the last straw. He simply didn't want to give up his secretary, and everyone in the company knew it.

With all that was going on, I began to miss Woodside—much to my surprise. I visited my family often enough, even participating in our St. Paddy's Day tradition of going to lunch at the Woodside Steakhouse on 61st and Roosevelt Avenue. It was a few blocks away from where my mom worked, so my mom's coworker friends would join my mom, Melissa, and me. It was a good time—eating corned beef and cabbage or steak and getting drunk.

My dad had found me an apartment there—just around the corner from where my family still lived. It was twice the size of the place I shared with Wendy and about half the rent. It sounded good to me; I wanted to be close to my family again.

"I'm going to miss you so much," Wendy said. "I really wish you didn't have to go."

But going from place to place, job to job, situation to situation, was my pattern.

HOME AGAIN

My plans to move back to the neighborhood included my new friend Elizabeth, another administrative assistant at work who had agreed to move in with me. She wanted to live in Manhattan, not Queens, but she said she'd give it a try.

Elizabeth had light brown, shoulder-length hair and a smile that reached her serene blue eyes. Her voice was gentle and soothing, and her cheeks turned pink when she laughed. Whenever she spoke, she carefully measured her words. I admired her manners, her grace, and her essence.

We bonded as two introverts. We laughed about meeting room scenarios where they go around the room, asking you to talk a little bit about yourself. As far as we were concerned, that was terrifying and humiliating—the same as bringing coffee into a meeting room. Neither one of us was a "small talk" person. We preferred to be among those with whom we'd established an immediate intimacy, and we tended to jump from one conversation to the next. We both loved eating in old-fashioned diners, preferably in nice, cushioned booths.

Over the summer, her family invited me to a lake house owned by their friends. Elizabeth and I took a rowboat across the lake. It was light when we left and dark when we returned, but it was such a serene, blissful day, mostly because Elizabeth was so Zen and genuine. I was completely at ease in her presence from day one, and I knew I could tell her anything. She made me feel normal, and that never ceased to amaze me. That is not to say that other people acted as if I was strange. It was just more or less how I felt with anyone other than Elizabeth at that particular time in my life.

Elizabeth and I were together at the office holiday parties with our cups of whatever liquor they had. We'd roam around, sipping, chatting, and giggling.

There was a nice afternoon, too, where we attended a ballet performance and had lunch at a little French bistro.

The six-story building we moved into was on a pretty block with a lot more trees than the one I'd grown up on—right around the corner. It was a nice elevator building with an intercom system.

We rented a two-bedroom apartment on the second floor with a living room outside the small second bedroom and a dining area next to the kitchen. It was a cute kitchen—large enough for the table and four chairs I bought. The red brick wall tiles, light brown cabinetry, and square terracotta floor tiles gave it a warm vibe. It also had a window pass for handing things to someone in the dining room. The master bedroom was huge and carpeted wall to wall in the same azure blue as the second bedroom. I arranged it with dark wood bedroom furniture and the amber glass shade lamp I'd been moving from place to place with since my marriage.

Elizabeth's small room had only her mattress and belongings. She didn't stay long enough to buy anything else. Unfortunately, Woodside wasn't for her, but we remained close.

Ian Taylor visited me there after she'd gone. Blaise had filed for divorce, and I'd signed the papers with no issue. I cooked dinner for Ian, and we remained at the kitchen table for a bit, making casual conversation.

I showed him my model's portfolio since he hadn't seen it yet. He said the pictures were good and agreed when I told him the photographer had called them amazing, but all I saw when I looked at them were eyes filled with anger. Pitiful sadness reflected in my eyes and my smile.

Aside from praising the photos and the dinner I'd made, he seemed to be withholding other compliments deliberately. I said something about it because, of course, I would.

His response was, "You're so addicted to all this praise and flattery you solicit from everyone else that if I sat here and insulted you for ten minutes, you'd probably jump out a window."

My jaw dropped. I'd never realized it until then, but I knew he was spot on. While I recognized how awful that was, I had to laugh.

Not long after uttering those words, he became seductive, affectionate, and loving. Things were fantastic from then on, and he spent the night.

After he'd gone, I was devastated.

Had I placed him on a pedestal as well?

It seemed that way because the entire time we were apart, I focused only on the good memories of him, the positives, and that was what I craved. When we were face to face, and as hard as I tried to ignore it, he was somehow shattering my illusions of him. I didn't want that.

I was beginning to see, however, that, as we keep someone upon that throne we designed for them, we continue to want the same thing from them. We don't even realize it when we're not enjoying it anymore. We still crave it. The moments of comfort and bliss are more and more fleeting. A sense of emptiness prevails, and it hurts. It hurts a lot. We sense we are in bondage, and we are because we are at the mercy of our obsession.

Unfortunately, as with any other addiction, our perception gets clouded, and our judgment is impaired, so, we are confused. The unrealistic expectations we harbor lead to our devastating disappointment.

MITCH

Oddly enough, I'd accompanied friends to AA (Alcoholics Anonymous) meetings since I was a teenager as a show of support for them. I'd been to a couple of ACOA (Adult Children of Alcoholics) meetings as well.

Some of the members in the AA group came around to me during the breaks and asked, "Are you new? How long have you been sober?"

I'd be taken aback. "I'm not an alcoholic," I'd say. "I'm here with (so and so)."

The next question was always, "So, you don't drink?"

It was meant to confuse me, I think. Plenty of people drink and are not alcoholics.

Once, a friend of mine pointed at me and told another member, "Her story's worse than mine. Ask her to tell it to you."

I thought that was funny, but I didn't for a moment take it seriously.

Meanwhile, I accompanied my friends to a New Year's Eve AA sober dance in downtown Manhattan to welcome in 1984.

My friends hit the dance floor the moment we got there, but I remained on the sidelines, observing. Rooted to that spot, I shook my head each time a guy came over to ask me to dance.

One particular guy kept an eye on me while the others were turned away one by one. He smiled at me, shaking his head. He had medium-length wavy hair—a golden blond that curled at the ends. His smile was to die for, and he got one back from me in return.

He approached me. "Do you want to dance?" His eyes were a vivid, sparkling blue.

I didn't really have "a type." Hair, skin, and eye colors were beautiful in every shade, and while I might have said I preferred tall guys, most of the ones I had dated were average height, and I didn't like them any less. This guy, too, was no taller than five-nine.

"No, thank you," I said. Then, before he slipped away, I added, "But you don't have to leave."

He spun around.

"If you like dancing, and you want to find someone to dance with, I understand," I stammered.

"I like dancing," he said. "But I don't have to dance."

His name was Mitch. He lived in Franklin Square on Long Island—the suburbs of New York City. He hated the job he'd had for fifteen years and wanted to study computer programming. He was in both NA (Narcotics Anonymous) and AA, and he was a born-again Christian.

"I used to do drugs," I told him. "I don't anymore."

It was true, although, obviously, I still drank. If I ventured out with Melissa, I'd have a few margaritas or opt for a Brandy Alexander. On occasion, I made Tequila Sunrises at home or picked up a bottle of Baileys Irish Cream on the way home from work.

Mitch and I found a quiet corner where we huddled together, talking and laughing the entire night. He was quite charismatic with his soothing voice and hearty laughter. In him, I saw a gentle person with such a kind heart. He was beautiful to me—and irresistible.

He shared with me the guilt he felt over a friend's death. "It happened in ninth grade. He OD'ed. We should have brought him home, but we left him to sleep it off on the couch. We didn't know the right way to help him."

I gave him a hug.

We exchanged phone numbers that night, and he said he'd call me in the morning. We kissed—a deep and rhapsodic encounter—and then we hugged each other tight.

The following morning, I'd just gotten out of the shower when the phone rang.

I yelled. "Ara, can you get that please?"

Ara, a tall, Korean-born graduate student, was my new roommate.

In my haste, I threw a towel over my head, knocking a decorative glass bottle off a bathroom wall shelf. Dark red blood came gushing out of my foot. I had broken the glass, cutting open a vein.

Ara was knocking on the door. "It's Mitch."

After wrapping myself in a towel, I barely managed to hop to the bathroom door.

"No, she hurt her foot," I heard her say. She covered the mouthpiece. "He doesn't believe me."

"Okay, give me the phone." I explained the situation to him myself.

"If you want, I can come get you and take you to an emergency room," he said.

I had no car. After selling the old one, I never bought a new one because when I was with Blaise, we used his car. I didn't need one living in Manhattan. Ara didn't have a car, either.

"Are you sure?" It didn't sound fun to me.

"Be right there," he said.

Ara worked at wrapping and suppressing my wound, and I got dressed but couldn't put my injured foot on the floor. I had to hobble.

Mitch took me to three different emergency rooms because they were all crowded. Well, it was New Year's Day. The one time I found a place to sit, a doctor came out to tell me the bench was reserved for psychiatric patients.

Mitch kept holding me. He kept me laughing. Declaring the emergency room situation "bullshit," he decided to find an available doctor. I didn't see how it was possible on this holiday, but he did it. The doctor he found gave me a tetanus shot, treated the injury, and properly bandaged my foot.

Ara wasn't home when we got back to the apartment, so Mitch ordered Chinese food. His favorite was shrimp with lobster sauce. Back then, whenever I ordered Chinese, it was chicken chow mein. (Thank goodness that now I'm always trying different things!)

"Sit and relax," Mitch insisted. "I don't want you getting hurt." He rummaged through my kitchen cabinets and set the table.

After dinner, he lay beside me on my neatly made bed. While we kissed, I had to keep my foot in its white brace off to the side. For some reason, that kept making us laugh. There was so much affection between us—and so much joy. I adored him.

Even so, I had to put on the breaks. Mitch said his sponsor had concerns because nine months of substance abuse abstinence on Mitch's part wasn't a long time. I had to be honest, too, about Ian. We weren't exclusive or committed to each other, but we weren't exactly over. He'd soon be in New York again and would want to get together.

"At least for now, I need time and space," I told Mitch. I was straightforward about why.

He was crushed, I could tell, but he respected my decision and agreed I should sort things out with Ian.

A few weeks later, Ian and I discussed the situation at the bar of a midtown Manhattan restaurant.

We were sitting there having a drink when Ian said, "I have a bad feeling about this."

"Mitch is a really good person," I insisted.

Ian focused on his drink. "I didn't say he wasn't."

"But you think since he's an addict, he may relapse."

He shrugged. "That's not unrealistic. Look, I realize it isn't fair to ask this of you while I'm 3,000 miles away, living around the corner from my ex and my kids, with not much more to offer you, but it's either him or me."

Ian appeared grounded, and he was successful, but Mitch was on his way to a better life, too. Besides, Ian intimidated me. My feelings for him hadn't lessened, but I was certain that I'd never truly have him—that I never truly had him in the first place—and that I wouldn't know how to handle him if I did. So, nothing he said mattered. I was going to do what I wanted regardless of what anyone had to say about it. I'd been doing that all of my life.

"If you're asking me to choose, I choose *him*," I said.

I saw a flush to Ian's cheeks when he responded with, "Sorry to hear that."

I stood. "Time for me to go."

"Please be careful getting involved with him."

Ignoring his warning, I hurried out the door and called Mitch the moment I got home. "I miss you," I said.

"Yeah?" I imagined he wanted to make sure.

"Yeah." I couldn't believe how much.

"I miss you, too," he replied.

"Can you come meet me?" I wouldn't have blamed him if he'd said no.

"Be there in fifteen minutes."

"Fifteen minutes?" I laughed. "You going to fly?"

"Something like that."

We talked about what happened with Ian, and he was happy I'd chosen him. Right away, he wanted me to meet his parents, so he invited me to dinner with them.

LET'S TRY THIS AGAIN

Mitch was agitated. "I told them not to make spaghetti and meatballs with Ragu. 'She's Italian,' I said. But my father went and did it—the spaghetti and meatballs. I hope you don't mind."

"Not at all," I said.

His family lived on a nice, shady block in a Cape Cod house with a well-manicured lawn. Inside were simple furnishings. The family room had plaid throws and old, comfortable chairs. There were baskets of fruit in the cozy little kitchen and a backyard door that led to a flower garden.

As soon as we arrived, Mitch hustled over to the stove and "doctored" the simmering sauce, afraid I would not approve.

His father was a bit gruff. "I don't care if she's the Queen of England," he said loud enough for me to hear. "It's what I made, and if it's good enough for me and my wife and kids, it's good enough for her." He eyed me peripherally and grinned.

At dinner, his father boasted that Mitch was a football hero in high school and played quarterback—and he'd made the local paper more than once.

His mom was passive-aggressive. She'd do things in my presence like casually reflect on how nice Mitch's ex-girlfriend was—the one he had right before me.

Although Mitch was only five years older than me, his parents appeared much older than mine. His mom's hair was grey, his father's white, but his dad had the same beautiful blue eyes that Mitch had.

They were wary of me, I suppose, but that didn't matter. After that night, Mitch and I became inseparable. He loved cruising in his van with me by his side. He'd show me beautiful neighborhoods and mansions on Long Island, and those reminded me of when I was a kid in Woodside, searching for magical places. I sang a lot with the radio while he drove, and I'd sing for him at my apartment when we were alone. He loved the performances.

He'd also ask me to read him the stuff I wrote, and he was always impressed. What a boost to my confidence that was! Suffice it to say, Mitch made me happy, and we agreed on almost everything.

I teased him about how sexy he was in his jeans whether shirtless or in one of those muscle tees. He had a nice, muscular body and a forearm tattoo. All he had to do was twist the lid off a jar I'd been struggling with, and I was in awe.

He cautioned me about the purple wall-to-wall carpet in my bathroom that matched the smaller rugs. "Bad idea," he said. "If, for any reason, you have flooding in here, it's going to stink, and you'll have to rip it out."

And that's exactly what happened when the neighbor upstairs had a plumbing issue that leaked into our apartment. Mitch ripped the carpet out for me and got it to the dumpster. "Use small area rugs," he said. "You can throw them in the wash, at least."

I was seriously impressed.

In some odd way, being with Mitch was comforting and a relief. Because of the people I'd grown accustomed to in my life, he was familiar. I could be myself and be confident. He was content to let me be who I was and wear what I liked.

Mitch had a way of endearing himself to others. He was quick to lend a hand, and his smile put people at his ease. He sat and talked with older people like my grandparents, asking them questions about their lives and making their eyes light up. He noticed how my grandmother always took her little purse when taking a stroll, even if she wasn't going to buy anything. It was part of the outfit she wore. And how my grandfather sat in the same spot and in the same way on the end of the porch bench, facing the street with his elbows resting on the surrounding gate. Mitch wanted people to know they mattered, and he gave them his attention. His interest was genuine because he enjoyed people.

"Most of my life, I didn't want to live," he confided in me. "I never told anyone that. Whatever I was doing, those things were distractions— diversions. When I met you, I thought—maybe. Maybe I could do this. Maybe I can have a wife, then a child, and I'd commit to this life. It would change everything. It would be real. It would be love. That's all I ever wanted."

Mitch's sponsor, however, was growing more and more concerned. "He says my priority right now has to be staying clean and sober," Mitch explained. "Make ninety meetings in ninety days, work The Twelve Steps."

"So, do that," I said.

"He also says no major changes in my life for the first year."

I admit I was clueless about recovery. To me, nine months clean and sober was a long time. Naïvely, I thought his struggle was over, as mine seemingly was. Besides, he *did* attend a meeting a night. He'd also started to gather the information he needed for returning to college.

Meanwhile, Ara saw that he and I were growing closer, and she said it made her uncomfortable to come home and find him sitting in the kitchen.

I offered alternatives—that he be at the apartment when she wasn't expected or we'd avoid hanging out there together entirely, but she adamantly declined my offers.

"I'd never ask that of you," she said. "It's your place, and I'm in the way here. I don't want to be in the way."

So, she moved out, and Mitch moved in.

He and I talked about going to Greece and cruising the Aegean Sea. It was my idea, but he thought it was great. We took the train into Manhattan and stood in line for over an hour to get passports but ultimately decided to put off traveling and buy furniture instead.

We bought living and dining room sets, area rugs, and a coffee table. The dining room table was long enough to seat twelve people with the extensions. I always insisted we buy everything—silverware, dinnerware—in sets to serve twelve.

"Who are these twelve people we're going to be entertaining?" he asked, shaking his head.

I laughed and shrugged. My head lived in a fantasy world. Like Greece—that was never going to happen.

It was a cozy setup, though. The bookshelves in our bedroom were filled with my favorite books. We had TVs in the living room and bedroom, and even a little one in the kitchen. When he was lying on the sofa, watching *M*A*S*H*, one of his favorite shows, it warmed my heart. There was a contentedness I hadn't experienced in any other relationship.

Mitch loved to cook, so we took turns making dinner. He was a great cook. When he made baked ziti, it was perfection.

In the evenings, when I came home from work and collapsed on the couch in my suit, wanting to do nothing but sleep, I didn't question why—but he did. He observed that it happened two weeks before my menstrual cycle, and he'd help me out of my suit. It never occurred to me to consider the reason why I was suddenly so exhausted. I was out of touch with my own body.

With all of this domestic bliss, I didn't forget how much my freedom had meant to me in the past, and how I didn't want obstacles in the path of other pursuits.

"You can balance work and romance," friends had insisted.

At the time, I thought, *Yes, people need to tell themselves that. They don't think you can be happy without the fairytale love, but I can.*

I never wanted to own anyone or to be troubled by the jealousies involved. I didn't want anyone telling me what to do or calling me constantly, wanting me to account for my time.

In past relationships, either the men tried to dominate me, or I tried to dominate them. Mitch and I were different. We'd wrestle a little for dominance, and then we'd laugh about it when it happened, but we respected each other. He didn't suffocate me. He truly was my equal and my best friend. We co-existed in a way I couldn't with anyone else, and I *did* want to marry him.

Now, if I were planning a wedding for someone else, I'd delight in choosing the music—Bach's "Air," Schubert's "Ave Maria," Pachelbel's "Canon," Beethoven's "Ode to Joy," and Jeremiah Clarke's "Trumpet Voluntary in D Major." To this day, I cherish that music. But, for this wedding, there was no music or church.

Mitch and I stood side by side in the foyer of a judge's Long Island mansion—us, the judge, and the judge's wife as a witness. He and I giggled throughout as though we were high school kids. Still, I thought it was perfect.

CHANGES

I'd had enough of Dr. Alden at the publishing company, so I quit after nearly four and a half years and began looking for a new job. Mitch rode the train with me to the city when I had an interview at the offices of Bijan NY on Fifth Avenue and 55th Street. On the train, I was nauseated and ready to faint.

"Put your head down," Mitch said, "below your heart. Stay that way for a while."

I was fine just before we parted ways and throughout the interview, but I didn't get the job.

Weeks later, Clairol Appliances hired me as an administrative assistant in their new technology department. Clairol was housed in the massive Bristol Myers skyscraper on Park Avenue, near 52nd Street. It was a pretty area—only two blocks away from St. Patrick's Cathedral. The guy I'd be working for seemed nice. He said the goal was to get me on the same trajectory as the promising career I'd had at the publishing company. Funny thing, I was there less than a month when a former co-worker called to tell me that Dr. Alden was fired from his job. Now, I regretted leaving there, but I was committed to giving this new place a chance.

There was one little problem, however: I was pregnant. For once, I was aware that something was going on with my body, and I knew it was that. So did Mitch. A home pregnancy test validated our suspicions, and by the end of the month, a doctor on Long Island confirmed it.

It thrilled me to realize that this little life growing inside me had been doing okay there for months. It seemed incredible, and I was ecstatic. I embraced the situation without hesitation because I truly wanted and loved this baby and his dad.

Mitch told me his mother worried that I'd make our child too smart with books, force him to speak proper English, and, thus, turn him into a snob who'd think he was too good for them. That had me shaking my head. He wasn't going to be a snob because he read books and spoke proper English. Mitch thought it was crazy, too.

During the first trimester, I was hardly ever sick but always tired. Still, the pregnancy was wonderful—one of the best experiences of my life. I wanted to be a good mother, a good wife, daughter, sister, and friend. And Mitch was a treasure to me. I loved being married to him. We laughed like crazy over baby names we never agreed on, and he bought a new light blue metallic Nissan Sentra for our little family.

He also said things that surprised me, such as, "When you're with your family, you're not the same. You're more lost and confused, kind of like a kid."

"Really?" I was aware of times when he and I returned home from visiting them, and I'd be a mess. I was so sensitive to everything they said to me and easily hurt. But I didn't realize I was a different person with them.

"Would you say they love you?" he asked.

"Of course, they love me!" I didn't even have to think about it.

Sure, stuff had happened between me and my dad, but I maintained we were all close. They showed their love in many ways. Whenever I needed help from my parents, they didn't hesitate, especially my dad. He'd come running. They were always there for me, same as Melissa, and Bridget, too, if I asked.

"I never felt loved growing up," Mitch explained. "My parents didn't tell us they loved us. Maybe they figured we knew. Maybe it's how they were raised, but their concern was providing for us, seeing that us kids learned and behaved and that we'd make something of ourselves. They believed in a God that wanted His children to fear Him. That was the way they loved us, teaching us to fear Him and fear them, but that message of love never came across to me. I thought my parents felt obligated to love me and believed they did, but they were always disappointed in me."

I knew by then that his father had abused him both physically and emotionally, so I hugged him tight. "I'm so sorry."

"It breaks my heart to watch you with them," he went on. "I see how much you want to earn their love and respect, and it breaks you. That's why you come home shattered. I have no doubt that the thing you want your dad to say is that he loves you. Because, deep inside, you don't think he does."

That made me cry.

"Baby, I don't believe God wants us to be fearful," he said. "He wants us to be sure He loves us. He is a kind and forgiving God, and He doesn't want us to be afraid." Mitch quoted the Bible then. "'There is no fear in love; but perfect love casteth out fear: because fear hath torment. He that feareth is not made perfect in love.'"

I wasn't sure what to make of that, but the one thing I was certain of was that Mitch and I were okay. I wasn't, though, and neither was he. At some point, he'd gotten tired of meetings. He'd go twice a week, then once a week, and then whenever. Once he was sick; the other times, he was too tired.

Even though street drugs and their consequences hadn't been part of my life for over a decade, I was still an untreated addict living with another primarily untreated addict, and neither of us had a clue how to navigate that. When triggered, I was at my craziest—at my wit's end—and I wasn't in touch with why. I suppose my brain was beginning to process the lingering pain, fear, and anger I'd kept a lid on for so long.

The trouble began that winter of my pregnancy. Mitch vehemently hated winter, and he was having dental work done, another thing he hated. He couldn't tolerate the pain, so he got a doctor to prescribe painkillers for him. He'd be flying high after every appointment with the nodding, mumbling, and slurred speech. That led to horrendous fights where I threw everything around me clear across the room. Those were codependent tantrums. I didn't realize then that the vicious cycle of making him feel bad about himself provided him with the next excuse he needed to get high.

"Please don't be angry," he said gently.

"I have a right to be angry!" I roared.

He remained calm. "That's a lousy right to fight for, if you ask me, but if that's the right you want, keep fighting."

"What do you expect me to do?" I asked.

"Anger is fear."Surprisingly, he was still calm. "You want to know why I don't get angry? If I allowed myself to get angry, I'd lose control. You won't see me angry. I'll walk out the door before that ever happens, and I won't come back until the anger is gone."

The morning after our fight, I awakened before he did and made a pot of coffee for him. He usually made it himself because he left earlier for work.

When he walked into the kitchen, I could see clearly that he was touched by my gesture because he reached for me. I pulled away. My anger hadn't fully waned, so when he tried to hold me in place, I instinctively swung to free myself, hitting him in the mouth.

He stood there, stunned, as he grazed his lips with his fingers. There was blood that had splashed from his lip to his teeth, making it seem like an awful lot of blood. Terrified, I ran to the bathroom and locked myself in.

He knocked. "Open the door, please."

I hesitated.

"I'm not going to hurt you," he said. "I need something to stop the bleeding."

"I'm so sorry." I opened the door.

He rinsed his lip off over the sink. "Why'd you run?"

"Because I thought you'd kill me?" I got ice for him, apologizing again.

He shook his head. "I'd never hurt you."

"I didn't mean for that to happen, I swear." I felt awful. I'd given him a fat lip.

"Don't worry about it," he assured me. "It'll be fine."

Another time, my father wanted to help us buy a house, but after speaking to Mitch on the phone, he quickly changed his mind. Mitch was high again—so high he could barely hold a conversation.

My dad was concerned. "I don't want you and the baby out there somewhere with him the way he is now. Stay where you are, close to home."

MIND BLOWN

My seventh month of pregnancy was in February, at which time, Clairol laid off my entire department. At this point, I was "showing" enough, finally, to make people wonder whether to offer me a seat on the train. It was close enough to my delivery date, so, rather than go on job interviews, I thought I'd collect unemployment for a while and stay home. I thought I'd even start writing again.

The funny thing was, I was so used to interacting with people by then that it was weird being home alone while Mitch was at work. I'd sit at my desk to write, and I'd want to call someone to chat instead. I couldn't readjust to thriving in isolation the way I had in the past.

When Mitch came home from work early one day, I was pleasantly surprised. Half an hour or so later, while he was in the bathtub, I knocked on the bathroom door to ask him what he wanted for lunch. He didn't respond.

I figured he couldn't hear over the running tub water, so I knocked harder. Still, there was no response and no sound except for the eerie gushing of water. There was a brief sense of dread, which I quickly dismissed before turning the door handle, and, when I opened the door, my jaw dropped.

He was holding a syringe aimed at his inner thigh, and, at that moment, it fell from his hand and into the water. For a split second, I thought I imagined it. He sat there in the tub, staring back at me with glazed eyes but said nothing.

I panicked, first storming out of the bathroom and then immediately rushing back in. He lay there now with the bath water reaching his shoulders. His eyes were closed. I couldn't wake him, so I shut the water off and called 911.

"Is he conscious?" the dispatcher asked.

"No. I mean, he's not awake." I was so scared.

Paramedics arrived. Their voices seemed to echo in an otherwise silent room, and I watched nervously as they revived him. Clearly, they perceived the degree of my shock while also noting my pregnancy.

"It was a heroin overdose," one of them said. "Did you realize he was shooting dope?"

I shook my head, still grappling with the horror of this reality. I felt unbelievably foolish.

"He's been doing it a while," another one divulged. "He's got track marks, old and new."

I'd never noticed the track marks. Oddly, I'd never *seen* anyone shooting street drugs into their veins because I was never there when they did it. Nor did I examine people's bodies. Still, I couldn't fathom how I'd missed that.

"Don't blame yourself," one of the paramedics said. "Happens a lot. Anyway, we gave him Narcan, but we'll take him to the hospital. Listen, if you hadn't called, he'd be dead now."

They helped him out of the bathtub, steadying him as he stood. When his eyes met mine, there was a familiar sadness in them, and his expression conveyed his remorse.

The next conversation the paramedics had with the two of us was about where Mitch would go once the hospital released him. He alluded that he wanted to come back to me, so they asked me if I wanted that.

"No." I was adamant.

Their focus shifted back to him. "Do you have somewhere to go?"

I could tell he was ashamed, but, given the circumstances, he didn't push the issue. "I'll stay with my parents for now." Before they led him out the door, he told me he loved me.

It was heartbreaking because when that man was straight, you couldn't have asked for a better friend or partner, or a kinder, more compassionate man to love. Now, though, as distressed as I was, I felt relief that he was gone.

Naturally, I empathized with Mitch. Among other things, he was plagued by that friend's death years ago—how it might not have happened if he and his friends had known what to do at the time. That was compounded by more guilt for being unable to stop using drugs after his friend's death. He thought it was the ultimate kick in the ass to his friend.

We'd talked about that. He blamed himself for his disease. I realized, too, that, on top of everything, it would kill him not to be with me and our soon-to-be-born baby. I was afraid he'd get discouraged, lose hope, and then go back out there and kill himself.

The next day, my father accompanied me to the unemployment office. I was still in shock over the mess my life had become, but he was there for me, as was the rest of my family.

Mitch and I spoke on the phone. He was remorseful and apologetic. He professed his love for me and our baby, and he vowed to listen to his sponsor and get back on track.

I did love him. We were friends above everything, so I couldn't walk away or give up on him. I do regret how the consequences of being involved with him affected the people I love, and I wish, in many circumstances, that the outcome had been different, but I've never regretted my choice to be with him.

My conditions for taking him back included the ninety meetings in ninety days. I also told him that, for the foreseeable future, we wouldn't be having sex. Bridget told me that people relapsing around that time were getting the HIV virus from needles. "Be careful," she'd said.

As for my pregnancy, I had to get the Rho(D) immune globulin shot because I am Rh negative and didn't have the Rh factor marker to mix with Rh-positive blood. If I hadn't done that, and my child was born Rh positive, my immune system would have created antibodies to reject what it detected as a foreign invasion by attacking the baby's red blood cells.

I spent a good amount of time reading parenting books, and I often played classical music or sang Linda Ronstadt's "Blue Bayou" because that's what soothed me then. I hoped my little child in the womb found it soothing as well.

In my ninth month, Mitch brought me to my surprise baby shower, organized by my mother and sisters. Elizabeth was there, too. There was so much love, I thought—mine for them and theirs for me. I hoped the worst was behind me.

After the shower and the gifts I'd been given, the baby's room was complete with a rocking chair and rocking horse. There was a high chair in the kitchen and a playpen between the living and dining rooms. We childproofed everything. My due date was Mother's Day, although we'd somehow miscalculated. Still, the doctor said our baby was in the right position, making his or her way to the birth canal. I tried to picture that. It just seemed so adorable and amazing.

A week after Mother's Day, I had an unconventional labor. My contractions came faster and faster but not in any consistent pattern. The doctor thought it was false labor. He told Mitch, "If you want, take her to the hospital anyway. They can give her a sedative to help her sleep."

The hospital was Winthrop University Hospital (now renamed NYU Langone Health) in the Long Island village of Mineola. When we got there, I was already five centimeters dilated. They admitted me and gave Mitch his scrubs. He was there with me the entire time, calming me, making me laugh, and allowing me to squeeze the life out of his hand. It was three-thirty in the afternoon when they admitted me, and, at six-thirty p. M., I gave birth to a seven-pound, eight-ounce baby boy.

Bridget later told me that she and Missy had yelled out the window of my parents' house, *It's a boy! It's a boy!*

And that was the most glorious day of my life.

DAVID

For the purposes of this book, I'll be referring to my son as David.

No one brought him to me after his initial examination or at any other point that first night.

"Where's my baby?" I kept asking.

In response, Mitch and the nurses insisted I get some rest.

How could I rest? I ached for the child I'd given birth to. I was worried sick. "Why isn't he here? Is he okay?"

Nothing around me registered except the solemn faces of the nursing staff. "We'll bring him to you tomorrow morning," one said. She offered me a sedative, which I refused until around midnight. Though I was exhausted, it was the only way I was going to sleep. Mitch was there with me for as long as he could be, assuring me everything was fine, but he refused to give me answers.

Come morning, there were clicks, clangs, and the squeaky wheels of passing carts—but no baby.

Mitch was there bright and early. "The baby's okay," he said. "They wanted to monitor him overnight because when the nurse tried to feed him for the first time, he held his breath and turned blue."

I immediately panicked. "*What?*"

"Relax, he's fine. They were taking extra precautions."

"I might have rested a lot easier knowing it was a precaution, and that he'd be fine," I said. "Why didn't you tell me? Why didn't anyone tell me? You saw how worried I was!"

"Sorry, babe. I was, too," he admitted. "I was scared. They thought if I told you, you wouldn't get any rest."

A nurse brought David to me shortly afterward. He was this beautiful, sweet-smelling tiny creature with fuzzy blond hair and the pinkest little face. He gurgled, grunted, and peeped at me through sleepy eyes, and it was the most wonderful thing in the world. When I fed him, he didn't hold his breath or turn blue.

Once we were home, Mitch chuckled while watching him in the bassinet, his tiny body and his tiny little feet. David made my husband's eyes sparkle with light. He amazed us, and we loved him so much.

Now, the little guy would be gazing at me when I sang softly to him. I sang "Blue Bayou" and many other songs.

My mom laughed when I said the midnight feeding took hours because David would fall asleep without finishing, and I'd hold him until he'd awaken and finish. I simply wasn't sure he'd drunk enough milk. In the meantime, he slept soundly in my arms, the only light coming from the blaring TV. It wasn't too loud, just the voices of David Letterman and his guests.

"You don't wait for him to wake up!" my mother exclaimed. "When he stops, you put him to sleep! And that's that!"

Well, there was a learning curve, but after a few months, I had a handle on it. Thanks to the infant CPR class I took at the hospital, I was even able to save the little guy from choking once.

Unsurprisingly, when my in-laws questioned my ability or judgment as a mother, I was sensitive. For example, I couldn't understand why it mattered to my mother-in-law how much I packed in the diaper bag, but she'd go on and on about it. She got flustered, too, each time I made her wait while I fastened the seatbelt on David's car seat.

"We never used car seats with any of our kids," she'd tell me.

"There's a reason they made it a law," I replied.

One day she told me to go out and have fun at the neighbor's pool and said she'd watch David. Next thing I knew, she was tending to the garden in her yard, going about her business of weeding and pruning without a care in the world.

I approached the fence. "Where's David?"

She grinned at me. "In the house."

After lifting the latch and opening the gate, I was in her yard. Without another word, I climbed the steps, swung through the backdoor, and passed from the kitchen to her bedroom. David was lying in the middle of the bed with nothing to protect him from rolling over and falling from the bed to the floor. I didn't like that one bit. David's pediatrician had cautioned me to prevent that sort of thing from happening, and I was determined to adhere to his advice.

She crept up behind me. "God watches the children."

I lifted my baby and held him.

"Go on. Go to the pool and have fun," she said again. "I'll watch him."

When I didn't budge, she clenched her teeth. "For goodness' sake, I'll stay here."

But I wasn't going to fall for that again. And I don't regret that. Concerning some of the other things, however, I do wish I'd had more of a sense of humor then. For example, when his mom complained that I had everything in that diaper bag but the kitchen sink, I wish I'd just laughed and said, "Oh, you know, you're right! We should go back and get it."Instead, when Mitch and I were alone, I cried.

The odd thing is I really did love his parents. My mother-in-law collected roosters and told me everyone collected something, so I decided that I liked little house figurines, especially ones with a bulb inside, so they could be lit around Christmas. She gave me a little English cottage to start my collection, and I was delighted.

I loved watching her and my father-in-law get down on the rug and play with David. They gave him so much attention and so much love that I was usually able to put aside whatever hurt I felt and let them enjoy their grandson. When we all sat around chatting about current events, we had great conversations. They weren't prejudiced or narrow-minded, so talking to them was easy. We laughed. We had fun. I wanted so much to be like another daughter to them and part of their family.

As for Mitch, he changed his share of diapers and warmed bottles to feed David whenever he took a shift. He paced back and forth until the bottles were ready and then made sure the formula wasn't too hot. Although he was great with the baby and seemed happy, he still made me nervous, so I started smoking again—something I hadn't done in a while. Mitch smoked as well, but whoever wanted a cigarette smoked it outside the apartment, away from the baby.

David was eight months old when I underwent another surgical biopsy for bilateral breast tumors—this time at Winthrop University Hospital. Again, the tumors were benign, so there was no mastectomy, chemo, or anything else.

A month later, Mitch was sick with the flu, and he couldn't shake it. When he got better, I got bronchitis. At one point, I coughed so hard that air escaped from my lungs. There was no doubt something was terribly wrong. Mitch quickly found a pulmonary specialist and drove me there. Initially, the doctor was skeptical about my insistence that air was continuing to escape from my lungs. He pointed to a chart of the lungs on his office wall and told me how they work. He took X-rays. After the X-rays, he confirmed I had punctured a lung and was right about what I'd described.

He sent me to the hospital where he'd planned to keep me overnight, but when he and I were alone in the room, I begged him from my hospital bed to let me go home. A nurse hooked me up to an IV, and the monitor's rhythmic beating made me groan.

Now panicked, I pleaded with the doctor. "Please, no, I can't—"

I told him the truth. "I can't leave my husband alone with the baby." Something told me that, in terms of being sober and clean, Mitch was hanging on by a thread.

"If you keep coughing that way, your lungs will collapse, and you'll die," the doctor insisted.

"I won't die." I was certain of it because my heart told me what to do, the same as it had when I'd saved Mitch's life and others back in my drug abuse days. "I won't because I can't leave David."

Miraculously, he believed me. "I'll send you home with a strong cough medicine, but you need to take care of yourself. No smoking, and if there's any problem, go straight to the ER."

I didn't smoke. I prayed. And Mitch took good care of me the whole night. He pretty much saved my life that day, and he also helped me realize that I could do anything for David.

BLISS AND TROUBLE

Mitch's genuine concern for David melted me.

"If he doesn't want to play sports, I'm not forcing him," he said. "If he enjoys it, fine. And whatever you do, don't scream at him or humiliate him. My father did that to me. Both of my parents yelled at me. Teachers yelled at me. Other people's parents yelled at me. It's as bad as anyone hitting him, maybe worse."

When we went Christmas shopping together, he led me away from the cute turtleneck sweaters I wanted to buy for David. "He won't get his head through those."

We talked about not spoiling our son. "If he wants something, get it for him," Mitch said. "But he has to appreciate what he has."

"Yes," I replied. "I've seen kids on Christmas ripping through packages and throwing them aside to get to the next one. If he gets that way, we cut back."

It worked. David continued to be the kind of kid who cherished and appreciated what anyone gave him, and he took good care of his things.

One night after a party where David had eaten two very sugary cookies, he was jumpier than usual at bath time.

Mitch heard the stress in my voice. "Get out of here," he said. "I'll give him a bath. You're too tired."

I got tired early most nights because I took temporary jobs to supplement our income. My sisters and grandmother rotated babysitting duties. Bridget and Missy had flexible schedules then, and my grandmother had retired. My mom worked full-time, but every once in a while, she was also available.

So, for two months, I worked at an architectural firm. After that, I spent nearly a month at the Orion Pictures production company. It was nice to be working again, but I always missed David and Mitch.

The reality was that Mitch and I had these beautiful moments where we were a typical, happy family. But sometimes, when Mitch was late coming home from work, it was inevitable that he'd be high. On those nights, I couldn't bring myself to get a single pot on the stove to start dinner. With my stomach in knots, I focused on taking care of David.

I remember my happy little boy bouncing in his jumper excitedly. He smiled, pointing to the Christmas tree. "Ball! Lights!"

"Yes, lights!" I smiled through tears because he was so innocent, and I was terrified for him as I braced myself for the jingling of Mitch's keys in the door.

The worst of it came after the New Year. Mitch came home in the late afternoon, an hour or so after the usual time, and he was high again. I didn't argue with him in front of David, but I'm sure my expression conveyed my feelings.

David, now eighteen months old, was thrilled that his father was home.

Mitch swept him up and hugged him tight. "Let's go bowling!" he said.

In retrospect, Mitch may have been bipolar or something. He had these manic phases where he was over the top, threw caution to the wind, and believed he could do anything with one hand tied behind his back. While in those moods, he wasn't his calm, practical self, and he was not rational. The drugs he took exacerbated that.

A familiar feeling of dread and doom took hold of me. "We're not going bowling."

When he couldn't convince me to go, he decided he'd just take David.

"No!" Without hesitation, I grabbed David from his arms. "You're in no condition to drive."

"I'm fine. How do you think I got here? Come on—he's my son, too!" He reached for David. "I'm taking the boy bowling."

Alarmed, I took a few steps back, holding David tighter against me. "Over my dead body."

We stared at each other for what seemed an eternity. The entire time, I trembled.

At last, he spun around and walked out, slamming the door behind him, and of course, it vibrated—highlighting another sober reality.

He caused an accident on the road that night and totaled the car. Thankfully, no one was hurt. He merely sprained his arm and got it bandaged.

"If our son had been in that car, he might not be alive now," I said.

"Wrong. I'd never drive that way if David was in the car." I'm sure he believed that. Addicts can convince themselves of anything. I understand that now. His denial was as powerful and lethal as my own had been for many, many years.

"So, it was your intention to drive recklessly because David wasn't in the car?" I put the question to him.

"No!" he replied.

He could have argued that if I'd allowed him to take David, he wouldn't have been shaken and therefore distracted, but he didn't. He didn't because people don't usually intend to drive recklessly, and being high is just as distracting as being distraught —probably more so.

Anyway, I was done. I wanted out of the marriage and met with a divorce lawyer.

"You have no grounds for divorce," the lawyer said, "His addiction is a disease."

The thing was, I had to protect my child. That was my responsibility, so I decided to tell Mitch I wanted a divorce.

"I understand your concern, and I don't blame you," he said. "I don't want to make you unhappy. Babe, I'll do anything you ask. I'd do anything for you. Tell me what to do, and I'll do it."

Mitch had a doctor's appointment a couple of days later, one he'd made before our fight. I didn't go with him. He wasn't high when he came home, but the expression on his face was solemn when he asked me to sit down on the couch, and he didn't mince words.

"I tested positive for HIV." He appeared genuinely shocked. If he wasn't, he was the greatest actor in the world. Even if he wasn't merely deep in denial, the reality astounded him. "My T-cell count was fifty-two, so they diagnosed me with AIDS."

In that heart-stopping moment, I hugged him.

"The doctor says a lot of people think they're buying a new, clean set of works, and they're not," he explained. "Those things are used and repackaged. I had no idea. I wouldn't have done it if I knew." Another thing addicts might tell themselves but they are living in helpless bondage.

I remembered then, that time he was sick with the flu. Going into the fifth week, he began wondering if it was cancer. Then he watched a segment on TV about AIDS and worried it might be that.

"Why jump to the conclusion that it's cancer or AIDS?" I'd asked him then. "You can't just guess what it is. You have to go to the doctor." I was surprisingly calm about it.

His voice brought me back to the present now.

"I'll leave if that's what you want," he was saying. "I wouldn't blame you."

I shuddered, processing the weight of what he'd told me, but making him leave now was crazy to me. In sickness and in health, as they say.

"No." We were in this together now. I'd never let him go through that alone.

"You'll have to get tested," he reminded me. "I'm sure you're fine, since we haven't had sex for a long time, and we used protection when we did, but we have to make sure."

"Okay." The shock hadn't worn off yet, but I had sobering chills.

"And David will have to be tested, too."

That gave me a jolt. "David!" My eyes welled up with tears. I gave in and cried now, my heart beating wildly.

Mitch held me. "I'm sure David doesn't have it. The doctor told me a little baby has an underdeveloped immune system. He wouldn't have survived if he had it."

"But he turned blue," I recalled. "Oh, God, what if—?"

"No, no, look at him; he's fine," Mitch said. "He's perfectly healthy."

That was true, but, in that moment, even Mitch was the picture of health. No one would have guessed he was ill.

He held me to his chest. "Hey, my one comfort is knowing you and David are safe, and that you'll be there to raise him when I won't."

Thoughts of David overwhelmed me now. I was completely shattered.

COPING

I was with Mitch when he told his parents. We were at Halls Pond Park in West Hempstead, a couple of miles from where his parents lived on Long Island. Mitch chose the place because he loved it, especially the duck pond where he'd taken me before and wanted to take David. The park was gorgeous in the spring with its charming footbridge and the most beautiful old trees. Besides the ducks, there were swans and Canadian geese.

We were gathered by the gate near the water. Mitch told his parents he had something to tell them.

With ducks quacking nearby and the bustling of a springtime breeze, he came out with it. "I have AIDS."

His mother gasped. "Oh, gosh!"She covered her mouth. "Good Lord!"

His father groaned with eyes suddenly downcast. "Whatever you need, we're here."

They both hugged him.

Mitch was with me when I went for my test. I was scared, and he continued to reassure me I'd test negative.

I remember sitting in a chair in someone's office. Mitch stood close by. I don't remember what the place was or what it even looked like.

"You tested positive," a voice told me. As I write this, I recall only that the person who relayed this news to me was a woman. Ordinarily, I clearly visualize the faces of people I'd met, going back to childhood, but this woman's face I can't recall.

Tears came in response to the news, I'm sure. They may have simply welled up in my eyes. I just don't remember if I cried. If I did, it wasn't audible or with my face in my hands, but I was certainly shocked.

Mitch was crushed by my test result. My being positive compounded his guilt. For me, the more crushing news was what it meant for David. Now, his getting tested "as a precaution" became a lot more terrifying.

This was 1987, and, at the time, there was so much we didn't know about HIV/AIDS. I recalled something that had happened while I was working at the architectural firm over the summer. One of the managers, who happened to be gay, suddenly died. He was young and such a nice person. People said he was HIV positive but didn't have AIDS yet—he simply got pneumonia and died. Someone later told me that the guy was probably immunocompromised, likely with a T-cell count of below 200. Ever since I can remember, a count that low met the criteria for AIDS.

Nevertheless, I wouldn't know how sick I was or wasn't until I saw a doctor.

Accepting I was probably going to die soon was easier than I'd imagined, but realizing I wouldn't be there for David was gut-wrenching. It was the worst, most agonizing, and torturous thing I'd ever experienced. I could bear the unbearable—but not that.

The first person I told was Elizabeth. We were sitting across from each other in a cushioned booth at a diner, and she responded pretty much as I'd expected.

"I love you," she said. "I'm here for you, anything you need. You're going to be okay."

My parents were also caring and kind. Missy was shocked and in tears, absolutely beside herself. She was afraid but loving and supportive. Bridget was shocked but also supportive.

Sadly, though, some people on Mitch's side of the family were unbelievably callous.

His brother told him, "If it happened to me, I'd kill myself."

His paternal aunt called me one afternoon and said, "Throw him out. He's done this to himself. He's done this to you. Kick him out *now!*"

I heard a lot about how it was a punishment from God, too, and people had to suffer the consequences of their bad choices. By this time, I had some understanding of what a powerful enemy addiction is. It cripples you. It blinds you. You're the prisoner, and despite all of the risks, it's hard to break the chains. You tell yourself it will be okay. You believe what you need to believe. You lie to yourself because the disease lies to you.

Besides that, plenty of heroin users or former heroin users didn't get HIV/AIDS, and bad things happened to people that have nothing to do with their choices—even children. It's not personal. People get sick; none of it is personal.

It truly saddens me how some individuals distort religion to serve as a reason to shun, bully, shame, and claim superiority over others and to justify their persecution and mistreatment of their fellow human beings.

If you are not one hundred percent on board with their beliefs, they reject you, even if only in passive-aggressive ways. In the worst-case scenarios, like believing God created HIV/AIDS to punish the LGBT+ community and drug addicts, the results are more direct and aggressive.

Even though I didn't believe this particular illness was a punishment from God, it still hurt to know that some people did. And what about my family, my child? If I was hearing those things, they would, too.

The same people probably later went on to credit God for helping doctors and scientists provide the life-saving drug treatments that have led to people with HIV/AIDS living longer and more normal lives and becoming undetectable. So, which is it?

Note, too, that in this ridiculous scenario, God didn't include serial killers and child molesters in the "chosen" groups to punish. He must have only had a problem with gay people on that day. Besides, if you are a powerful God and want to eradicate or annihilate a population, you have the means to do it in one fell swoop. So, none of that argument makes any sense.

There were people from all walks of life in this situation. Heterosexual transmission was on the rise. The LGBT+ community, from the very beginning, acted as frontline warriors in creating awareness and providing resources for people with HIV and AIDs. The Gay Men's Health Crisis (GMHC), in particular, extended itself to people beyond its community. They were a lifeline.

At the time, however, I didn't quite grasp how this impacted my family. What I wanted from them was a guarantee that David would be loved and treated well—welcomed and embraced by the family. I ached for the comfort of someone convincingly saying, "Don't worry. We'll take care of him." I tried to get commitments from them, and they said yes, but they'd continue to assure me, "Nothing's going to happen to you."

That stressed me out to the max because I didn't expect to survive. I took it as an unwillingness to commit. I realize now that my immediate family didn't want to lose me, and that was why they continued to assure me nothing was going to happen. I also realize it was hard for everyone, not just me. None of them had wanted this outcome for my life.

My hyperfocus on David's wellbeing, present and future, gave me tunnel vision. Nothing was more important to me than my child. He had to be okay no matter what happened to me.

One social worker told us, "Babies are born with their mother's immune system, meaning David had a 50/50 chance of being positive at birth. But he would've shown signs by now if he was infected. He wouldn't be well."

Another, on a different occasion, said, "He'll probably test positive, too. I've seen this situation before. You were infected while pregnant, and his immune system was so weak—there's no way he didn't get it."

David saw his pediatrician regularly. He was thriving and had such a sweet spirit. People said he got more and more beautiful as he grew, and he favored his father's side of the family. Mitch was half Polish and half Russian. David had blue eyes and the lightest blond hair. He'd had so little hair at birth that we'd decided to let it grow to shoulder-length, and it grew fast.

David hated needles when he was little. It took four doctors holding him down to take his blood for the HIV antibody test. He screamed, fought, and cried. I was in tears, thinking, *This is my fault.*

When we returned for the results, the waiting was so much harder than when I'd waited for mine. The doctor we were supposed to meet with scooted by half a dozen times. She'd glance in my direction and hold up the index finger of her right hand as if to say, "Be right with you." Her expression each time was solemn. I figured it had to be bad news. If she had smiled even once, I'd have relaxed some. I had so much anguish and fear.

But David was negative. I thanked God, and my tears then were happy ones.

LIFE GOES ON

Just about every day, David ate breakfast while watching *Romper Room* and *Zoobilee Zoo*. Then we'd go to Windmuller Park, which ran from 52nd Street to 54th Street in Woodside. They had a fantastic playground. On the way back, we'd hit the stores. David loved to walk and would go anywhere. He enjoyed every vision, every encounter. Once home, he ate lunch while still babbling and giggling in his highchair. After that, he was so tired that he took a three-hour nap.

Bridget lived out of state by then, but Melissa hung out with David and me whenever possible. I have great memories of those days, most of them sunny and gorgeous. We laughed so much. We took David to Central Park Zoo, to our favorite pizza place, and wherever else we went. He was always eager to go around the corner to visit his grandparents and to walk to the candy store with my mom. Mitch and I took him to an amusement park on Long Island, indoor play arenas, and the Big Apple Circus at Lincoln Center. There were play dates and kids' movies. The three of us also traveled to Florida for the holidays to visit Mitch's parents, who'd since moved there.

To prevent the transmission of HIV, Mitch and I were cautious around David and everyone else. Of course, we would not allow anyone to come in contact with our bodily fluids. The primary risk in non-sexual relations was blood transmission, so, if we were bleeding, we first isolated ourselves and then promptly stopped the bleeding. And while we routinely disinfected surfaces and floors, we also immediately cleaned any surfaces that may have come in contact with our blood. At the time, nurses told us to use household bleach for that.

Mitch was often tired or experiencing malaise. He had swollen lymph nodes in his neck and had to deal with muscle aches, joint pain, and stiffness. Sometimes, he had an appetite; sometimes, he didn't. He didn't usually appear unhealthy, but his vision was increasingly impaired, and he thought he was going blind. He saw several doctors, including emergency room physicians as a last resort, and no one could diagnose the problem. It must have terrified him, but he tried so hard not to be afraid.

He was eventually diagnosed with AIDS-related Cytomegalovirus (CMV), which compromised his light-sensitive receptors, but there was nothing to give him for it. The HAART (Highly Active Antiretroviral Therapy) cocktail patients receive now to treat this virus was not yet available.

A drug had been approved to treat the AIDS virus, though—AZT, a nucleoside analog reverse-transcriptase inhibitor also known by its common name, Retrovir. I was with Mitch the first time he presented his prescription for that to a pharmacist.

The pharmacist sneered at him, saying "We don't have that here."

So, merely getting the script filled was a chore.

When he finally did, he wasn't able to tolerate the medication. Doctors prescribed it in megadoses at the time, and it was too powerful for him. It made him sick.

Then, after dealing with the backlash of his diagnosis from his boss and coworkers, he was fired. I got angry at the way people treated him, but he said, "It's fear. They don't understand."

He applied for disability. He prayed.

I shopped daily because I had to be careful about how much I spent. In a moment of desperation, I asked my father for a loan. It was hard to do. I'd never asked before, but he turned me down on principle. Still, Mitch and I remained optimistic, and we had our laughs.

Once, David and I were at the Woodside Bakery getting a birthday cake. David, seated in his stroller, blurted out, "I can't stand these people! They make me sick!"

The people around us laughed. David had no clue what that meant. He must have heard me say it about people blocking the aisles when we were in the supermarket. Of course, Mitch laughed about that as much as I did.

Another time, Mitch and I were hanging out in front of our building with David, and a passerby stopped to admire our child. "How cute!" she said. "He has blond hair like his mother."

Mitch unexpectedly replied, "Hers is fake."

I erupted into laughter. "Yes, that's true. My husband is the real blond."

She didn't know quite what to do with his response or mine.

The truth is, I'd found that while navigating the obstacle course of life, having a sense of humor helped tremendously. My mother always said I was the first to start laughing and the last one to stop.

Not quite so amusing was my back going out right around that time. It was as if the punishing pain pulling, stabbing, and shooting through my lower back was equivalent to the unbearable emotional pain that came in waves when I let myself think. It reminded me of Bob Dylan's song "Like a Rolling Stone," about someone who'd fallen hard. It wouldn't have applied or have seemed bizarre if it happened to me many years before, but it happened after I hadn't touched street drugs in seven years, and after I'd gotten the *good* jobs and a promising career.

Nevertheless, I saw a Long Island chiropractor for a couple of weeks and then began my search for a permanent full-time job. We found a babysitter a block away from us. She had two preschool-age daughters and took care of two additional kids.

It didn't take long for me to find a job—this time at Memorial Sloan-Kettering Cancer Center on York Avenue near East 68th Street, a block away from Manhattan's East River. It was an administrative assistant position.

A few times while I was at work, Mitch showed up at the babysitter's house to get David, wanting to spend the day with him. The babysitter wouldn't allow it without my permission, so it hurt him to leave without his son. Granted, he loved his little family. He was proud of us and felt so blessed, but what I observed about him convinced me he wasn't well enough to care for David the whole day and to be alone with him. For example, he took meds to take the edge off his pain, and then he'd lie on the couch smoking and often fall asleep.

I started going to Al-Anon meetings to learn how to better cope with the disease of addiction. It helped, but now that I worked full-time, it seemed impossible to fit those meetings into my schedule

When David got chickenpox, Mitch got shingles from that. He was in so much pain and yet willing to do laundry because I was at work. I shouldn't have been surprised. When he was in one of his manic phases, high as a kite, he'd decide to clean the bathroom like a frenzied madman, so it was sparkling when I got home.

"I worry so much about you," I'd tell him.

His response was, "Even if I was in the best health and ate nothing but vegetables, I could be crossing the street tomorrow and get hit by a bus. Don't worry. Let's live."

When David climbed out of his crib for the first time and came shuffling into the living room, we were both equally amused. We shopped for his new bed that same day. We had it built for him—a captain's bed crafted of handmade wood. It had storage drawers and matched his oak dresser and rocking chair. I decorated it with a blue Peter Cottontail bed set that matched the rug and warm blue drapes on the windows, topping it off with his posse of stuffed bears.

Mitch bought him a book called *Teaching God's Word to Children* by L. Craig Martindale. He asked me to give it to David when he was old enough to read and understand. He wrote in it for him and signed it.

Despite the circumstances, Mitch and I were closer than we'd ever been, and my husband's heart never soured due to his predicament. He sponsored a child from Save the Children and gave to St. Jude's. He had a pension fund that had been accumulating because he'd started at his job when he was eighteen and stayed there. He wanted to put it in my name.

"I want you to be able to write full-time," he said.

But I didn't want to talk about him dying. I didn't want him to die.

"Do you mind if I put it in David's name then? I do want him to go to college. I figured you'd take care of that if I left it to you, but it might be better this way."

"Yes, because we both know I love to spend money," I joked. "Yes, put it in David's name. That's perfect."

Mitch got three denials for Social Security Disability even though he was literally dying. When he finally got it, we made a tough decision. David's safety was of the utmost importance, and, while I had to work full-time to support us, Mitch required constant care. His parents were available. He'd also have his sisters and their families, as they lived in Florida, too, not far from where his parents lived. One of his sisters was a nurse and knew the best hospital for him to get treatment. She also knew the most knowledgeable and capable doctors to treat him. The weather in Florida was better for him, as well.

We weren't getting divorced; I planned to visit him as often as possible, with David, and I was thinking about moving there if it worked out to be the best option.

Meanwhile, I asked my dad if he'd let me move back home for a while with David, and he said no again on principle.

Undeterred, I quit smoking. I'd tried hypnosis and other things, but what worked for me was a book called *You Can Stop Smoking* distributed by Smoke Enders. Since the day I stopped, I've never had the desire to smoke again. Simply put, I love being a non-smoker more than I've ever loved smoking. Doctors later told me that quitting probably doubled my lifespan. And while I highly recommend that book, I suspect that no method will work until you're truly ready to quit.

Mitch, with his competitive streak, wanted to prove he could quit, too, so he tried, and things seemed to be improving all around.

After a year at the hospital, I was promoted to Paralegal Assistant in the Insurance Claims office, where, in addition to administrative support, I organized and maintained a database of statistics, initiated author correspondence, and fielded telephone inquiries. My boss put me in charge of handling subpoenas, too. My job was to notify the deponents, namely doctors, and assist them through the process. I learned to read medical charts and became a notary public for the staff. I loved it and ultimately stayed for three and a half years.

My back issues, however, complicated things. Once, in the restroom, I literally fell to my knees because of the pain. It may have been symbolic of the fear I had, but I was eventually diagnosed with a lumbar spine disc condition. X-rays showed that the disc was shot, so surgery wasn't an option. The bad episodes happened when I overdid it physically, so I continued to seek relief from chiropractors.

I swear it was David who gave me the will to keep fighting. I'm a fighter anyway, but at home, it was just him and me now, so I became a warrior.

When I fell asleep playing with him, he'd still be there in the same spot playing quietly when I opened my eyes, and I'd realize how much I treasured him. Reading him stories, I couldn't miss a beat. During one of his favorites, *Peter Cottontail,* I got a little lost when I was tired, and he corrected me. "No! He lost one shoe amongst the cabbages and another shoe amongst the potatoes!" It was important to get the story right!

Wherever we went, he was completely fascinated with trains and stopped dead in his tracks to watch in awe as they arrived and departed. I got him train sets for the holidays, and he helped me put them together.

At the age of four, he had memorized *Winnie the Pooh and the Honey Tree.* He sang along with Rod Stewart on the stereo to "You're in My Heart," and, if you told him a joke, even a long one, he'd retell it brilliantly, delivering the punchline with ease. He did it in Florida when we visited Mitch and his family. He had Mitch, his grandparents, his aunts, and his cousins in stitches.

He wasn't shy. He was full of enthusiasm and love. He was happy.

ELMHURST

Mitch and I had a mutual friend in Vinny—the neighbor who lived two floors above us. Vinny was aware of Mitch's diagnosis and mine and wanted to help. He and I remained friends when Mitch moved to Florida. He would do things like bring me a bucket of chicken from his favorite place on Roosevelt Avenue.

"You got to try this," he'd said. "It's the best."

As tenants, he and I were concerned that our apartment building was under new management. The rent kept increasing—not that it was worth it. Woodside was becoming more and more dangerous. Three men were attacked and stabbed while walking together at night—right on Woodside Avenue. My dad's car was broken into or stolen a total of six times. My mother and grandmother, during separate incidents, got mugged in broad daylight. Burglaries happened in the middle of the day. Another tenant in our building found intruders in her apartment when she returned from the laundry room. There was even an incident where a mugger knocked an infant child from his mother's arms to grab her purse.

An available apartment in Elmhurst was $100 cheaper for rent. It wasn't the best neighborhood, but despite having the same formidable urban vibe as Woodside, it was better at the time and more diverse. As a teen, I'd hung around Elmhurst for quite a while, so, perhaps, nostalgia brought me back.

The available apartment was on the second floor of a salmon-colored, three-family Center Hall with a silver gate around the property. It was across the street from a high school housed in a five-spire, baroque-style building. Teens from the school sat on nearby cars or leaned against them. They'd lay on one of the hoods, laughing and kissing. Occasionally, they'd sit on the steps outside the door of this place I was checking out.

Two blocks away, on both ends of the street, there were churches—one an Episcopal church, the other a reformed Dutch church with an ancient graveyard. Both churches were centuries old. So, the neighborhood was pretty and had character.

The owner of the three-family house lived on the first floor with his wife. Both of them were tiny with white hair and glasses, except he'd lost half of his hair, and she had fluffy, snow-white curls. The hall smelled of her Italian cooking or of the equally delicious pastries she baked, giving the place a homey, family-like vibe. They grew herbs and vegetables in the small backyard—a yard we'd be free to use.

Two of the three bedrooms had wall-to-wall carpet. The living room had lovely hardwood floors, as did the master bedroom, which also had a little nook I'd use as a den.

I was ready to go.

Vinny offered to help with the move, and, on different days, he or my dad helped me arrange and rearrange furniture. They helped me hang and assemble things, like the new desk I'd built with my dad. Vinny put my window gates from Woodside on the windows here, and, now, I also had an ADT security system plus deadbolt locks on the door.

I purchased a brass bed and snowy white sheets with Victorian lace trim. I had a floral three-way lamp and kept rose floral trinket boxes on my dark wood dressers, along with vanity trays for perfume bottles and my musical jewelry box with the dancing ballerina. There was a TV and of course, in the nearby alcove, my bookcase full of books accompanied by my brand-new desk set.

There was a relatively small room with brown wall paneling and a rose-colored carpet. We put an off-white sleeper sofa there, a dart board, and a TV. It was where I hung my old *The Taming of the Shrew* poster I'd bought with Wendy in Manhattan.

For the kitchen, we got a white oval table and chairs cushioned in yellow and white, yellow placemats, and a centerpiece of blue silk roses.

The wall-to-wall carpet in David's room was bright green. The previous tenant left a three-level unit of white shelves about four feet high and six feet wide. We used it for his toys. I added a laundry basketball hoop and a behavior chart. We had this great star system where he lost privileges for defiance but had a chance to earn them back with good behavior. It made sense to him, so he was on board with it.

Honestly, David was such a good kid. I'd figured out early that he was acutely logical, and the best way to appeal to him was with logic. Things had to make sense to him.

Melissa bought him his first video game system, which we hooked up to his room TV. We had a blast playing with him—Melissa, my mom, and me.

So, we were good. On the surface, things seemed normal. The place was always clean. I did laundry every week. I cooked a lot.

I enrolled David in Sunday school, and we also attended Mass on Sundays. I intended to give David a spiritual foundation and then let him sort it out for himself further down the road.

My rationale was that exploring is essential—especially having that freedom to explore. I always felt that children must also be allowed to think for themselves and form their own opinions. I'd learned the hard way that they need to know they will be unconditionally loved and accepted without buying into their parents' total mindset and having to live the exact life their parents envisioned for them.

But I was surely relying on my original faith back then. For church, I chose a nice suit or a demure dress. When the priest spoke, I listened intently, sometimes moved to tears at the notion of hope for our family. When Mass was over, we proceeded to the altar, where David and I knelt side by side to pray.

I thanked God I was able to work and care for my son. Wiping away tears so my little boy wouldn't notice, I begged God to let me stay with David until he was old enough to take care of himself or for however long he needed me. I prayed to be able to watch him grow up and find happiness, for his dreams to come true—and for him to eventually find someone who'd support him and share in his happiness.

While in his presence, I easily held it together, but it was a different story when I was alone—for instance, riding home on the train. The dingy yellow light, the people, and the honking of the train's horn got to me after a while. I'd suddenly think, *I'm going to die. My heart's going to explode. I'm going to lose my mind.* Sometimes, I got off the train, sat on a bench on the platform, and took in some deep breaths.

I continued to have chiropractic treatment for my back issues. It was a vicious cycle where back pain led to anxiety and anxiety led to more back pain.

When David was asleep, I'd lie awake worrying about him, and I'd cry. The truth is, there's never a day you don't think about being HIV positive, and I was flying by the seat of my pants. A panic attack came over me unexpectedly one day as I stood in my kitchen, getting ready to put together a meal. Oddly enough, I called my dad.

"What's happening?" he asked cheerfully. "What's new? Everything all right?"

I was aching to say, "Help me, Daddy. No matter what happened between us in the past, I love you so much, and I need you." My heart felt as though it had been shattered to bits. The anguish was harrowing, and I just wanted him to hold me, love me, and make it all better.

Instead, I hesitated before saying, "Yeah."

"You sure?" he asked.

"Yeah," I assured him. "I just wanted to say hello."

He said something like, "I'm washing the dishes. You want to talk to your mother?"

"It's okay," I replied. "I need to get dinner started."

Another time, I called Vinny, and he managed to calm me. It was easier to tell him what I was going through because I knew it wouldn't hurt him that I wasn't okay—not the way it might hurt my dad or someone else in my family. And I certainly didn't want to burden Mitch; he had enough on his plate.

The problem with Vinny was, he had more on his mind than friendship, and I knew it, but I was so desperate in those days to hang on to any life raft I could find.

He stared at me once with his intense brown eyes, consumed with anger and hurt. "The sad thing is, I'm willing to accept your situation and make a life with you," he said, "but you don't care half as much about me as I care about you." A slight head toss tousled his dark, wavy hair.

I said, "And that's why, even if I were single, which I'm not, I'd never initiate or allow anything beyond friendship. We don't even have to be friends if you don't want to be."

He shook his head, smiling. "I'm your friend, and whatever else you want me to be, okay?"

Sometime around then, I visited my mom, and she gave me a gift that soothed me more than Vinny's words ever could.

She rummaged through her closet and pulled out a familiar black cashmere coat with a red collar. "It's too small for me now," she said. "See if it fits you."

I was sitting on her bed, and I stood to take the coat. "Really?" When I tried it on, it was a perfect fit, and it smelled like Arpege Lanvin—her favorite perfume. After a swing around before the mirror, I took it off and handed it back.

"It's beautiful," I said.

"Keep it," she told me.

"Wow! Thank you!" It meant so much to me at the time. It was as if I could take part of her with me to Elmhurst, and, God knows, I needed her. Granted, we were little more than a mile away from each other, and she'd soon get a job working at the Queens Center mall, half a mile from my new place, but I still missed being around the corner from her and the rest of my family.

AZT

My new internist had an office in Woodhaven, Queens. Dr. Lettiere was tall, with brown hair and eyes and a chevron mustache. He was easy to talk to, compassionate, and kind. He said my T-cell count was 560, which was relatively good. He diagnosed me with asymptomatic HIV, not ARC (AIDS-related complex), and not AIDS, but he wanted to start me on AZT, so he wrote a prescription.

Aware of what Mitch experienced, I was reluctant to begin on the medication. I was scared to even present the prescription to a pharmacist while in a public place. There was a drugstore I passed walking home after work from the train station. It was a small store, and the pharmacist's counter was in the back. When I peeked in the window, as I did several times, I had a clear view of the pharmacist in his white lab coat. David was with me those times because I had picked him up from the babysitter.

Eventually, I ventured in to browse the three tiny aisles, observing how this pharmacist interacted with customers. I noted his slight, unimposing build, his gentle voice, and his warm smile. The kindness he showed others impressed me. His name was Sajeel, but people called him Saj. We were about the same age and height. He had light brown skin, a full head of dark, curly hair, and a face as beautiful as his heart.

He greeted me with a warm hello on the day I summoned the courage to hand him my prescription.

When he read it, he met my gaze fearlessly, his big, brown eyes reflecting not pity but compassion. "I have to order this for you," he said. "I'll have it for you tomorrow."

"Thank you." I smiled. "I appreciate it."

"Of course," he replied, returning the smile.

It was the beginning of the sweetest friendship, and, as long as I lived in Elmhurst, I'd never get my prescriptions filled anywhere else.

The AZT was brutal, though. One day, I'd planned to take David to a carnival but couldn't get it together. I didn't feel well; I was tired. Everything inside me wanted to shut down, but it was a one-day event, and I really wanted to go. Unfortunately, by the time we got out of the house, it was already mid-afternoon. The day was warm, sunny, and beautiful, so I started out cheerfully and bursting with enthusiasm. Along the way, however, I was dizzy, short of breath, and nauseated.

We were by the Queens Center mall.

"I need something to drink," I told David. I thought something cold and refreshing might help—Sprite, maybe, or ginger ale.

"Okay." He obligingly held my hand as we dashed inside the mall.

I bought one for him as well, grabbing two straws.

The drink helped a little, but it was four o'clock when we got to the carnival, and, by then, they were taking the whole thing apart. It was awful, but David took it in stride. He didn't complain when we turned around and journeyed home again. He simply loved going anywhere with me. Still, it saddened me that he'd missed the carnival.

Once home, he rushed to his room to play. I turned on the AC and took refuge in mine, closing the door. My face in the mirror was pale. Overheated and sweating, I couldn't get out of my clothes fast enough. It helped to change into something cool—a tank top and shorts. I lay sprawled across my bed just long enough to gather the strength and then called my doctor.

His nurse answered. "Are you taking the AZT?" It was her first question when I told her what happened.

"Yes. I didn't know if it was the virus or the medication."

"It's the AZT," she said. "Hold on, I'll get Dr. Lettiere."

"Keep taking it," he said when he got on the phone. "Your body will adjust."

Now, it made even more sense to me why Mitch couldn't tolerate this drug in his much weaker state. That saddened me.

Poor Mitch. Poor David.

It was as if I had some inside knowledge that it was tougher on them than on me.

PARENTING

During family visits on holidays, Sundays, and birthday celebrations, it was easy to chat, listen, tell a funny story, or laugh at the hilarious things my family said. I managed to disregard the painful realities, memories, and emotions in those treasured moments.

It helped, too, that David brought out my maternal instincts. (I swear you don't realize all of the things you can handle with ease and how, amazingly, you can find stuff in a heartbeat that no one else seems able to find—and even find room for things that others insist won't fit!)

There you are, leaning over to tie tiny shoes, fix a meal, or remove a splinter, and all the while you're melting over the earnestness in your little boy's eyes as he watches you. He trusts you to make everything better. When you're unsure how to do something, you figure it out. It's when everything's quiet, you're entirely alone, and there's nothing to fix, nothing to do, and nothing to explain that it just hits you and clutches your heart like an iron fist. The tears come, and they don't stop. It's brief but intense.

Whenever I was home, I utilized the TV as background noise. I'm sure I did it because of those Saturdays I'd stayed home, writing alone in the house where I grew up. The quiet at that time was the loudest, most disruptive, most disturbing quiet I could imagine. I also did it because my limited attention span made the usual tasks like cleaning and laundry so tedious that I had to break the monotony with disruptions. Watching or listening to television did the trick, and singing with the music on my stereo worked as well. Giving my attention to those things broke up the chores so I could manage them more efficiently.

For me, the most important thing was to cherish each moment I had with David, and it was easy to do because I loved him so much.

I didn't forget the book Mitch provided for him—*Teaching God's Word to Children.* It provided cute and humorous analogies to help a child understand the concepts. There was one about a hamburger that David found highly amusing. He laughed a lot whenever I read that part, and hearing him laugh, of course, was everything.

Mitch and I decided to put him in preschool while I worked. We chose

Forest Park School in Rego Park. A kind, white-haired rabbi ran the place, but it didn't matter that we weren't Jewish. They welcomed us, and after observing how wonderful they were with the kids in their care, I was sold. When David first started, I picked him up and dropped him off going to and from work, but they eventually offered door-to-door bus service, which helped tremendously.

When we spoke on the phone, Mitch was thrilled to hear the details. He was excited and wanted to plan a visit to New York, but his mother interceded.

"Let me talk to her," she pleaded with him in the gentlest of tones. After cheerful greetings, she said, "Tell him no. He's not doing well. He's not in any shape to travel."

"Okay." I hesitated, allowing that reality to sink in. "We'll come there."

Mitch and his parents lived in a two-bedroom co-op with a screened-in patio. It was a nice place in south Florida—open, airy, sunny, and full of light. New York, by comparison, seemed murkier and greyer, with more heaviness and overall darkness. Still, the latter was always home to me.

Mitch was slimmer than usual. He was handsome, though, with his fresh haircut and shave, which accentuated his prominent cheekbones and brought out the vividness in his pretty blue eyes. Unfortunately, he was back to smoking, and, aside from raspberry and lemon sherbet, he didn't eat much. His mother often handed him a can of Ensure, and he drank it to please her.

He took me out to dinner the first night—the two of us alone, having a date. It was a seafood place, and he did eat a little then. For me, the intimate evening reinforced how much I loved him—loved talking to him, laughing with him, being with him. And I wondered how much longer I'd get to do that.

When I finally broke down in tears, he said, "I'm not going anywhere. I'm not dying."

"But this virus…you can't take the medication, and—"

"Nah." He shook his head. "This won't take me out."

I remember smiling sadly in response. Sometimes, I was numb, maybe shell-shocked. Other times, my heart bled for him.

"Anyway, if it does, my sister's going to take over my sponsorship of the little boy from the children's fund. We talked about it. She promised to make the monthly payments and write to him the way I did. And, of course, I know you'll take good care of David."

That night, Mitch and I shared a bedroom at his parents' place. David's bed was assembled in the living room. It was wonderful to hold my husband, hug him, and sleep with him after months of not being together.

I imagine Mitch, as well as most other people, loved whatever there was to love about being in Florida. For me, it was nice for a while—traipsing over to the nearby pool in shorts and a swimsuit top, and it was a quick drive to the ocean. I enjoyed being out on the patio and having coffee with others at eight o'clock in the morning. The palm trees, warm sun, and lazy lounging by the pool were nothing I'd ever complain about. We ate at I-Hop and Pizza Hut, and one day, we set out for Disney World.

The temperature dropped to a cloudy thirty degrees that day. No one had coats, so we bought hooded Mickey Mouse sweatshirts, and each of us wore two. We got Mitch a wheelchair. He looked gaunt and didn't feel well. I saw in his face how sick he was.

David and his cousins were blissfully oblivious on their quest to find Mickey himself, and Mitch wouldn't let anyone quit the search. When we finally found the mouse, David rushed headlong into Mickey's arms and hugged him.

We got early evening tickets to Medieval Times in Kissimmee. I loved the medieval atmosphere, and the show during dinner was fun. Fascinated as we were with the fire-eater, David was even more thrilled that they served a four-course meal. Whenever they cleared the table, he kept looking for the waiter, highly anticipating what would come out next. The food was great, and it was a wonderful time.

TRAGEDY

Our next visit to Florida was in July of 1989. When David and I arrived, Mitch was lying on the couch, disoriented, with his father circling and his mother sitting beside him, wiping his face with a damp cloth.

"I've been taking his temperature since early this morning," she said. "Last time, it was 106."

"He can't fight a high fever," I told her. "His immune system is so weak."

Mitch shivered when I held him. His skin was clammy, and beads of sweat coated his face.

I sighed heavily. "We have to get him to the hospital."

His father, eyes filled with tears, nodded. He and I balanced Mitch when he got on his feet and then kept a tight grip on him as he stumbled out the door. We helped him in and out of the car while my mother-in-law held on to David.

Other patients and hospital staff did double-takes when we came through the emergency room doors. Mitch was so pale and thin. His cheekbones were sunken, and his eyes were barely open. Nurses rushed toward us and quickly whisked him away. They placed him in a private room with an IV drip of antibiotics, fluids, and medication. After about twenty minutes of us huddling in the corridor, a nurse told my mother-in-law it was okay to go in to visit him and to bring four-year-old David.

Mitch was sitting up in bed when I peeked in, and he was as beautiful as he ever was—even more so. His eyes glistened when he glanced my way. There was a light in them I'd never seen before. It was as if peace and serenity enshrouded him. I thought it was a miraculous gift, perhaps for David's sake.

I took David's tiny hand, and, together, we approached Mitch's bed. His parents stood on the other side.

There was a lunch tray there already. Mitch hadn't touched it.

His mother said, "Go on, Mitch. At least eat your cake."

David's eyes shifted to her in a heartbeat. He said, "Grandma, ask him,

'Do you want *David* to eat it?'"

We all laughed, including Mitch.

"I want David to eat it," Mitch replied. "Give it to the boy."

David happily ate the cake.

In between hospital visits, however, emotions ran high in his family.

"You probably believe *he* gave it to *you*, but what makes you so sure *you* didn't give it to *him?*" his father asked me. We were seated on the sofa in their apartment.

His wife lowered her eyes but said nothing.

That hurt, but I struggled to remain calm. The man was upset. Maybe he needed someone to blame. Maybe they thought I blamed Mitch. I didn't, though—that's the thing. I felt bad that I wasn't equipped to handle his disease in a way that would have helped him, and that I had recklessly assumed I was up for the task.

"If that were the case, I'd be as sick as he is or sicker," I replied.

"Not necessarily," he argued.

On our next visit to the hospital, I mentioned it to the doctor in private.

"You are correct. What you're seeing with him—this is eight to ten years progression," the doctor explained.

I wanted to be sure. "Meaning he had this for eight or ten years?"

"I'd say so."

"I didn't even know him then!" I was still processing the information. "But I doubt he knew when we met."

"I very much doubt he did."

For most, it might have become a question of *When did he know?* My guess was that, for some time, it was a fear deep down. But again, denial is such a powerful thing. It takes over time and time again, so we can hope and survive and possibly get that happily-ever-after ending. And the idea of what "happily ever after" means is also a sort of fantasy, often only taking into account what we're *supposed* to want.

Denial has a price, and it's often quite steep. I learned that the hard way, and I continue to see its cost in the world on a daily basis. I'd never again underestimate its power to destroy lives, institutions, and, well, everything. That's why getting to the truth is essential.

"How is he doing?" I asked the doctor next.

"He's been in and out of consciousness," came his reply, "but he's been awake for the past hour or so."

A nurse was checking Mitch's vitals when I slipped into the room. He was shivering from chills. He was weak, short of breath, couldn't walk unassisted, and was experiencing fewer lucid moments. His family and I took turns sitting or standing beside him or staying outside with David.

I saw the love his parents and siblings showed to him in his time of need. At the same time, his parents were racked with shame and guilt.

"We were hard on him," his mother said. "We didn't show him enough how we felt. We were that way with all of them." I got the impression that she saw her constant efforts to show him that love now was proving too little too late, but she amazed me, really—taking responsibility for the mistakes they'd made.

One thing I was certain of was that he didn't love himself, and when it came to self-love, I had plenty of work to do on myself.

They had Mitch reclining in bed one day. His sisters were there, along with his parents. He was lucid but mostly stared straight ahead. I realized he couldn't see us, but his other senses were heightened. One by one, his loved ones left the room, crying. His father didn't want to leave, so he and I were the only ones left. Mitch then asked for a moment alone with me. His father quickly obliged.

I leaned forward on the bed until I was practically lying with him, and I held him.

"Goodbye, foxy lady," he said.

For some reason, the first thing that came to my mind was, "You still think that?"

He laughed. "Hell yeah."

I hugged him, then rested my head on his chest, and I cried. I felt his weak but soothing hand combing through my hair.

That night, he was taken to hospice for palliative care. No one knew how long he'd be there, but I realized his goodbye to me was final. He was aware that he'd run out of time. As silly as our last conversation may have been, it was meant to be a letting go without the heaviness. I believe, too, that those were the last of his lucid moments.

Unfortunately, my boss expected me to return to work. I had to go.

As heavy as my heart was, I was happy to see New York again. Mitch's mom called me shortly after I got home to tell me he rarely opened his eyes anymore. His breathing was labored. His hands and feet were cold.

A couple of weeks later, Mitch passed away. I didn't cry when I got the call; I was too numb. I wasn't really processing the information. It was his brother-in-law who called me, so I just said thank you and hung up the phone.

My response was a sigh. The inevitable deep despair one feels under these circumstances was buried well beneath the surface. My goal was to focus on David, do whatever was necessary to spare him from one tragedy after another, and give him the best life that I could. Little else mattered.

PART II
THE ROAD BACK

AFTERMATH

For me, everything in my apartment had to be clean and welcoming. In the bathroom, there was the ensemble of snug little rugs, baskets for essentials, and clusters of African violets in miniature bowls. Sometimes, before taking a bath, I hooked up my twelve-inch TV or set fragrant tea light candles around the room.

The black silk convertible sofa in the living room was overstuffed and comfortable, with pretty pillows to add a splash of color. On one side of it were a halogen torchiere floor lamp and a black butterfly chair. On the other side were a reclining leather chair and ottoman, and a floral urn upon a wood stand filled with branches of dried dogwood.

I bought a gorgeous chess set with scalloped edges of dark wood and soapstone chessmen in light green and burgundy.

It wasn't as if I had a lot of money to spend on all of this stuff. Perusing catalogs was one of my favorite pastimes, and I was impulsive—always ready with one credit card or another. It served as an escape from reality.

Now, the holiday season was upon us, so we also had a tree with unique ornaments, multicolored lights, garland, tinsel, and little Santa Clause chocolates wrapped in foil. We strung popcorn. Under the tree, beside the nativity set, I had my Charles Dickens's *Christmas Carol* village, arranged with my collection of figurines that included Scrooge himself. The tiny houses had lights, and I loved it when the entire apartment was lit only by the tree and the other decorative pieces. The kitchen had a red holly and pine candle centerpiece, which also lit up, and I always hung stockings for David and me.

For the most part, I was enjoying the holidays. That year, Elizabeth and I began a tradition of seeing the lit-up Rockefeller tree together. First, we took in a movie—Disney's animated adaptation of *Beauty and the Beast*. After that, we had lunch and then strolled around Midtown. By evening, the illuminated Rockefeller Center tree was a marvel with its lighted golden angels and brass trumpets. We lingered over the skating rink where the gilded bronze sculpture of Prometheus loomed, and we were filled with the spirit of Christmas, as they say. Being with Elizabeth was heartwarming and fun. She was just so sweet and kind, and little things like that meant the world to me.

Meanwhile, David was in awe of a train set he saw in Saj's drugstore window. Saj's dad was at the register one night, and I asked him to ring up the train set and put it in the bag while I distracted David. David was easy to distract because he was interested in everything. So, we pulled it off spectacularly.

In the days that followed, one of David's preschool teachers called me.

"I can't believe how smart he is," she gushed. "You have to come in one day to observe how he is on a typical day. I mean, we love him."

I did, and when I entered the classroom, David was seated on top of his desk, singing Linda Ronstadt's "Blue Bayou" for the class and getting them to sing along. He had no inhibition whatsoever, and the sight of it moved me to tears. I wished Mitch could've seen him; he'd have been so proud.

About that train set—David's eyes filled with delight as he unwrapped it, and they stayed that way the entire time he and I sat cross-legged on the rug, trying to get it going.

I'd seen a few different therapists by then but wasn't satisfied with the recommended ones, so I found a therapy center in Forest Hills where David and I each saw individual therapists. David's therapist merely watched him play and spoke with him casually. He didn't see any problems and thought David was adjusting pretty well. We went on Saturdays. After therapy, David and I ate lunch at a nearby Roy Rogers. Sometimes, we also saw a movie at the Midway on Queens Boulevard. He was always a happy camper.

Since this was our first holiday season without Mitch, I thought David and I should spend some time in Florida as well. I figured we'd all bring each other comfort. Well, David certainly cheered them up. As for me, I said all the wrong things, and some of my transgressions included what I *didn't* say or do. I didn't ask to go to the cemetery to visit Mitch. It never occurred to me that it might be nice to ask them to go, and I wouldn't have wanted to impose.

Then there were the bikinis I wore to the pool. They thought I should have been more modest and reserved since I'd been a widow for merely five months. They didn't think I ever loved Mitch, and, the truth is, I loved him the best way I knew how at the time, and if what they said was true, I'd have been long gone.

My mother-in-law complained, too, that I took too many vitamins and showers. (I took one shower a day and four or five daily vitamins).

There had to be a villain—someone to receive their wrath—and I was ripe for the picking because, on the outside, I seemed invulnerable, whereas, inside, I was a mess. It never escaped my mind that I'd be raising a child alone while waiting for the same illness that killed his father to kill me.

Even during our trip to Epcot Center, there was undeniable tension, and it concerned me that David might pick up on it.

Both of Mitch's parents are now deceased, but we'd apologized to each other long before then. We kept in touch for a while, and they visited a couple of times. We'd always arrive at an impasse, with them asking if David could stay with them in Florida for a week or two. It wouldn't have been a problem if I trusted them to take proper care of him, but I didn't.

"How's he supposed to get there?" I remember asking since they hadn't invited me.

"Just put him on a plane," my mother-in-law told me. "We'll get him at the airport."

"He's a little kid," I reasoned. "Who's going to watch him until he gets there?"

"The stewardess will watch him," she said.

Yeah, and God watched him while she was digging around in her garden, leaving David in the house by himself. It doesn't work that way, and that's why people have parents and hire babysitters.

The other problem was that David remembered a lot of things. He didn't want to go. It was hard enough to get him to take the phone when his grandmother asked to talk to him. He'd be sweet and polite, but he didn't like it.

Many nights, I dreamt of Mitch. In those dreams, he'd never fail to tell me he was okay. Each time, I assured him that I'd been taking good care of David, and he'd respond with, "I know." In one version, Mitch and I talked on the phone, and when I woke up, I saw the red light flashing on my answering machine, but there weren't any messages.

At about two in the morning on Christmas Day, I suddenly sensed his presence. I was on the sofa by the lit tree, wrapping the last gift, and it spooked me. As I nervously continued wrapping, I was unsettled and even a bit scared. I wanted him to stay because his tenderness tugged at my heartstrings, but I didn't want him to suffer anymore; I wanted him at peace.

With him gone, he'd taken a part of me with him. Besides that, he was the only one who understood what I felt—especially the pain of what our fates meant for David. I wished he was there to make me laugh, hug me, and remind me again why life had to be so cruel to an innocent child.

I loved Mitch dearly and always would. There were songs I'd sing in the middle of cooking or cleaning, while I was listening to music. One was Whitney Houston's "Didn't We Almost Have It All?" Another one was "Miss You Like Crazy" by Natalie Cole. Both songs would always remind me of him.

DEALING WITH MEN AND RELATIONSHIPS

When I was ten and went bowling with friends, older guys were already staring at us and sporting a lewd kind of smile. Of course, you want to know you are pretty and not the hideous freak you'd accepted you were, but you're also wary of the danger of attracting attention either way. That never changes, and, in terms of behavior, not much surprises you after a while, but during my first few years of living as a single mom with HIV, people *did* surprise me.

For example, doctor inappropriateness wasn't uncommon. They were aware of my medical situation, which may have emboldened some of them. I saw a breast specialist in downtown Manhattan because I had dense breast tissue, making self-examination more complicated. Before I switched doctors, he fondled my breasts as if it was the most normal thing in the world. An orthopedist I saw for my back problems made lewd comments and implied that I must "really enjoy sex." There was a time I disassociated when a therapist talked to me in graphic language about sex. After a few sentences, his lips moved, but I couldn't hear him anymore. Mentally, I had checked out.

Meanwhile, a couple of women advised me not to tell a man about my child or my illness until I hooked the guy! Similarly, I sat in a support group where a man openly admitted that he waited to tell women about his HIV status until *after* they'd slept with him. During the support group incident, I judged harshly without saying a word despite it being a nonjudgmental space, according to group rules. Aside from frowning and rolling my eyes, I let the moderator handle it, and she did a good job.

Honestly, my mind can work out why people say these things. For most, sex and companionship are essential and high on life's priority list. When a set of circumstances threatens to take that possibility away forever, people get desperate and scared. I'd liken it to a toddler hearing, "You can't have it." Now you've given them something to prove—that they can. I knew, personally, I could have it because people are human and vulnerable—as I was. Still, I continued to overcompensate in different ways to prove to myself I was worthy.

That included my ongoing quest for physical perfection—clothes, hair, jewelry, makeup, and daily workouts. A small part of me thought, *You don't have the right to solicit attention.* In fact, I stopped wearing perfume! It made me feel like I was sending out invites I had no right to send. I know it's ridiculous; people don't necessarily wear fragrances to signal that they are available. It makes them feel good, the way nice clothes do. That didn't matter to me. I usually had up to six perfume bottles on my dresser tray and couldn't bring myself to use any of them.

At the same time, I sought constant reassurance that I was attractive and desirable. It was essential to my survival that I feel young and alive and good about myself because putting off my romantic, emotional, and sexual death kept me from embracing my physical death. It was also a diversion. It was a message I kept sending myself: *This isn't over. Fight any way you can. Whatever works, whatever it takes, as long as you're not hurting anyone.*

So, I wanted men to fall for me, but I also wanted to protect them from me, and I did.

In my opinion, considering physical intimacy with someone falls under the "need to know" category. If I were to put the man off sexually until he fell in love and *then* told him, the deception and manipulation would seem cruel to me. In addition, hiding such a huge secret created a wall between us which, in my view, meant the "relationship" wasn't authentic.

As for hiding my kid, my response was, "Why would I want someone who doesn't want my kid?" Seriously, if someone doesn't enjoy or want kids, he should be in a situation he finds more comfortable. My reality was, I have this illness, and I have a kid. My general belief is that if somebody is genuinely interested in you, they're not scared off so easily. If they're not genuinely interested, any excuse to bolt will do.

Of course, I hoped to eventually find someone who'd be a good father to David, but someone who might do more harm than good wasn't an option. David was my priority, so it had to be the right person for both of us, not to mention someone we could trust.

I once agreed to a lunch date with an architect I'd worked for over the summer. Randy was a stocky, six-four, dark olive-complected man with brown hair and eyes, and he was a charmer. It didn't take long for him to start flirting with me.

I asked him flat out, "How are you handling being a single guy dating in this era of HIV/AIDS?"

His answer was, "Oh, I can tell. For instance, you're young, beautiful—a healthy-looking single mom, so I know *you're* safe."

He was fascinated when I told him what the deal was, and he was also full of questions. That's when people admit they'd been scared to get tested themselves because of risks they'd taken, and, so, they jump on the opportunity to talk to someone else about it.

He asked if I regretted my relationship with Mitch. "I can't," I told him. "I can't regret him or anything about that part of my life. I wouldn't have David, and he's the best thing that ever happened to me."

My relationship with Mitch had its ups and downs, for sure. Some of it was terrible, and some moments were more beautiful than I can ever explain. He taught me so much. I learned so much. And having this illness, I learned a lot about myself and about people. It's opened my heart in ways you'd never imagine.

I didn't get into all of that with Randy, but it wouldn't have mattered. He was on to the next thought. "It's almost impossible for a female to give it to a male," he reasoned. "Even if that weren't true, there's a lot of other stuff we can do."

And here I was not talking about sex or thinking about having it with him, but because I had HIV, he must've assumed I was eager for the opportunity. I saw the wheels turning in his head.

I'd heard people in support groups say, "We're both positive, so we can be together." Yeah, they can, but they need to be cautious as well. Many of them seemed unaware that one person can re-infect the other with a worse virus strain than the one they already have.

As far as I'm concerned, the situation is complicated. A person has to understand what they're signing up for and be prepared to educate themselves about what's true and what isn't. They have to deal with the issues appropriately and maturely. It's the denial that worries me.

Guys like Randy are fully aware that you sharing this big "secret" with them can create intimacy and even a bond. They think, too, that maybe they will have an edge because you're afraid that being HIV positive, no one else will want you.

Some may say these "Randy" guys probably wouldn't follow through with intimacy, but I figured out early that the promise of sex is a powerful thing, leading many to throw caution to the wind. Finding a person who truly loves you is the hard part, and it's what most people want above anything.

Unfortunately, unresolved issues will put us at the mercy of others. We project our yearnings through body language and in things we say or do, appealing to those who prey on weaknesses and who manipulate others to get what they want.

Often, too, when people have an illness or a secret that they're afraid to disclose, they don't realize people may decide that, despite everything, you're worth it. We project a lot of insecurities, and that often determines an outcome.

Anyway, there *was* someone I considered for a while. Steve, my chiropractor, was a handsome guy with dark hair and eyes. But it wasn't his appearance so much. I loved his energy. It hit me as soon as he would slip into a room. He was also a warm, compassionate man, charismatic and intelligent, sexy and sweet.

Steve was genuinely concerned when I first walked into his reception area with Melissa holding my arm. His demeanor said, "Don't worry, I got this."

He provided enormous comfort with everything he did to soothe and relax me and everything he did to make me better. His confidence strengthened me and gave me hope, something I needed at the time. My attraction to him was evident in how I gazed into his eyes and spoke to him—although I always did so respectfully.

If I want someone or something, I don't hide it. And if I love someone on any level, they know. To his credit, he practiced restraint while blushing and smiling until he tried to kiss me right there in his office.

I didn't let him. As tempting as it was, I turned my face away. It occurred to me that what was happening between us was inappropriate. The issue of proper boundaries seemed more important than ever now. I mean, I was crazy about the guy, but I reminded myself that if it was that easy for me to get him to kiss me right there in his office, I probably wasn't the only one. So, I put an end to that.

It goes without saying that as a rule, doctors are not supposed to get romantically involved with their patients. But with single people interested in romance, vulnerability is necessary to trust, right? We have to take some risks.

The truth is, we want to heal and grow to bring people into our lives—people with whom we *can* be vulnerable. We have to move beyond having insatiable needs and find a partner who lives for more than just constant ego gratification. Some people have a lot more healing and growing to do before they get to that point.

And as *we* heal, our interest in others is far more genuine. More beauty and joy await us because we're truly ready to love and be loved.

Around that time, I also dealt with what many single moms experience when there's no man of the house—certain men who are in your home in a professional capacity leering at you or taking advantage workwise or moneywise. One of them put a cigarette butt out on my kitchen floor since I didn't own ashtrays. Another took a piss in my bathroom with the door wide open. I didn't realize it until I passed from the kitchen to the living room.

Every bit of it struck me as a relentless assault, so I was triggered by any man coming over unless I was familiar with the guy. I was too afraid at the time, too fragile, and I know they sensed my vulnerability.

One of my doctors at the time prescribed Xanax for me then, but I only took it when I was overly anxious.

Still, I got to a point where I'd had enough, seen enough. I wanted nothing more than to guide my kid through this predicament, help him navigate it, and watch him rise above everything.

Even now, since becoming confident and in charge, I'm still triggered by a sudden, loud rapping at my door or men coming over to fix things. Often, they are as nice as they can be, and I'm equally kind, but I'm not comfortable.

UPS AND DOWNS

My T-cells dropped to 270 at one point. That meant I was immunocompromised, but my count still wasn't low enough to meet the criteria for AIDS, and I continued to be asymptomatic. Nevertheless, in addition to the AZT, my doctor now had a nurse coming to my apartment twice a month. The nurse, male or female, would hook me up to an IV while I rested on my bed, and they'd remain at my side to supervise me the entire time they infused me with Pentamidine.

They did that because my body's reaction to the Pentamidine might have been life-threatening. It took a couple of hours from when they arrived to when they left. David was in school while this happened because I didn't ever want him to watch that. I had to store the IV pole and paraphernalia in my closet, and I was disgusted by its sight whenever I slid open the door because it was like my sordid little secret, and I was beginning to hate secrets.

Around this time, I developed irregular menstrual bleeding, and my gynecologist prescribed birth control pills to regulate my cycle. For my back, I wore a black support brace with adjustable suspenders or a white corset-type brace concealed under my clothing. I bought one with a Velcro strap and a pocket for an icepack to use at my desk. I did frequent "ice treatments," as I called them, usually lying on my stomach with a pillow elevating my pelvis and the pack of ice in its pocket sheath over my lower back. Whenever possible, I opted for high-back armchair support. For my seat at the kitchen table, I bought a seat cushion with a back made of medical-grade egg crate foam. The chiropractor was on speed dial, and I took a lot of Tylenol. On days I couldn't walk, I canceled appointments and missed important events.

I thought for certain my death was imminent, and committing to anything long-term seemed disingenuous, so I didn't. My greatest fear (well, one of them) was not being able to pick my son up from school, so I did whatever was necessary to ensure that never happened.

The dreams I had then were crazy. (Well, when were they not!?) However, in one that recurred, I was in bed but suspected someone was at the door, so I got up and peeked through the peephole. First, there'd be no one, but then I'd look again, and there'd be a strange man, almost faceless but with a black stovepipe hat. Suddenly, I'd start flying around my room in the dream, but I was unable to go in the direction I wanted. Perhaps that was the underlying fear—having no control over where things were going.

Recurring nightmares of somehow losing David weren't uncommon, either. It was the worst feeling I could imagine, and my panic in the dream was next-level cataclysmic.

There were nightmares about moving, as well. In each one, I'd never have enough time to gather my stuff. My things were all over the place, and the scene was chaotic. Maybe the dream was symbolic of my powerlessness. It was the same way I'd felt with the two rapists who had drugged and raped me as a teenager, the same way I felt rushing home in the dark and in many other situations.

At this time, Bridget had distanced herself from the family as she often did, but I didn't realize it was out of necessity. So, I'd usually be the one to get her on the phone and rein her back in. I didn't understand, as she did, that as a family, we'd become more and more collectively traumatized. The same metaphoric ghosts spooked us, and sometimes it was terrifying. I saw it as an unbreakable bond between us, and I was more apt to cling to her, even though we triggered feelings of inadequacy in one another and unintentionally reminded each other we weren't worthy or enough. And we weren't safe.

Being the older sibling, Bridget sometimes felt responsible for the safety and well-being of her younger siblings. At the same time, just taking care of herself overwhelmed her. With an impossible burden on her fragile shoulders, she tried. She both failed and succeeded, but she tried.

Those times I sought to rein her back in, she'd be cautious at first, but then she'd oblige. And if she surmised you were drowning, she'd throw you a life raft.

Now, I reached out again.

She told me about the motivational author Louise Hay and sent me Hay's book, *You Can Heal Your Life*. Bridget also recommended Hay's audiotapes to listen to when I couldn't sleep or to calm myself. She and I talked excitedly about it in many phone conversations, and she was very kind and caring.

David listened to the tapes with me sometimes, and he'd repeat the suggestions to me. "Mom, don't say 'should!' Louise Hay says not to 'should' anyone, not even yourself!"

Ms. Hay reminded me that attitude was everything. My mistakes might teach rather than hinder me. Broken things didn't have to stay broken if someone else didn't fix them.

I like to use this analogy: Say there is a computer problem. Certain people simply want it fixed and don't care how. They simply want it done for them. And then some people are the "fixers." Working in offices, I'd been tasked with figuring out computer issues and the ins and outs of programs we used. And if a copier jammed, I took it apart and resolved the problem. So, I was that person who wanted to know how to fix things, and I realized I could be equally resourceful when it came to my life.

Bridget also told me that Louise Hay and spiritual growth lecturer Marianne Williamson founded The Manhattan Center for Living on the Lower East Side. It was for people with terminal and chronic illnesses, and volunteers provided free massages, chiropractic treatment, therapy, and reiki sessions. They also had a large kitchen where they cooked macrobiotic meals for their clients.

It was open every day from nine a. M. to nine p. M., and I loved going there while David was in school, although I brought him with me quite a few times. I mainly went for chiropractic sessions and therapy. My ritual when going there was to leave home mid-morning, stop at McDonald's when I got off the train, and treat myself to a breakfast sandwich before my appointment. Yes, joining the others for the center's macrobiotic lunch was a better idea, but I needed some pacification.

The 6,000-square-foot center was warm and cozy—everything from the soft and soothing ambient lighting to the comfortable sofas and chairs. The practitioners could not have been nicer or more welcoming.

CONTROVERSY

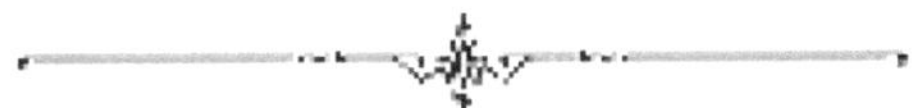

When David was in second grade, a controversy arose around a proposed age-appropriate school curriculum promoting inclusivity. They called the new curriculum *Children of the Rainbow*, and it promoted racial harmony.

The course material also addressed the reality that not all families consist of a man, a woman, and their children. Even as a single parent, I'd experienced some ostracization from other mothers. It didn't occur to people that you might be a widow, but, ultimately, it should not have mattered why you were a single parent. The program's overall intent was that regardless of what you think about someone having two moms or two dads, it has nothing to do with the child, yet the child might face ridicule, humiliation, and cruelty from other children who were taught that it was wrong.

The message was, primarily, "Love one another; love thy neighbor, etc.," but there was also an intention to encourage safety through HIV/AIDS awareness. Of course, I was immediately on board. Love and acceptance feel healthy and right to me. I want that for everyone, along with plenty of peace, happiness, and success to go around.

The *Children of the Rainbow* curriculum was available to read in its entirety in the principal's office of my son's school, and I was one of only two or three parents who bothered to read it. Its content was presented with age-appropriate material for each grade. So, there wasn't much, if anything, for the lowest grades. Those of us who read it thought it was a good, well-meaning program. Furthermore, no student could participate in it without their parent's consent, so there shouldn't have been any reason to object.

Angry parents and school board members, however, were not satisfied with keeping their own children from participating; they didn't want *anyone's* children to participate.

Yes, I realize that many people believe they are fighting a spiritual war to win back a "corrupt" nation and doing it on God's behalf. They may sincerely believe that, but from what I can tell, it's more like a war between love and hate. The burdens we share should inspire universal love and compassion, yet we've witnessed ever-increasing hate worldwide.

Regarding the curriculum, I, along with the other parents, received a letter from the school board president urging us to take action against the program. The letter referred to both the LGBT+ and HIV/AIDS communities as "the scorn of the earth."

It was painfully obvious to me then that many people never put themselves in someone else's place and say, "That could be me." Instead, they find reasons why that wouldn't happen to them because they always behave the right way or they are the "right" sort of person God wants them to be. It enables them to detach themselves emotionally. It's always this idea that people reap what they sow—until tragedy hits home.

Well, bigotry and discrimination have always been deal-breakers for me, so I went down to the school board with the letter in my hand.

"Don't ever send me this kind of letter again," I told the stunned author of its contents. "In fact, take me off your mailing list!"

It shocked her because she couldn't fathom why *I'd* care about those people she'd deemed "the scorn of the earth."

Protesting parents exaggerated and flat-out lied about the program, making statements such as, "They want to teach two-years-old kids how to use condoms."

Of course, there were no two-year-old kids in this elementary school, and teaching little kids to use condoms wasn't included.

I wondered why these people weren't secure in the notion that their children would come to them with questions about what they'd learned, whether from teachers or other kids. I was sure David would because he trusted me. Were they creating an environment that welcomed open communication? Or were they discouraging it?

While this played out at the school, NBC News arrived with their trucks, cameras, and microphones. They were interested in what I had to say since I was one of the few parents in support of the curriculum.

"I'll be the one to talk to my children about those things—especially sex," a man shouted from the crowd outside the school. "They're not talking to my kid about that stuff. *I* don't even talk to my child about that stuff."

Other parents were nodding and muttering in support of his argument. They acted like if they never mentioned sex to their children, the kids would remain unaware that there *was* such a thing.

"How do you prefer they learn about it?"I challenged him.

The guy shrugged and replied, "They'll learn it on the street, same as I did."

"The only thing to teach is abstinence," a woman stubbornly insisted.

"It's great to teach them that," I responded, "but a lot of kids don't obey when it comes to sex, so what if they're oblivious to the consequences of unsafe sex, and they contract a deadly disease? How will you feel then?"

The overall response was, "Well, that's their problem."

I didn't understand it. "So, you'd rather your kid obey or *die?*"

"Yes," one parent replied, and several others chimed in, agreeing.

The parents I spoke to didn't resent me for speaking out because they seemed more preoccupied with being ashamed of themselves. They knew they couldn't adequately articulate any reasonable justification for protesting without confessing their bias.

A few of them threatened the school chancellor's life for daring to promote this curriculum, so the debate raged on until the following spring, and the protesters ultimately got what they wanted. It made me realize that people's biases and fears would always be in the way of us achieving unity and understanding in the world, and that genuinely saddened me.

FRIENDSHIPS AND SURPRISES

I don't remember what prompted me to seek treatment at the Infectious Disease Department of Elmhurst Hospital while still a private patient of Dr. Lettiere's, but I did. I imagine his office was closed at the time, and something came up that couldn't wait for his return.

The first doctor I saw there was shocked upon learning I was on Pentamidine.

"Why are you on Pentamidine?" she asked. "You don't belong on Pentamidine. It's a last-resort treatment for patients with full-blown AIDS. You don't have AIDS."

I couldn't accept that Dr. Lettiere put me on something he shouldn't have, but she was determined to convince me. "Do you know why it's a last resort treatment?"

I shrugged. "I might have a bad reaction to it."

She shook her head. "Yeah, the bad reaction is your heart could stop in the middle of a transfusion."

I was scared to believe her and scared *not* to believe her. It's so hard to decide who to trust when your life is in their hands. Fortunately, I chose well in deciding to trust this doctor. She wanted me on a different regimen, so I switched to Elmhurst Hospital for my care. When they tested me, I had no symptoms of HIV. My T-cell count was 475.

"Not bad," the doctor said, "but we want to bring that up."

While I had some renewed hope, receiving care at Elmhurst was different from being treated by a private doctor, where it was usually me alone in the waiting room. Elmhurst Hospital's drab and packed waiting room had rows of folding chairs that were always fully occupied. Sometimes, you had to stand and wait until a patient got called in to see the doctor, and then you could take their seat. That was a good thing because the average wait time was an hour and a half to two hours. Over the next few years, David would often be at my side there, and sometimes, when the doctor came for me, our heads were resting on each other's shoulders.

It was a strange and challenging time, but it was also a time for which I have many cherished memories.

I'd remained friendly with Saj at the drug store and Cheryl, who worked the front end. Cheryl invited me to brunch at her apartment one day, and I readily accepted. (See, so I'd made progress!)

That morning, it snowed heavily. After dropping David off at school, I stopped at the florist to buy flowers for Cheryl and then headed to her place. It was freezing out, and I arrived at her door bundled in warm clothing. She was a mama bear—unbuttoning my down coat and helping me settle by taking off my fur-trimmed hat and gloves and setting them aside.

She gushed over the flowers while arranging them in a vase and placed the vase in the center of the table where our place settings waited, so she could admire the bouquet during our brunch. We talked about flowers and plants and Saj, and I swear she extolled on his virtues as a way of selling him to me—playing matchmaker. It didn't go anywhere because both Saj and I were hesitant and shy, harboring parallel crushes that made us blush the way a couple of school kids might. As for Cheryl, I always brought out her maternal instincts, and I imagine Saj did, too. At the time, no amount of nurturing was too much for me.

On the school front, I made another new friend. Zahra was a lovely woman with dark hair and eyes who most often wrapped her coarse hair in a tidy bun. Her husband's name was Caesar. Caesar and Zahra were honest people who worked hard to support their family, and I had tremendous respect and admiration for them.

They had two boys attending the same school as David—one a year older than David and the other a couple of years younger. The family lived in a one-bedroom apartment about six blocks from me.

Zahra and I took the kids to the movies, McDonald's, bowling, and into the city, visiting landmarks like FAO Schwartz. More often, we just sat in a neighborhood park talking, while the kids ran around playing. Sometimes, after dropping the kids off at school, Zahra and I had breakfast at the Georgia Diner on Queens Boulevard. David and I loved that place. Other times, she'd come over to my house, and I'd put on a pot of coffee and make egg sandwiches for the two of us, or she'd do the honors at her place. Zahra prepared meals in a small galley kitchen and kept a washer and dryer in the large dining area, where she also had a long dining table

I enjoyed her entire family, so, now and again, I had the whole bunch of them over for dinner. My apartment was now a haven where I nurtured dieffenbachia plants and begonias, a devil ivy plant in a faux stone urn, and a six-foot ficus tree in a hand-painted porcelain cache pot. Zahra always admired the plants and the flowers I'd buy for any occasion. I loved gladiolas for summer, white or orange ones I'd place in a hand-blown glass vase in the living room. For spring, I bought hyacinths and tulips. Year-round, I might have roses in one hue or another. The blush-colored roses were my favorite, and I'd place them in glass-fluted pedestal vases or the beautiful crystal vase that Zahra gave me.

Zahra shared things with me about her Islamic faith and her culture. Learning about other cultures and enjoying different cuisines have always been fascinating and wonderful to me. And Zahra was very much like me in that sense.

Despite my progress, and though I didn't realize it then, relationships were still challenging for me. A part of me tried to hold on to people by giving them things. For women, it might have been gifts and treats, buying a round of drinks, or picking up the tab in a restaurant. I'd been that way since I was very young. In the past, with men, if I wanted them, I'd give them the intimacy they sought. I never felt I was enough without overcompensating. On the bright side, making them happy genuinely filled me with joy. I never regretted what I willingly gave, no matter the outcome.

So, of course, I loved giving Zahra things. When I had an appointment with my chiropractor in Manhattan, David stayed with her and her kids, so, upon my return, I would bring pizza. It was like going home to family— especially on the drizzly gray days or snowy, cold ones.

Then, there were the parties. I decorated enthusiastically for Halloween and did my best to make the party fun. It worked because the kids didn't want to go home. They danced, too—even David. We would invite the entire class.

Zahra and I wanted to have a picnic once, but David didn't like picnics or bugs, and our conversation about that somehow led to me teasing him that I could fly.

"The only way you can fly is if you have wings," he argued.

I continued to tease him. "Well, maybe I'm just hiding my wings, and I can just make them sprout when I want to."

"With what technology?" He challenged me.

I grinned. "My technology of magic!"

"You think you can fly with wings so small that no one can see them." He shook his head. "Even if it were not physically impossible, microscopic wings would not get you off the ground."

"Yes, you're right," I said, laughing. "I'm just playing with you."

So, there wasn't any picnic, but, for Easter, Caesar came with Zahra and the kids to celebrate with us. They made latkes, and I made eggs, sausages, and bacon. We organized a treasure hunt, and Caesar taught me some great chess moves.

Zahra was a nurturing type like Cheryl, giving me her full attention, and always caring about anything I had to say. She was generous with her assessment of me—what I did, what I wore, how I looked. She saw a kindhearted person in me, so I believed I was at least a decent one. That was true of Cheryl and Elizabeth as well, but Zahra's confidence in me and enthusiasm for me remained unprecedented.

She was another lighthouse in a stormy sea. When I saw myself through her eyes, I had no doubt I was succeeding—perhaps thriving, despite the circumstances, which was a fantastic feeling.

SEEMINGLY DOWNWARD SPIRAL

Bridget had moved farther north with her husband and now lived several states away. Melissa was married, too, madly in love, and living her best life on Long Island. I was in therapy again, and I talked a lot about my family—sharing memories, especially of Melissa.

"You miss her, don't you?" my therapist asked. "You love her very much."

"I do."

I knew that wherever life led us, I'd never *not* love Melissa with every beat of my heart. I'd never *not* love Bridget, my mom, or my dad. Each of them had worked hard to secure the future they wanted, and they deserved to enjoy it.

David and I visited Bridget and Melissa at their respective homes, and we continued to visit my parents in Woodside and Elizabeth's family in Hastings-on-the-Hudson in Westchester County. Once, David and I met Elizabeth in the city and spent the day with her at Central Park, strolling through the zoo. Finally, we took a rowboat out on the lake, much as we had years earlier, except now we got to marvel at David's wonder and curiosity.

I spent a lot of time reading then. I became obsessed with Anne Rice's *Vampire Chronicles*, her *Sleeping Beauty* series, and many other horror books. Mostly, I found them at the library, and when the movie *Interview with the Vampire* came out, my mom saw it with me. I'm not sure how I talked her into that, but she simply loved getting out of the house and thought it was fun.

The OJ trial was going on then, so David and I watched some of it. More often, we watched classic sitcoms—both new and in syndication. I lost count of how often he and I saw the movie, *My Cousin Vinny*, but it made us laugh so much!

We got a home computer—a Mac. It was fascinating to me that there was this little underworld where you could talk to strangers around the globe. You didn't have to go anywhere, didn't have to meet them in person. If you were wary, you had total control of what people got to see and do—

or so it seemed. As far as I was concerned, it was perfect.

Around the holidays, Cheryl came over for brunch, and we exchanged gifts.

David and I were supposed to spend Christmas with my parents, but on Christmas Eve, my dad called to say, "It's snowing, Diane; stay home." He thought I was fragile even though I regularly slogged through Elmhurst's snow. He cared, though, and that meant a lot.

Once or twice, while David was in school, I went straight to the Elmhurst ER because of heart palpitations and pounding that I thought was a heart attack. It was another panic attack, but, this time, psychiatrists at Elmhurst had me experimenting with different medications to calm me.

By the end of that year, I got sick. I had a fever, chills, congestion, and a sore throat. I'd be shivering and absolutely convinced I'd freeze to death, but David was fine. Being sick, I didn't have much appetite, so my weight dropped significantly. My T-cells were supposedly good, over 500, which meant my immune system wasn't too weak to fight, but my viral load was in the highest range. That meant the virus was growing, frantically taking over, and that the medications I took to prevent that weren't working.

I spoke to a nurse at Elmhurst Hospital. She pulled my chart and told me, "Your white blood count is too low. Can you get to the hospital? Go to the hospital as soon as you can."

So, I asked my family to care for David, and they complied without hesitation.

When the hospital admitted me, I was put on IV antibiotics and given two blood transfusions. Later, doctors were standing at my bed, asking, "What's wrong with you?"

"Shouldn't I be asking you that?" I was confused. "I thought I had sinusitis or something."

They acknowledged that I had a fever and scribbled down the other symptoms I described, but they didn't seem sure about what was going on.

Meanwhile, I couldn't stomach the hospital food, so one nurse brought me orange juice with crushed ice, and it tasted so good. It reminded me of Mitch and the sherbet.

Melissa tried to bring David to my room, but he was too young and refused to lie about his age. That kid was and always would be honest to a fault, but he didn't understand what was happening.

Melissa took him to IHOP instead, and, for months on end, he laughed at the recollection of her saying, "I don't know how you can eat pancakes with all them frickin' chocolate chips at eight o'clock in the morning."

"It was the way she *said* it," he insists to this day.

But Missy—she was the angel of angels, worrying, holding my hand, offering words of comfort, and cheering me up with our shared sense of humor. What I remember more than anything are her tears. She later told me that when she first visited, she left my room and slid down the wall in the hallway, crying into her hands.

This is it, she'd thought at the time. *She's going to die.*

I got better, though.

The hospital staff hesitated to release me, but I was anxious to leave that suffocating room of rhythmic monitors and unsettling blood work visits, so I bolted. The freedom of combing the urban Elmhurst streets in the cold of January was exhilarating—so much so that I'd left my winter jacket open to the breeze.

I had recovered from the sinusitis. The nurse who'd summoned me to the hospital eventually called to say the white blood count read was an error, but they were still concerned about the high viral load. Thus, they changed my medication.

SOBRIETY

After much coaxing, I accepted an invitation to join a party at a bar with male and female bikers from an online chat group. It was the middle of January 1996. I wore a leather motorcycle jacket over a black tank top with a short skirt and boots, and my hair was blonder than ever. Why was I even there, though? I wasn't a biker. I'd just decided to join a biker chat group and got to know these people by interacting with them on the internet.

Well, I got the attention I must have wanted—the fix of praise and admiration from the guys. They seemed in awe of me. Sure, after a couple of margaritas, I was flirty and fun while still fully able to say no. It was a public place, and nothing even remotely dangerous happened, so I should have been thrilled. But during the drive back home, I was entirely disgusted with myself.

It wasn't any one thing. The drinks, the outfit, the flirting—out of the equation, there was nothing wrong with any of those things. Similarly, you don't have to be a lampshade-wearing drunk or fighting barroom drunk for the whole drinking mindset to be a potential problem.

Up until that night, I thought just backing off street drugs was the end of that forbidden road. I didn't fully understand why people said it was "one day at a time." If you're not *abusing* alcohol or any other substance, and you're never even close to relapsing, you're good, right? You've got this. But that's not how it works.

Addiction, I learned, is a disease of the body, mind, and spirit, and emotional sobriety while abstaining is also an ongoing one-day-at-a-time battle.

On the emotional end, it's been referred to as the "disease of the attitudes."

Most of us who've resorted to substance abuse have "fleas" from narcissistic abuse, usually from people who were also living through the aftermath of narcissistic abuse. On top of all of that, many of us are trauma survivors who've dealt with physical, emotional, or sexual abuse—quite often all of those things.

Under these circumstances, we've co-opted the shame-based coping and survival skills of our abusers. They are skills that have kept us alive and emotionally intact while also putting us at significant risk over and over again. So, we've been wandering around doing things we weren't aware of to block out the pain or create a pacifying illusion of safety.

This is why, on some level of our consciousness, our needs seem urgent, making us unusually vulnerable. We crave attention, validation, and praise, and it's another drug, a temporary fix whenever someone complies. It doesn't work for long because, as with any other drug, the euphoria fades, and we remember the pain of what we genuinely fear—that we're not special, or that no one loves or cares about us. Hence, we crave one fix after another.

We convince ourselves that certain relationships are about selflessness and love when they are more often tainted by our dysfunction. We may love people the best way we are able to, but it can only be as genuine as we are.

During our lifelong frenzy, we often become con artists while attempting to survive the madness. Often, too, we lack empathy. We are self-obsessed and often unable to put ourselves in someone else's place. We've lost the connection where we assimilate what others are experiencing.

Without realizing it, we may become bullies, always hyperaware of any perceived threat, frequently compelled to do damage control. We're fiercely determined to preserve our delusions and denials and protect our "secrets." We attempt to control everything, including how others perceive us. So, drama is very much a part of our lives.

We are always waiting for the other shoe to drop. We dread it when the phone rings, and there is an automatic response of *what now?* And we don't hold ourselves accountable for our actions. Instead of learning from our mistakes, we make excuses.

Despite having developed a shaky trust in others, we still trust the wrong people at times because those types are familiar to us. We form toxic relationships that can put us in or keep us in dangerous situations, often with severe consequences. As a result, people inclined to use our fragility against us instinctively take advantage, and, at the same time, we unintentionally draw them to us.

Sometimes, they suffer from the same affliction, and their desperation is so great that they can't discern beyond it. Neither can we.

Whatever the deal is, addiction is an obsession. In its active state, it impairs our judgment and clouds our perception. It robs us of clarity, which returns and continues to improve only with consistent physical and emotional sobriety. Meanwhile, the pressing urges of codependency will consistently override any willingness to be authentic.

Even at our lowest and most desperate times, most of us believe we are honest. The trouble is, we can't be honest with others until we are honest with ourselves. And we can't be honest with ourselves until we can discern what is true—until we confront it, accept it, and deal with it however we must.

The point is, we can abstain and still be a hot mess. When we come to our moment of surrender, we are broken and quite fragile in our vulnerability. Our self-esteem has been gutted. We feel unworthy of anything good. We lack the tools or coping skills for dealing with life on life's terms. There continues to be unrelenting self-sabotage and self-loathing.

So, I realized that night that abstaining from one drug and not another may work for some people, but it wouldn't work for me. That's when I decided I might as well stop drinking, too, and adhere to the 12-Step Program.

It was only the beginning of my surrender.

Recovery is a long road for us, during which we are often tormented by guilt. I still cringe, embarrassed, when I remember things I said or did, and, at one time, it was hard for me to find any empathy for the person I was.

My dear friend, Elizabeth, reminded me not to be so hard on myself. "That girl was just trying to survive," she said.

It's hard to believe that merely trying to survive can be so catastrophic, but we're not perfect. We struggle, and if we continue to put in the effort to become the best people we can be, we never stop getting better. The most important thing to me is continual recovery in every regard.

As long as we're still here, we have a chance to fight for our lives. I'll never stop fighting, and I'm always grateful for another day to wake up and thrive.

IN ANOTHER WORLD

When David was fourteen or so, Crixivan, one of the antiviral medications I took, caused me to develop a kidney stone, at which time I was rushed to the ER by ambulance. No one mentioned to me that you need to drink lots of extra water while taking it.

Meanwhile, a psychiatrist at Elmhurst Hospital placed me on Wellbutrin, an anti-depressant, which made me fall asleep in the middle of the day. It was difficult to awaken me when that happened, so the doctor discontinued it at my request.

He also prescribed Klonopin (only .05 mg two or three times per day), and he monitored me monthly. He said it was a mild muscle relaxant, and when I took it, it did relax me and eventually helped me regain the weight I'd lost.

That psychiatrist soon left Elmhurst Hospital, and a new psychiatrist took his place. When the second psychiatrist ultimately moved on, the pharmacy I used continued to deliver Klonopin right to my door, per the internist's orders. No psychiatrist monitored me at this point.

For my back problem, I no longer went to Steve for chiropractic care. I'd found a new chiropractor who told me, "There's nothing I can do that's going to fix your back problem. You realize that, right? I'm just making sure you don't expect miracles. I can provide temporary relief, nothing more. You'll probably end up in a wheelchair."

It was the last time I saw *that* doctor. I had no intention of ending up in a wheelchair, and I wasn't going to subject myself to his negativity. His words had an impact, though, along with everything else. I isolated myself more, and my disease of addiction found a new way to manifest itself—the computer. I'd found a respite from reality, a way to cope. Add in the calming medication, and I was at peace in my own little world.

I loved online roleplay—acting in a fictional parallel universe. It was great for creative people, and it sufficed for me since I'd lost the motivation for writing novels and poetry. I couldn't focus long enough to read a book, let alone continue to work on abandoned novels gathering dust on my shelves. In the roleplay world, one got to learn other professions and lifestyles to fulfill fantasies—creating characters who were healers, swordsmen, warriors, etc. It seemed as if you could explore that world fearlessly without any real consequences.

There were and still are dangers for the many who are unhealed from their traumas and vulnerable. Predators are known to hone in on others' weaknesses, which they discern quickly since they seemingly have all the time in the world to perfect their game. The stakes are alarmingly high for some— people who maybe never had a chance to be noticed, get attention, and be popular. They'd concoct elaborate schemes and manipulations, stopping at nothing to take down perceived rivals.

As for me, I felt estranged from society in general, and I had tenebrous moments of feeling cursed or damned. I remember one chat room troll who thought of me as her rival. In one of her rants, she told me if I didn't accept and support everything the Bible said, I was a "cherry picker." It ruffled my feathers at the time, even though most people I knew cherry-picked, too, because they wanted to "believe" while also having empathy for themselves and others.

So, even though I still wanted to connect with people, I had to keep them at a distance. It was fun talking to the ones who were kind and cool, even for an hour or two on the phone—as long as I didn't have to meet them in person.

My mantra at the time would have been this: *Hold on loosely, but don't let go.*

Otherwise, it was great to chat with people from other parts of the world and with those of different backgrounds and faiths. I was particularly fascinated with Wiccan and pagan beliefs.

The Internet was a distraction that enabled me to stay in the moment. Getting absorbed in online chat room drama highly amused me.

I also enjoyed the challenge of figuring out how to do things on my computer—create websites, add music, create forums, you name it.

Here's what I wrote at the time (a parody of The Twelve Steps with only ten steps):

GADGETS ANONYMOUS

An easy little program with ten steps!

1. I admitted I am powerless over gadgets.
2. I have come to believe that a power greater than myself could restore me to sanity by removing this obsession with gadgets.
3. Just for today, I will not download plug-ins, smileys, toolbars, etc., install chat rooms, find cool layouts, or do anything else whatsoever to enhance my online experience or yours.

4. I will make a list of all of the persons I blew off while I was in the frenzy of searching for, installing, and/or playing with the gadgets mentioned above.
5. I will make direct amends to such people wherever possible, except when doing so would injure them or others or would involve another gadget.
6. I will continue to take personal inventory and admit it when I see that a gadget has caught my fancy. I will blindfold myself and tie my hands together.
7. I will pray!
8. I will turn off the computer regularly.
9. I will go OUTSIDE and play.
10. Having had a spiritual awakening as the result of these steps, I will carry this message to other "gadget-holics."

By that time, my grandfather had passed away, so my parents sold the house in Woodside. They bought a house on Long Island and had lived there with my grandmother for two years before I decided to move there as well. I found an apartment that was six blocks away from them. David and I received a monthly allowance from Mitch's pension fund, so I was able to take a much-needed leave of absence from work.

Thanks to Klonopin and staying home for the time being, I didn't have the vicious cycle of anxiety leading to back pain and back pain causing further stress, so it was easier to manage. I didn't use a back brace, take Tylenol, or resort to ice treatments unless I felt an unbearable strain.

Five times a week, I worked out at home—Pilates, weight training, cardio, and overall muscle toning. I looked forward to glamorizing myself a couple of days a week for grocery shopping, doctor appointments, or getting haircuts, but I preferred to spend the day in boxers and a tank top, playing on the computer where I had a false sense that everything was fine.

I did date an attorney I'd met in a real-world scenario, instantly disclosing my HIV status. It was only for two or three months, but we'd have dinner and lunch dates, go to movies, and pal around at the mall, always laughing. He wanted a physical relationship; I didn't. He wanted us to be together more; I preferred once a week. I didn't want to devote the time and energy required to go beyond that, and it wasn't fair to string him along, so I ended it.

It was a time when I also became increasingly uncomfortable at extended family events. I withdrew as much as I was able to. Excluding David, there had to be limits on my time with people. If I didn't want to go somewhere, I simply canceled. It became more difficult for me to judge time, so, when I did show up somewhere, I was often late. Before long, I often ignored the phone ringing and rarely opened my snail mail. Most of the time I'd be kind and attentive, and always to David, but "Diane" was lost somewhere inside me where no one other than David could get to her.

As I've mentioned previously, I still find it hard to forgive myself for some of the coping strategies I employed then, even though I did whatever it took to get to the next moment. We're strategists, concocting scheme after scheme to hold it together, and we don't realize we're doing it, but it's instinctive.

Sometimes, visuals popped into my head of things that could happen to people I cared about, or I'd agonize over the pain they or others might, at any given moment, endure and, in general, how people worldwide suffered unbearably. In moments when songs like "We Are the World" reached my ears, or Princess Diana appeared on television hugging little children with AIDS, I believe those tears were mine, the real me. It moved me to no end. When Princess Diana died, I cried.

My family had no clue what was happening to me, and it took me a while to see it myself. A little bell began to go off in my head when my mind could no longer figure out how to do certain things I used to do with ease. Sometimes, I even struggled to open a car door from one of those high seats in a taxi van. It was as if my mind was scrambled.

ONE CHRISTMAS

My parents' new home was a charming hi-ranch of brick/frame construction on a .09-acre lot. It was no more than twenty years old when they moved in and had the most beautiful bay windows overlooking pretty flowerbeds.

The new house had two floors. The lower level was primarily my grandmother's new place, and my dad had a garage and a wine cellar on that floor as well, right next to the laundry room. Patio doors on the other end of it led to the yard, where there was a sizable canopied patio set and a barbecue grill.

Upstairs, where my parents spent most of their time, the décor was still a bit French Provincial but a bit cozier now. The floral sofa was situated across from a soft recliner, and both had fringed throws. The carpeting was a gorgeous shade of blue.

It was where we celebrated Christmas Eve from then on, and my mom loved decorating for *any* holiday, so she had it all—a sparkling tree, a nativity set, window lights, decorations, wrapped presents, and stuffed stockings for each of us.

The music played from the moment we arrived—Christmas classics by Bing Crosby, Frank Sinatra, Dean Martin, Nat King Cole, Brenda Lee, etc. And, of course, there were the Italian classics. Lou Monte's "C'è La Luna Mezzo Mare" and "Dominick the Donkey" were turned up high to begin with but got progressively louder after the wine and champagne began to flow. I didn't drink wine or champagne, but I thoroughly enjoyed the merriment and the glorious aroma of my mom's Christmas Eve dinner wafting through the air.

Since childhood, our tradition was the Feast of the Seven Fishes on Christmas Eve. Initially, my grandmother did the honors. My mother ultimately took over, but, by now, we were down to four fishes—fried shrimp, scallops, flounder, and calamari—the most popular ones, with plenty of spaghetti, salad, and bread.

After coffee and dessert, Melissa, David, and I played board games with my mom in the dining room while the others watched TV in the living room. No doubt, we disturbed them just a bit with our cackling, giggling, and sometimes hysterical laughter.

My mother was good at games—the reigning queen at Checkers *and Parcheesi*, an all-around cunning strategist. But when we introduced the *Who Wants to Be a Millionaire game*, pop culture references and American slang put her at a disadvantage.

One question was essentially asking, "What breakfast drink do the letters O. J. stand for?"

Disregarding the choices provided, and before Melissa even finished reading them, my mom yelled out, "Piña Colada!"

"Piña Colada!" Melissa shouted. "Where'd you come up with that? It's not even one of the choices!"

My mom said she thought the question was, "What does O. J. Simpson drink with breakfast?" But even then, Piña Colada? I think she explained it that way because she didn't fully understand the question. It might have been the language barrier, the fact that she never drank orange juice with breakfast, and, possibly, that she'd had too much wine.

Her responses surprised us because she was generally sharp, wise, and intuitive—certainly not unintelligent. For that reason, we laughed so hard, and my mom giggled along with us, her little shoulders shaking.

I think I take after her in more ways than one, but especially when I'm left wondering why I said something that I fully realize made no sense. Now and then, it happens.

Anyway, on one of those fun Christmas Eves, my dad came away from the window, bellowing, "Man, it's snowing hard out there!" He smiled, feeling good, I imagine, after plenty of wine.

The heaviest snow fell from two p.m. through nine p.m., leaving two to five inches per hour. David and I wanted to walk the six blocks home.

My father roared. "*Are you kidding?* There's more than a foot of snow, and the winds are gusting thirty to forty miles an hour! You can't even see with that blowing snow! Stay *here.*"

"We'll be fine, Dad," I assured him.

I'd never hiked through a blustery blizzard at night. The fallen snow whitened the sky, and the stretch of gleaming snow for miles ahead seemed to have no beginning or end—as if you were wandering into a white void. It was this hushed world but for the whistling wind and hardly another soul in sight. I felt like we were on a different planet—one that belonged to us alone. It didn't matter that it was windy and freezing, and the snow continued to fall. It was breathtakingly beautiful.

"It's like walking on Jupiter!" I joked.

"You cannot walk on Jupiter," David scoffed. "What part of 'Jupiter is a giant ball of gas' did you not understand?"

I couldn't help laughing. "I know that. I don't suppose you could suspend logic for a moment and let your imagination wander? The weather there is too extreme, as well. I'm aware."

"That would be the least of your worries," he replied. "But you don't have to worry about any of it because the pressure would crush any spacecraft that got close enough and reduce it to a melted puddle. And if it were possible that you should succeed in getting past all that, there's nowhere to land or stand on Jupiter, and the gas and radiation would kill you."

I laughed so much at that.

It's one of my favorite memories for different reasons—the main one being that I was fearless and felt free and happy. During that walk home, I ran and spun and shouted, "Merry Christmas!" And when I fell in the snow, I, again, laughed so hard.

My dad called after we got home, wanting to ensure we'd arrived safely.

"It was fun," I told him.

He laughed. "If you say so."

Yes, I said so.

The power went out soon after that. We lit candles, and I was just grateful to be safe and warm.

BIRTHS AND DEATHS

In 1999, Bridget became a mother. She had a baby girl. About a year and a half later, Melissa had a boy. My grandmother was gravely ill by then and passed away in July of 2001.

Two months after my grandmother's death, I watched on television as two planes hit the World Trade Center. The first appeared intentional; the second merely confirmed it. David was ready to go out the door and catch the school bus, but I stopped him. I wanted to keep him home that day.

For nearly a week, the mood across the country was expectedly grave. Collectively, we felt violated and vulnerable, and our illusion of safety was completely shattered.

My personal fearlessness waned, too, and my trust was dwindling, but whenever my now sixteen-year-old son saw a tough situation, he'd say that we must "soldier on."

I laughed. "Soldier on?"

"Yeah," he replied. "No use worrying or panicking. You just soldier on!"

I was pretty impressed and grateful for the reminder.

Another friendship was born and blossomed that year when I met another wise soul in a recovery chat room on the AOL web portal.

Jace was an artist with twenty-two years of sobriety. He was divorced, had two kids, and owned a profitable business. For years, he and I often chatted on AOL Instant Messenger and sometimes on the phone. Before long, there wasn't a single topic we couldn't discuss.

In photos he'd sent me, he had dark brown, shoulder-length hair and dark, sparkling eyes. One of the pictures showed him crouched in front of his motorcycle. He was a big guy, six-five, with a robust physique. He had a sly smile, and I thought he was cute.

What I loved most about him, though, was his mind. By then, I'd become something of a sapiosexual—enraptured by brilliance—and what I loved second most was how incredibly funny he was. We made each other laugh a lot. I can't thoroughly depict it here, not in a way that I could do it justice, but I will recall some of our relevant conversations.

For starters, I'd always thought of myself as honest to a fault, but as I continued chatting with Jace, I realized that wasn't true. More aptly, I'd gotten myself into a tangled web where my truth became shrouded in veils.

I told him about the writing, modeling, and everything else—and precisely why I thought the modeling clashed with my writing.

"Maybe you're conflicted because of the stereotypical images you have of writers, models, and whatever," he said. "I used to have my own perception of what an artist was. Then, as I continued to meet other artists, I found the generalizations to be unreliable. There are writers who never drank the way Hemingway or Fitzgerald did in the historical accounts. Expecting all writers to fit that drunkard image is almost the same as expecting all artists to have one ear and a loose grip. Self-destructive people exist in both creative and non-creative dispositions. Creativity is a process shaped by experience, but pain is not mandatory for its existence. Everybody experiences pain, but there are people who go on for decades making creative contributions to the world, and they are no more tormented than the next guy.

"Seriously, I would hate for you to buy into this myth, romanticizing the pain, the torture, and the never-ending drama," he went on. "It's masochistic, and what it can do is create a self-fulfilling prophecy. You don't have to be negative or miserable to share your gifts with the world. As for modeling and anything else you want to do in life, you have to know who you are and have confidence in that knowledge, and you have to realize that you can't control what others say or do and that it doesn't really matter." He hesitated before adding, "You seem to be at war with yourself."

Although that wasn't one of them, we had a lot of flirty conversations. We crushed on each other so hard that it was often romantic and beautiful, and we talked about the possibility of a relationship beyond friendship. It was only fair to tell him about my HIV status, but I knew it wouldn't be as easy as past disclosures. It was different now because it was Jace. I had to work out a way to lead up to it.

I began one of our private messages with, "I feel like I have a lot to explain to you. Just bear with me, please, because this will be hard."

He was calm. "Then don't explain it until you're comfortable."

"I have to," I insisted.

"You either want to explain it or you don't," he said. "It's up to you. If you want to tell me something, you will in your own time."

"I said that I *have* to tell you, didn't I? And I have to tell you *now.*"

"Yes, but you are clearly torn."

The anguish I felt overwhelmed me. "I don't want you to be angry with me."

"I'm not angry with you. I'm a little impatient with you at the moment but not angry."

"I don't want you to *become* angry at me."

"And, so, what if I did?" he asked. "I'd manage it but not at your expense."

My heart was frantically beating and bleeding. In retrospect, I can hardly believe how difficult that was. "Do you have any idea how painful this is?"

"No, I don't," he said. "How could I? I don't have any idea what you're talking about."

"I am so scared of everything, and somehow, when you are around, it comforts me." I was rambling. "You are brilliant, talented, and confident. You have such a good heart and an old soul. You're everything—mischievous, fun, caring, loving, exciting, fascinating. I mean, you're powerful."

He didn't seem at all surprised by the praise I lavished upon him. "You were sold before you sat in the car."

"What?" I was floored by this response and struggled to regain my composure. "Why are you so skeptical?"

"I'm overly trusting by nature," he said. "I have to work at being skeptical."

"Well, in my book, you are the first true hero I've come across in my life."

That seemed to amuse him. "You have me seated at the throne of the gods."

Now, *I* was becoming impatient. "You're not making this easier."

"I told you; you don't have to explain anything to me."

"No, I do."

"I'm not asking you to."

"I know you're not."

"Okay."

"But I need you to help with this."

"No, I can't help you with it, and you need to see that. I can't do this for you. Just tell me. After everything…after all this time, give me a little credit and a little trust."

"I can't."

"Then don't."

I certainly didn't like how that went and didn't know what to make of it. Was my manner of going about this bound to make a man who had always been patient with me suddenly impatient? Not that I could blame him.

DON'T SAY IT IN A POEM

My next scheme was to write a poem about it—about him. Except I'd spun my thoughts into a fantasy tale. To be fair, though, that's often how poets explain things.

Shadows of My Soul
Reality to me is the dusk.
Prevalence in the shadows.
It is cloaking,
Grasping,
Discerning
In a world of darkness.
It is torment.
It is restraint.
The disturbing notion
That one must taste a normal
Subsistence,
An existence so mundane and
Unremarkable.
Part of me scorns it—
The contrived,
The unnatural kismet—
And so, loves being
Unbounded.
But, the beauty of the peaceful lull
Amid the trees just before sunrise
Lies in contrast with the hazy tumult
Of my self-inflicted tomb.
I have lived, and I have died.
Life, as I knew it, is over.
Still, I am happier than I have ever been.
I know love.
I know peace.

I am in awe of every vision.
I bask in the passion of every caress.
Every bit of air I breathe is a godsend.
I could listen to the stillness of the ocean
Before daybreak,
To the waves amid a blue-violet sky.
I could dance with flair to the music
With a glow that illuminates me.
What I long to say,
I hesitate to say it.
There is the danger,
The allure
As my hand reaches out to touch your face.
Can I hold you
And resist all temptation?
Can I ever set you free?
To protect you is to leave you when I must,
To silence you when you probe,
To evade,
To elude.
I can sense your presence,
Always,
Before I see you.
And, I kiss the earth you swagger upon!
We can only be hurt if I love you.
It's all been said before,
No doubt.
I might have said it all sooner,
Had I not been savoring every moment
Of getting to know you.
Wishing that carefree innocence never would
Cease.
There is no one else I'd rather be—
Unless it was to love you.
You are all that I crave.

He asked me to e-mail it to him, and I did.

"Okay," he said after he'd taken a quick glance. "There's a lot said here. I need time to digest it."

Days later, I told him we needed to talk about the poem.

"Not now," he said.

That stung. *What was this "not now" business? Who tells me, "Not now?"*

"Fine," I said. "You know what? I am so done with you!"

What that, I vanished from social media.

I was having another codependent tantrum. It pained me to give Jace time to cope with his emotions because I didn't know how to manage my own. I didn't understand boundaries because mine were so weak. And I didn't fully understand that he led a busy life where he dealt with many people because I chose to deal with very few. There was an urgency for me that didn't exist for him, and I had to remind myself that although my drama may have been my priority, it wasn't his.

Fearing that I didn't have any hold on Jace and that he could easily slide through my fingers, I tossed myself across my bed in defeat. It seemed pathetic to lie there clutching my pillow and crying like some teenage girl. But I gripped the pillow tighter as the tears continued to fall.

There was some masochistic high I felt with the helplessness of it all. It was as if someone had injected me with something that filled me with the most profound anguish, the deepest pain, and torture. And yet, I craved more.

I absolutely *ached* for him, and, squeezing my eyes shut, I called out to him in my head, a silent agony.

In the middle of that, he called me.

"The next time you choose to have a hissy fit and pull a vanishing act, kindly let me know before I spend half an hour responding to you in an e-mail," he said.

"Jace!" I sat up in an instant. "I know. I'm sorry. Listen, I'm a dramatist when I write. I mean, I do feel that way, but what I write—some of it is pure nonsense."

That threw him for a loop. "What does what you write have to do with me?"

"I wrote it so you'd have a better understanding of me."

He said, "Sounds to me like you have no idea what you want on a day-to-day basis."

"No," I replied. "That's not true."

He held his ground. "I'm telling you how it sounds to me. I'm not sure what you want, either, if that's any help. You want me but don't want to get involved. You don't see a fundamental contradiction in those two statements?"

My poem expressed my desire to protect him from me, but Jace took it as rejection—me telling him to go away. Like I was this femme fatale dismissing the "not good enough" guy when, in my eyes, I was the unworthy one standing in awe of him, and all the while I was hoping he'd fight for me.

"Yes, there is a conflict," I admitted. "That's why I wrote the poem."

"A poem is for the poet," he argued. "It's a lousy way to communicate because it's open to interpretation, and you may expect one interpretation then get mad when it's not what you get. I don't want to critique a poem that is allegedly about me. Don't you see that? In all probability, it's not even about me but this manifested icon. And for all I can tell, you'll find some other passing fancy in a matter of months."

"Ouch," I said. I knew what he meant about the manifested icon—that pedestal thing. "I suppose I deserve that one."

"No. Look, I'm not saying this to hurt you," he explained. "It is an incredibly awkward position to put someone in."

"I trust your judgment," I said.

"My judgment is that I'm not objective. You're mixing up emotional stuff with work stuff, and it's a bad combination for you critically and an impossible situation for me."

We talked a lot about it, but one of the things we discussed had to do with the femme fatale aspect that I never related to at any point in my life.

"I was a goofy kid," I told him. "When I got older, I wanted to stand out in a good way."

"Never to be ignored again," he said. "Come here. Go away."

That surprised me. "Wow! But I don't do that."

"Yes, you do."

"It wasn't…it isn't intentional."

He disagreed. "Maybe not consciously, but it certainly was and is, considering what your goal was."

I let out a sigh. "I can admit I wanted you, always, to find me irresistible. There's nothing wrong with that."

"No, there isn't," he agreed.

I continued trying to make sense of it. "You misunderstood me, though. I also wanted you to care."

"If I didn't care about you, we wouldn't be having this conversation." There was weariness in his voice.

"Yes," I admitted. "That's true." But I was more confused than ever.

After all that, I told him flat out—about Mitch, about HIV—everything.

"Okay," he said. "And that's what you were so scared to tell me?"

"Yes."

"It doesn't change anything."

I relaxed, breathing a bit easier. "Well, good. I didn't think it would, but it sounds so awful when I say it. And people never believe me at first when I *do* say it. They think they can tell by looking at you."

"You're very brave," he said.

That earned him a chuckle. "What choice did I have?"

"Oh, there were many," he replied. "You know that."

"What I know is I'm lucky to be alive."

"Me, too," he said. "Me, too."

"Coming on to someone with HIV is not what anyone plans," I pointed out.

"No, but, to me, it's similar to someone telling me they have cancer," he said. "Right, we don't look for less-than-ideal situations in romance, but if it so happens that the circumstances are challenging, I'd approach it with the understanding that whatever burdens lie ahead are my burdens, too, and I've chosen that. With HIV, you have the additional challenge of being intimate with one another and finding the safest ways to do that. But if you love someone, it's worth it, isn't it? I don't have to tell you that because you were in it for the long haul with Mitch, and you deserve nothing less than that kind of commitment."

"I'm pretty much a recluse," I replied after giving thought to what he said.

We made plans to meet several times after that conversation, but, each time, one of us would ultimately chicken out. He was afraid I'd created such a fantasy of him in my mind that I'd be disappointed. I got the impression that he'd expect sex to be the next phase once we met face to face simply because he brought it up so much. That scared me.

THE TIP OF THE ICEBERG

Not expecting to be around much longer, I wanted David to have my family as a strong support system once I was gone. So, I got the idea to move into my parent's new house on Long Island—the bottom floor that my grandmother had previously occupied. They had a new cat, Figaro. We had a cat, Armand. We were all cat people.

My father and I worked out a deal where I'd pay rent, and I would pay for our utility bills and groceries. It wasn't the ideal solution, but I was obsessed with worrying about what would happen to David if he lost his only remaining parent. At the time, I was in touch with LIACC, a Long Island nonprofit agency that provided services and support for people with HIV/AIDS and their loved ones. Their legal department helped me create a last will and testament free of charge.

I found a new HIV doctor who is world-renowned in the field of infectious diseases. He was concerned that I'd been on just about every cocktail combination but assured me that new medicines continued to be approved by the FDA. Under his care, my numbers improved dramatically, albeit with a few side effects. One particular medication caused low bone density and a permanent loss of some muscle mass. He eventually got me off of that and on to something else.

Around that time, another doctor convinced me to undergo one more surgery for my left eye. It was a complete success. It didn't matter anymore if I was tired and makeup-free, my eyes were perfectly straight. But my need for constant reassurance and validation hadn't waned. I had to do the shadow work, the healing work.

David was eighteen by then, and you can imagine how thrilled I was that I'd made it to his eighteenth birthday. He'd gotten partial scholarships for different colleges and started part-time work at a local supermarket. David had grown to be such a wonderful and handsome young man, six feet tall, with hair still blondish reaching past his shoulders.

We had a lot of laughs in those early, almost celebratory, days on Long Island.

My mom came to me one day with an old clothes iron she wanted to give me. "It doesn't work right," she explained. "Well, it works, but the water doesn't come out." She hesitated. "Maybe if you push the button."

"Okay." I had an iron that did work, but I was curious. "Does the water come out when you push the button?"

"Try it." She shrugged. "If you don't want it, you can throw it out."

My father entered the dining room where we were holding this conversation. "Oh, no, you don't!" he bellowed. "There's nothing wrong with that iron."

He turned to me. "She made me buy another iron, and there's nothing wrong with the one she's got."

Ah, my mom simply wanted a new iron.

She started again, innocently. "The water doesn't come out."

"Then it's no good," I said.

"But maybe if you push the button."

I laughed. "Okay, we're going around and around in circles here. Give me the iron."

I tried it, and it worked fine.

My father said, "I told you! She made me buy another one."

I couldn't resist. "Did she get one where the water comes out if you don't push the button?"

He shook his head in exasperation.

He sure loved her, though, and he was hardly one to talk with his quest for the perfect toaster. He bought one after another, checking Consumer Reports for the highly recommended ones, but he was never quite satisfied. We got at least one free toaster from his rejects.

In another hilarious conversation we had, my dad didn't get the concept of "potluck" events.

"If I invite someone to my home, everything they want is going to be there—more than enough!" he roared. "If they bring something, you say thank you and put it on the table. I never heard of anything where you tell people to bring corn and this and that. If you can't afford to have the party, don't have it. That's it."

"He's so delightful," my mom said, shaking her head.

She helped as we tried to explain it to him. "They don't do it because they can't afford it, Dad. It's a fun thing where everyone gets to contribute something."

He scowled in response, unconvinced.

Meanwhile, the online world was still a sort of refuge for me. I created a MySpace page for HIV/AIDS advocacy and awareness, sharing information, photos, and songs. Soon, thousands of people followed the page, truly appreciating it, but it was a labor of love.

I also met a sweet woman online with seven years of sobriety under her belt, and we chatted often. She was in a precarious situation, so I worried about her.

"Be careful," Jace said. "She can suck you dry. You're a sucker for a hard luck story."

"I am?"

"You are."

"My heart just breaks for her, but you're probably right," I said. "She fell in love with this guy and uprooted her kids and put them into a school in his state, but then this guy wanted nothing to do with her, so she took the kids out of school again and flew back home."

"I hear this kind of story a lot," Jace replied. "Or slightly altered versions of it. They all end with wrecking a kid's life. Your assignment for the day is to find one female friend who has her shit together and do something social with her."

"So, you don't think my new friend has her shit together?" I teased him now because I already knew the answer.

"No, baby, I don't. Ill-fated plan, not that there was much planning to begin with, and she read the situation completely wrong. Look what happened in such a short period of time, and she didn't even see it coming. It's drinking behavior."

"Don't worry," I joked. "I will not invite her to move in with me."

"No, you won't."

Admittedly, I did have enough problems of my own.

I'd had two more surgical procedures for bilateral breast tumors, including a core needle biopsy. Even though they were benign again and again, I found myself less cheerful and calm with each procedure and more emotional, if not traumatized.

Uterine bleeding was another ongoing issue for me with periods now lasting two weeks. So, most of the time, I was either bleeding or going through PMS. My gynecologist diagnosed me with endometriosis, and I underwent a dilation and curettage surgical procedure to remove any abnormal tissues. I took prescribed birth control pills to correct my cycle and Midol for the symptoms, but the hormonal imbalance affected my temperament and increased my anxiety. It was probably another reason why I preferred to be home and have limited contact with others.

Ultimately, I was diagnosed with endometrial pre-cancer and advised that surgery wasn't necessary yet, but they'd continue to monitor it. I got a second opinion that confirmed the diagnosis.

The good news was, even though I had a severe, multidrug-resistant strain of the HIV virus, the medication my doctor prescribed ultimately led to undetectable virus levels and a T-cell count in the 900 range. Yes, the HIV virus became undetectable in my system after thirty years of living with HIV!

"You won't die from this virus," my doctor said, "but it does make you more susceptible to other illnesses, particularly ones that run in your family. I wouldn't worry too much about it; you take excellent care of yourself, so keep doing what you're doing."

According to the experts, you can't transmit the virus by having sex when you're undetectable, but I'd gotten used to avoiding risk.

Jace was happy for me when I told him about my medical progress.

That led to a conversation about Mitch.

Jace asked if I felt Mitch had manipulated me. "Yes, of course," I answered. "It's part of the disease, and I've done the same thing in other situations. We don't realize we're doing it. I mean, I guess some people do. I'm not sure *he* realized it. He was in a desperate phase where everything threatened to come crashing down around him."

"When the shit starts hitting the fan," Jace acknowledged.

"Right. I still feel guilty because I thought I understood the disease of addiction," I said. "But I never learned enough to help him."

Jace went on to explain that most of us dealing with addictions aren't experts in that field, and even as we learn more about it, we're incredibly vulnerable while personally involved. "And you had a kid to worry about," he said. "It was a lot. You couldn't have saved him."

"I barely saved myself," I replied with a laugh.

"But you *did* save yourself, and you saved David."

"Well, time will tell," I said. "But I hope so."

He reminded me of one of the 12-Step Program slogans. "You didn't cause it, and you can't cure it. And you were suffering from the same disease; you were just on the other side of it. At the time, his addiction was drugs. Your addiction was him."

It occurred to me then that there is a question we often have to ask ourselves: *What is the payoff for our denial?* Because there is one. An issue we weren't aware of made us vulnerable in this situation. We were addicted to at least one thing this liaison provided, and it's doing a lot more harm than good. It's a disaster waiting to happen because when reality kicks in, and it will, the pedestal crumbles, and it's a heart-wrenching plummet to the bottom.

THOSE MEETINGS

One group I liked had AA meetings in a pre-war building on East 37th Street, not far from the Empire State Building. I went only a handful of times because I hated going to *any* kind of meetings—Al-Anon, AA, or whatever. I read the literature, absorbed it, worked the steps, and was keen on putting it into practice, but when I walked into those rooms, my social anxiety took over. I dreaded introducing myself or the speaker calling on me, and I hated fighting back the tears. It bothered me that some people took swipes at previous speakers who shared. Opposing philosophies about God and alcohol v. narcotics led to some harsh judgments.

At the end of each meeting, I dutifully participated in holding hands with the people closest to me and prayed with them, though I dreaded that, too. It was every bit as uncomfortable as shaking hands while offering the sign of peace to others when I went to Mass back in the day.

"Of course, you're not comfortable," Jace said. "If you stick to what's comfortable for you, you will miss a lot of opportunities to learn and grow."

He reminded me that we—especially addicts—don't like being uncomfortable. It's why we turn to other methods of coping with reality.

Online recovery seemed easier, so I participated in it for about four years. It wasn't easier though. It was worse, but I kept trying.

Compared to other members, I was a "candy ass," considered to have had a "high bottom" as opposed to a low one. Unlike many of the others, I never had my child taken away from me due to neglect or abuse. I'd never been to jail or detox, had never been homeless, driven drunk, or experienced a blackout. I'd never even had a hangover! I felt like an outsider because I never felt that sense of belonging, fellowship, and camaraderie the rest of the group undoubtedly cherished.

At some point, too, I came to believe that there wasn't any sort of God or higher power and could find no "happy place" in my mind when I was at the end of my rope. There's nothing wrong with not believing, of course, but it wasn't very comforting to others in the group, and because of it, they challenged not only my moral conscience but my sobriety as well.

That said, despite my general empathy for others, it's painfully obvious in retrospect that I was missing a sensitivity chip. For all I know, it may result from how autism affects me. I'm known to be very direct, which is fine, but, at times, I said the wrong thing and hurt someone unwittingly.

Even worse, my privileges made someone else's struggle unrelatable to me, and I admit that, at times, I was slightly judgmental. I took for granted that I'd had good jobs and promising career paths and that in my recovery from substance abuse, I wasn't struggling the way others were.

Many would say, well, you worked for those things. Yeah, I did, but the fact that I was able to shouldn't have blinded me to the reality that it was hard and damn near impossible for those who didn't have the advantages I had while growing up. My expectations of others at the time were unrealistically high.

During harsh confrontations, I'd tell myself I was merely resolving a conflict when I was, in fact, breathing fire. I've since had to work on all of that because I never want to hurt anyone, intentionally or not.

Unfortunately, however, in the online recovery environment, there were a lot of people almost anonymously competing for attention, pointing fingers at others for having the same character defects we are all supposed to be working on and using known vulnerabilities to manipulate others. For the most part, that was what I responded to in anger because the endgame was often to seduce someone or take somebody down. The culprits may have had many years of sobriety and talked a good talk, but they were acting out of their own untreated narcissistic abuse.

Here's the problem: Survivors of narcissistic abuse derive from their experiences that there's not enough of what's good to go around, which may even be the case in their family environment. They then take that fear out into the world, believing, again—perhaps only subconsciously—that there's a limited amount of love, attention, money, success, fame, and so on, no matter where they go. More for you means less for them; therefore, everything becomes a competition.

Perceived threats can be enviable traits, such as someone else's popularity and influence, or even unenviable traits, such as an illness or disorder. People begin to pay more attention to the afflicted or popular ones, which can trigger an alarm for them. It compels them to redirect the attention they're not getting so the focus is back on them.

Somehow, I achieved that level of power and influence while creating and managing one of those online recovery sites. That was when I learned that character assassination is most definitely in the wheelhouse of many who have suffered narcissistic abuse, and they excel at it. Out of the woodwork crawled enemies I never knew I had, and they got me good.

I was quite sensitive then, so, at the end of that online meeting phase, I had a nervous breakdown.

The truth is recovery is an ongoing, permanent pursuit requiring a daily commitment to better choices and continuous reminders that "that's not the way we do things anymore." We are never above reproach or incapable of making mistakes, bad judgments, or reverting to old patterns. You can be physically sober for decades and still be an ass.

If you're doing the work, the healing continues. You deal with different things at different stages of recovery when you are ready to deal with them. And becoming comfortable in your skin, soberly, is a journey, as well.

Eventually, I learned to leave the type of unhealthy environments I described above, and I'd been called selfish for doing so. Sometimes, people don't realize that what they're asking you to do is tolerate their constant disrespect and abuse. But that's okay. I learned an important lesson: *Don't confuse someone you can save with someone you need to save yourself from.*

And work on your damn issues! Always!

Jace told me that he deliberately attended *all-men* AA meetings to avoid that kind of drama. He thought I should try an all-women group.

By now, he also knew about the various situations I'd been in with men, including the sexual harassment from employers and doctors, which led to an even more serious discussion.

"Certain obsessions and compulsions I've had come and go as if they no longer serve their purpose and then manifest in some other way," I divulged. "I mean, I remember walking in Manhattan, holding on to the wall, and wanting to call an ambulance for no reason."

"Not for no reason," he said. "Just no reason you could identify."

"Or maybe nothing I could talk about. When I told anyone, I always felt it was a mistake, but I realize I do have to talk about this stuff."

"Yes, you do."

"It will rush at me in waves," I divulged. "There was a long time when I told myself I never knew how to control anything, so I was always suddenly in over my head. I kept saying no to guys, sometimes screaming. That was when I was fifteen years old and again two years later—I kicked and fought a lot."

He typed, "That's way too young for that stuff."

"Yeah, the fallout from a lot of that made me feel crazy."

"No, baby, you're not crazy," he said. "You experienced betrayal in every sense. It's no small thing. You have a lot to overcome. It's painful. It's difficult. I've done the work. You're doing the work. It's going to be okay."

After a pause, he added, "You never have to worry about me trampling over your boundaries or bullying you. If I ever made you feel bullied at any time, pressuring you to meet me or whatever, I apologize."

"Jace, you are the last person in the world who needs to apologize to me," I said. "You've done nothing but try to help me."

"Yeah, but I can be insensitive sometimes. I make mistakes. And when I do, I want to be held accountable."

That made me smile. "Well, me, too."

I AM THE DRUG

Jace once asked me if, given a chance, I'd ever give up my looks in exchange for a healthy, happy relationship.

The question had me confused.

"Take your time," he said. "It's not an easy question, but it's been asked of me, and I'm curious what your answer would be."

How absurd, though, because it should have been an easy question.

My first mind-boggling thought was how much I'd taken for granted throughout my life. I had to reflect on how much of my power had to do with my appearance. I asked myself if I'd want someone who wouldn't love me if I didn't look the way I did.

The strangest thing was I couldn't answer that at the time. I couldn't answer it even though my look wasn't exactly among the most covetable.

I also knew, down deep, that my real power didn't have as much to do with my appearance as I might have once thought. That included the power of seduction and the power of my strength.

The truth of the matter is I was brainwashed. It should be enough that we are attractive and appealing in the most natural ways. That we are loved and cherished by those we hold dear.

That could be part of the problem. We don't feel loved, and we somehow think the way to get someone to love us is to dazzle them with our irresistible beauty.

"You want me to love you, don't you?" It was typical of me to come out with these out-of-nowhere proclamations.

Jace typed, "Why do you say that?"

"Many reasons."

"Interesting."

"You think I am wrong?" I asked.

"I'm not sure I think you're wrong," he replied. "My first reaction is, I don't want to influence your feelings in any way, tell you what to do or how to feel."

"How can you?"

"I can, only if you let me. If you think I'm making you want me, you've already given up a piece of yourself."

"You made me want you long ago," I told him. "Nobody could have made me want you but you."

"You wanted someone, and I fit the bill," he corrected me.

"I didn't want someone until I knew you."

"I didn't change anything. I just happen to have the characteristics you want."

"I wasn't looking for anyone, not consciously."I searched for the words to explain where I'd been going with all this. "I feel like I'm in a hypnotic trance with you sometimes. Like I'm under some kind of spell."

His response was, "You give me a lot of power."

"I do?"

"Unless you get to this state with others, then you'd be giving them a lot of power, too."

I was truly astonished by these perceptions—fascinated. "No, it's just you." I hesitated. "The trance feels good."

"Of course," he said.

That confused me even more. "Of course?"

"You are an addict. I am the drug."

I wanted to protest somehow, but I was at a loss for words.

"It's in your head," he said. "It's something you need and crave. I represent that something to you—the icon—and it makes you feel safe. It's not rational. It's symbolic."

"Are you serious?"

"Yes, very."

"So, you are my icon?"

He typed, "LOL…white horse, big sword, etcetera… No, seriously, you can get to someone's very soul by understanding their symbols. Steal it, in a sense. I mean that in the metaphorical and not familiar spiritual sense, but some might take advantage of that."

"And you understand my symbols?"

"I am beginning to."

"Hmm. Well, for someone who is out to steal my soul, you sure are arming me with a lot of information to keep that from happening."

"Yes!" he said.

He made me shiver now. "It just occurred to me, I was never afraid we would not like each other, but that we would."

"Right," he agreed. "That's where the problems start."

"So maybe I don't know you as well as I think I do."

"No, of course you don't."

BENZO MADNESS

I felt dizzy and nauseated one day from one of my HIV medications, Kaletra, and mentioned it to Jace. "I know; I shouldn't complain," I said almost instantly.

"Why can't you complain?" he asked.

"Well, I not only put myself in this predicament. I put David in it, too. Aside from that, I'm here, and Mitch isn't. Plus I have David and so much more. Listen, don't mind me. For some reason, I'm angry today."

"Good." After a pause, he began typing again. "I knew you were angry."

I laughed. "I knew you knew. Anyway, I'm starting to have panic attacks again, which is weird because they have me on Klonopin."

"Is that a benzo?" he typed.

"A what?"

"Benzodiazepine."

"I have no idea."

"I'm pretty sure it is," he said. "You did coke, hallucinogenic drugs, and amphetamines at one time, right?"

"Yes."

"You have no business being on benzos, kid. Someone I met in AA had a similar history, and the doctor refused to prescribe those to him."

Intrigued, I made a mental note to seek a professional opinion on the subject. After a pause, the conversation shifted to another difficult topic.

"By the way, how's the living situation?" Jace asked. "I've been meaning to ask you. From what you told me, I was concerned about you living there."

I instantly recalled the most recent shopping trip with my parents. I wore the black cashmere coat my mother gave me a while back—when I moved to Elmhurst. When we got out of the car, she stood before me in the parking lot, adjusting my collar. "It's warm for this coat," she said.

Then, as we headed toward the store, my father grabbed my arm. "Honey, why are you walking between the cars? You're going to get killed."

"He was really nice about it," I told Jace. "He meant well, but it seemed to me that he saw me as a helpless child."

"I do that with my kids," Jace said. "Put my arm in front of them when they're in the car, and some other driver does something stupid. It's reflexive."

"Your *kids,* exactly. I'm an adult and knew what I was doing."

But the coddling by my dad was common. "It's cold, Diane. You need a sweater," he'd say.

I told Jace, "He wants to keep me safe and alive and well. For that, I'm grateful, but the day before, he ranted and raved about the water bill being too high, even though I'm quick with showers—and he thinks I'm careless with money."

I parodied my dad lamenting, "'She doesn't even look at price tags. How much is it? A million dollars? Okay.'"

My father also took my reclusiveness personally, even though we often ate dinner together and had fun. I explained that to Jace and about how my mother and I would go to the village pool together at least once a week. I visited them often. So did David.

Although I didn't tell Jace this part, I got the impression that my dad was ashamed that I was back home, unemployed, and living with HIV. He didn't say those things outright, and he didn't say them to me, but David and I overheard a lot, now living directly below him. He was often drunker and louder than he realized.

"He destroyed her," he told my mother once, referring to Mitch.

"She's not destroyed," my mother argued. "She's going to be okay."

That conversation got my tears flowing. One thing was clear to me: We had to get out of that place. I was determined to get back to work and, almost immediately, updated my resume and began applying for jobs.

I set up a psyche evaluation as well since I hadn't had one in years. The psychiatrist I saw, Dr. Kozlov, was tall and blondish, with curly hair and blue eyes—handsome, well-built, and quite charismatic.

"I'm taking Klonopin but having anxiety again," I told him. "Does that mean I should be on a higher dose?"

He called this experience the "benzo-tolerance phase."

"The proper way to treat someone on this medication is monthly monitoring and a treatment plan with a goal for eventual weaning," he said. "You might have benefited more from taking it as necessary rather than preemptively. Anyway, the question is, what do you want, Diane?"

"I want my life back," I said.

He shrugged. "Then you need to get off this medication." He soon added, "That is not to say people can't take it if it's the right medication for them. You simply have to be careful, and this, evidently, is not the right medication for you."

He further explained that as people require medication, they sometimes unwittingly change at least part of their life and the goals they may have had. It becomes a different life, but one that works for them. In my particular case, if I wanted the life I'd lived before, it was time for weaning. So, I found an online forum for people tapering off psychotropic drugs. It was a great resource for learning the best ways to do it while getting support from others.

It occurred to me at some point that I might have to change my sobriety date. People in the program said I shouldn't because I took the medication as prescribed by a doctor and, besides that, I'd had no idea about benzos being off limits. They reminded me, too, that I wasn't even in AA when I began taking it, and that I didn't *get* sober in AA. AA came afterward.

HEAVEN AND HELL

Somehow, my dad became convinced that I'd had a more sinister motive for moving in with him and my mother, and that I didn't care about him. Contrary to what he believed, I wasn't interested in inheriting the house or anything else. I was sure I'd be the next person in my family to die anyway. Yet, he insisted that I'd never forgiven him for what had happened between us in the past. He was livid. His voice cracked as he spoke, and it was terrifying.

When I told Jace, he said, "He's a ticking time bomb."

In private, my mother told me, "Don't worry about what he says. I want you here with me."

Meanwhile, my doctor told me that my pre-cancer condition was now Stage 1 cancer, and I had to have surgery as soon as possible. When I told my father, he was still raging out of control. So, while they wheeled me into the hospital O. R., all I could think about was him, and I had tears rolling down my cheeks. Of course, I'd forgiven him for whatever had happened in the past. Forgiving him now was the issue—and forgiving myself for putting him, me, and David in this terrible situation. What hurt the most was that he had no idea how much I loved him.

Thankfully, my doctors were able to remove the cancer in its entirety, and there was no need for chemo or radiation. Losing my entire baby factory, ovaries included, was a small price to pay. I was lucky and in good spirits watching *Dancing with the Stars* from my hospital bed, all the while trusting that everything would be okay.

David and I got to packing our things pretty soon after the hospital released me. I began tapering off Klonopin as I continued to pursue a job and an apartment. Without anything to soothe my anxiety, I'd freeze momentarily at traffic lights. All I saw was the infinite mass of fuel-filled death machines cruising toward me, and I was sure one of them would kill me.

Withdrawal from Klonopin had many awful symptoms, including one called "jelly legs," where you feel you can't stand on your legs because they suddenly get shaky.

In the meantime, Jace and I continued to talk often, online or on the phone.

I said, "You think whatever happened to me in the past screwed with my head, don't you?"

He answered, "Yes, I do, baby, but you're growing and healing. You survived it and a lot more."

I had to give him credit. "You helped tremendously."

"You helped yourself," he said. "I didn't do anything but listen."

"You did a lot more than listen. You showed me the way."

"No, you were willing to see it, even though it's hard to see when you're in the middle of it. I was just waving a road sign I stole from some AA guru."

That made me laugh. "I hope you realize you'll always have a special place in my heart."

"You do, too, in mine," he said, "And that's all the mush you will get for today."

I typed, "LMAO, okay, so you don't like mush; I get it."

"No," he typed back, "but I understand the need for it."

"It's amazing how we can help each other," I marveled.

"No kidding," he said. "It's what we are supposed to do."

"But sometimes people are stuck, and they stay stuck. I didn't want to be one of those."

He typed, "Your magic wand was never broken, dear."

"Huh?"

"That was the moral of the story *Willow*," he said. "The point is, trite as it may sound, what you need is within you. We already have the power to heal. Success happens if you make it happen. Control your destiny. Don't wait for it."

"Yeah, I guess I've been procrastinating for a while."

"No," he said. "You've been fighting for your life."

As I write this, I am more and more convinced of how blessed I was, and how fortunate I am to have met people who planted the seeds for me to learn. I am ever grateful that I was able to gather the strength to move forward and figure out how to heal. Whether I've been in the right place at the right time, open to learning, or whatever the reason was that I stumbled onto a better path, I'll never take it for granted. I appreciate each precious moment I get to live and breathe, and I want to do anything I can that is good.

When it came to Jace, I had to fight to keep things in perspective. I was his friend who lived in another state, and he was attracted to me, interested, and wanted to know me better. He had family and friends he loved and who loved him. He had children who meant the world to him and a job that kept him busy. There were his dogs, too; he was as devoted to them as he was to his children, which was beautiful, and what we shared was so precious that I was determined not to do anything to harm it.

When he talked about his kids, I was compelled to say. "They are brilliant like their father."

"You still have an idealized version of me," he said. "I'm not brilliant—just pretty bright."

"Well, *I* think you are brilliant"

He typed, "LOL. Thanks. I'll start climbing up my pedestal now."

"I'm convinced there is a sweet and gentle soul in there somewhere."

I got another laugh response—this time LMFAO.

"Okay, now why are you laughing?" I typed. "Have you been fooling me?"

"No, baby," he said. "Trust your instincts."

"So, now I *can* trust my instincts. Does that mean I'm right in seeing you as so very generous with all of the time you spend talking to me?"

"It's not really very noble," he insisted. "I like talking to you. I always have."

"But you're honest, genuinely kind, and caring."

"You are not objective when it comes to me, but I do appreciate it."

I teased him. "Oh, damn. Why, oh why, do you torture me so?"

"I don't…ever."

"Yes, you do. You know I will go nuts trying to figure out how to say things to you. Or is it fun to watch me squirm?"

"No, it isn't," he said. "You know that. Why do you think I practice so much restraint with you?"

"I am not sure. I didn't know that you did."

"I did and do…I try not to say things that will be difficult for you. But you needed to come up for air."

I cringed. "I think most of it was very unselfish on your part."

"Not unselfish, baby. I'd rather be appreciated because a person knows me, not that I owned them because they created a false image. Does that make sense?"

"Yes," I admitted. "But you have always been a wonderful person to me, and you only become more attractive as an individual as I get to know you."

"But there's a difference between being attracted and being enslaved. The important part is that you see it."

I laughed. "Well, you're not an icon to me anymore."

He typed. "LOL, you sure?"

I was about to go to bed, so he ended our conversation by saying "Good night, beautiful," in Italian. He wasn't Italian, but he got it right.

My response was, "Ooh, good night yourself, handsome."

I was reeling—my head, my heart, my soul, and every other part of me.

We were getting closer, and something quite magical was happening. I fell asleep with happy thoughts of him.

We had a mutual online friend who was a huge supporter of our relationship.

"Never mind the bear roar and male rumbling," she cautioned me. "He's vulnerable because he is in love."

"I would like to believe that," I said, "but it seems overly optimistic. He's attracted. He's interested, and he wants to make sure I'm not merely obsessed with an icon that doesn't exist."

He was right to be concerned about that. If I had constructed him to become the perfect channel for what I required at the moment, what I'd constructed wasn't real. It was an obsession—a persistent, disturbing preoccupation with an unreasonable idea or feeling. It is anything but love and should never be mistaken for love. It would have meant that what I'd wanted was the fantasy—not the human being donning the costume.

We can be toxic when we are this fragile. We hurt people or put them in harm's way.

We put *ourselves* in harm's way because this idol we've manifested has become our dependency, our drug. They provide whatever we ache for— validation, attention, admiration, or something else entirely. If they want to take advantage of us, they'll give it to us in spades, and they'll instinctively know or learn to withhold it when necessary to regain control, so when it's dangled before us, we can't resist. And when deprived of it, we are mentally, emotionally, and sometimes physically sick. (If the drug were heroin, we'd go to detox and then abstain from the drug, hopefully working on ourselves so we may become free from our obsession.)

Unfortunately, too, we may find a "hero" whose behavior we would not ordinarily condone. That person could even admit to being a jerk, a bastard, or a bitch, and our first instinct is to contradict and comfort them. Sometimes, we figure because a person can be charming to us, we are the exception, the chosen one who will make it better. We're not, and we won't.

At the same time, our perception of this "hero" goes from one extreme to another. This paragon of the ideal either walks on water or is a monster. We decide they can't live without us, yet we fear we will lose them. We trust them; then we don't. Of course, we also swear that we love them to no end, but we can't love someone we don't see.

AWAKENING

Thankfully, things did work in my favor. Less than two months after my surgery, I had a new apartment and, soon after, a job.

The mid-size law firm that hired me kept me employed for the next eight years. They occupied two floors of a six-story building with glass doors and marble lobby floors, but, in stark contrast, they also had an eerie old elevator and your basic, colorless offices—nothing fancy. The area, however, had great restaurants.

My brain was fried, though. I doubted I'd be able to figure out how the equipment, programs, and systems worked—things I'd had a knack for in the past. My confidence and self-esteem had taken a plunge in recent years. I cried while blow-drying my hair each morning, rolling the old tapes in my head of everything my father had said to me. David wouldn't hear me crying above the buzzing noise.

The realization slowly sank in: *There's no cavalry riding up to save you. You don't sit around waiting for someone to rescue you. No one can fix this but you. You have to save yourself.*

Now and then, I'd turn the blow dryer off and say to myself, "I can't do this."

Thankfully, a little voice told me each time, "Yes, you can." So, I'd turn the dryer back on and continue, simply putting one foot in front of the other and continuing to do the next right thing.

Going back and forth to work, I'd say to myself, "How am I, this chick from Woodside Queens, suddenly wandering around on Long Island? What am I doing on Long Island?" Of course, the chain of events wasn't that sudden, but it seemed that way.

Once, I saw a squirrel crossing the street through two lanes of traffic. He got hit by a car and miraculously got up to make his way back to the curb only to get hit by a second car. It happened so fast, and the whole day, I couldn't stop thinking about him. I felt bad for him, but the weird thing was, I also somehow identified with him even though my circumstances were nowhere near as dire.

A wise friend taught me to always stay in the solution. Think about what you can do at that moment—not what you can't do. Control what you can. Of course, life would be so much easier if we could manage to stay in the moment. We wouldn't be worrying about what happened yesterday, an hour ago, or what's going to happen tomorrow. I had to constantly remind myself of that, which is not easy, especially when you're in a panic.

It helped tremendously when I told myself that life is an adventure. With that notion, I saw myself as one of many living things in a vast, astounding universe being given one opportunity after another for experience and adventure. I wanted to hang in for the ride. It made the warrior within me determined to keep rising above any challenge.

I'll admit, facing people at my new job was a challenge in itself. Either I didn't look them in the eye, or I did and broke contact immediately. When I finally got around to socializing, it was unbelievably awkward.

Klonopin withdrawal made me borderline claustrophobic—hesitant about getting into elevators and opting instead for the stairs. I couldn't stand being in confined spaces at the office, especially crowded staff parties in the kitchen where men blocked the one exit. I'd spot two of them talking in an enclosed space I had to pass through and go the other way, no matter how inconvenient. Was it the men or the enclosed area? It was probably both. I hated to pass men in the corridor unless I had achieved some level of comfort with their presence. If it had to do with the sexual trauma I'd experienced in the past, I suppose having been sedated one way or another for so long had helped with that.

At some point, I told Jace, "I've realized since I returned to work that I don't trust people much."

It was clear to me that I began life as an outgoing, overly trusting, and friendly kid who'd bought into the concept of life and whatever it had to offer. It's also true that I'd become increasingly introverted at a gradual but steady pace. Sure, it may have been a case of me playing with fire, repeatedly getting burned, and, eventually, not wanting to be anywhere near that fire. Add to that being "wired differently," as they say, and you feel compelled to keep to yourself for the most part, dreading the masses and gatherings. You're careful about who you interact with, and saying no isn't necessarily personal.

Although I hid it, I was quite often upset. Retreating to the ladies' room, I'd be shaking. There were moments I let the tears flow, or the tears flowed along the way home.

I imagined I'd always have an anxiety disorder, but I had to keep it from coming across to others as something negative. When attorneys came to me in hyper, flustered, or panicked states, their instructions about the assignments they gave me reached my ears as gibberish. They were under pressure with tight deadlines, so I'd be processing their energy along with their words, and I'd have to compartmentalize. It felt as if I'd recorded what they were saying in the innermost recesses of my mind. Their words didn't register or process until I worked on the assignment. The fact that I handed them a completed job that they were happy with, on time no less, was as much a surprise to me as it was to them.

The work itself was great, but the office environment—not so much. Some people were always ready to throw another person under the bus. That never changes. I watched them gossip and spread rumors about people—rumors they either knew were not true or had no idea if they were true or not. They didn't care; that was the problem. They had this idea that if you didn't trash others, particularly the boss, then you were a spy. So, according to a handful of them, I was a spy. I thought that was pretty funny. I still do.

The office manager who'd hired me—my boss—seemed to believe in me, and she eased me into the job at a good pace. She was happy with my work, and her presence was one of the few that calmed me. To me, she was an angel. The truth was, I managed all right as long as things ran smoothly and the way I'd planned or expected. Under continued pressure, I'd reach a breaking point and find myself in desperate need of a timeout to quell my fear and anxiety.

The *good* news was that, as the benzo fog lifted, it was as if my senses had been dulled for years, and I saw the outside world for the first time or, rather, with new eyes. I wanted to be outside simply to stroll and marvel. There was that balmy scent of summer, and everything was incredibly beautiful—cherry, maple oak, and dogwood trees, flowers, birds, butterflies, the sun's warm radiance, pillowy clouds, and blue summer skies. Equally fascinating were the rows of gorgeous Tudor homes with their magnificent half-timbered façades scattered throughout the neighborhood.

In the fall, it was the flocks of geese on the sprawling courthouse lawn that captivated me. Another time, it was coral clouds and a full golden moon in total darkness, leading the way and lighting my path.

I told David about the walks and how I loved the chirping birds. "They're singing and celebrating life," I mused.

"That's not what they're doing!" he quipped. "They just want to get laid."

I laughed so much about that.

DADDY FOURTH STEP

At this stage in my recovery, I should have been beyond "fighting everyone and everything." We use that phrase because that's what we do before we begin to heal. I was not fighting everyone and everything, but finding myself in conflict with my dad after so many years left me completely distraught. I also had to think a lot about forgiveness, which is quite complicated.

Early in my life, people told me, "You're a Scorpio; you hold grudges. You can't forgive." Astrology books confirmed it: We Scorpios aren't content with merely driving that dagger into an enemy's heart. We'll twist it from one end to another and carve out your guts. So, per the books, we diabolical Scorpios must punish others with mad vindictiveness. And yet, like so many other cases of preconceived expectations, this is simply not the case. Not all Scorpios are vindictive, and you don't have to be a Scorpio to be vindictive.

Put simply, I didn't want to be that way, and I knew I didn't have to be something I didn't want to be in life. I could not only forgive but become more generous with my forgiveness. When someone disappoints me, I remind myself that I've disappointed a lot of people in my life. I've hurt people with my decisions, and I'm sorry I hurt them.

At the same time, I'm not in the vengeance business. I realize some people have had their humanity stripped from them, thanks to the abuse of others. I also realize that while it seems people don't always pay for their misdeeds, we're unaware of their personal torment and turmoil. They are their own worst enemies, and, sooner or later, the piper needs to be paid.

As far as I'm concerned, their punishment is none of my business. That's between them and their higher power, whatever that higher power may be. (I'm not talking about crimes here where justice is sought. I'm talking specifically about everyday bullshit.)

Now, for whatever it's worth, my dad was a Scorpio, too.

Based on my concern about this conflict with him, another friend in recovery suggested I do a fourth step solely about my dad.

That meant taking an inventory of my role in whatever happened between us. Of course, a child isn't to blame when an adult is abusive in any way, and even as we get a little older, we may have played a small or innocent role. It's always about learning how there might have been a better outcome, and we tend to carry guilt anyway because of our love and devotion, so there is a shame so deep we're oblivious to how it derails us. Fearlessly assessing our motives is an ongoing part of our healing.

People often say, "What other people think of me is none of my business." And I agree with that in part. We still have to be accountable for our behavior, and it doesn't help to stubbornly insist we are fine, and that whatever we do is okay regardless of how many people say otherwise. It doesn't mean we have to believe every negative thing anyone says about us, either. It's more about the willingness to consider what others have to say, whether it's favorable to us or not.

So, in my room that night, I wrote feverishly, noting the most memorable incidents with my dad and what my reactions to them had been. Writing it out also led to more painful revelations about how my father made me feel, and what affected me most in that writing had to do with a poem I wrote for him when I was about twelve.

I'll preface this with a story about how I became a bona fide card-carrying poet in the first place.

Shortly after my tenth birthday, our English class had an assignment to write a poem, and, unbeknownst to me, the kid behind me had copied over my shoulder.

After we handed in our poems, the nun compared my poem to his.

"I'll ask you first," she said to him. "Where'd you get this poem? And stand when you answer me!"

His desk nearly toppled over as he maneuvered out from behind it. "I copied it from a book," he lied.

"What book?" she growled. "Where did you get the book?"

He pointed to me!

She fixed her angry eyes on me and wiggled her fingers. "Let's have the book. I want the book now!"

I was too frightened to say there wasn't any book, and the words wouldn't come. Instead, I frantically searched the large cubbyhole under my desk for a book that didn't exist, and I prayed for a miracle.

"She did not cheat!" A voice called out.

A second voice joined in. "She's a poet!"

These were children who'd been in my class since the first grade.

"She's a writer!" they insisted.

I was shocked by their unwavering faith in my ability, and it moved me to tears.

"Get up," she said to me.

I rose, shaking, thoroughly humiliated.

"Did you write this yourself?" she asked.

As I nodded, I wiped a fallen tear.

"Excellent work!" She gave my paper a gold star and immediately tacked it to the bulletin board.

My parents seemed as proud as I was when I showed them the paper on Parent/Teacher Day.

So, what prompted me, two years later, to write a poem for my dad?

Well, it was seeing him drunk and crying at our basement bar on New Year's Eve. Something triggered it, and I have no doubt there was residual pain from his upbringing and from being a soldier on the frontline in Korea, a sergeant decorated for his bravery. I heard him say he'd failed at being a father. It didn't have anything to do with me but something else that had happened. Still, it broke my heart. Going to comfort him might have embarrassed him, so I opted to write a poem in tribute to him, praising him to no end for what a good man and wonderful father he was. (Me and my poems, right?)

After I wrote it, I shuffled into the dining room, where he sat reading the newspaper. My mother was in the nearby kitchen, and she came over when I told him I'd written a poem for him and wanted him to read it.

"I'm busy now," he said.

"But it's about *you*!" I pleaded. "I wrote it for *you!*"

He held his place in the newspaper with an index finger, but his eyes didn't shift from the page. "Go ahead," he growled.

Aware that he was angry and impatient, I read nervously, stammering and fighting back the tears. As I read, his eyes never left his newspaper.

"Very, very nice," my mother said with a smile when I had finished.

My father simply said, "Thank you," and continued reading the paper.

To this day, I wonder—*What did I expect him to do? Did I expect he'd jump to his feet and hug me? Tell me he loved me? Did I think it would put an end to his pain? Did I think it would end mine?* Although I never explored it in therapy, the incident had to be symbolic of something, or it summed things up in a way because something snapped in me when I recalled this while doing that fourth step.

Suddenly, I cried and cried in a way I never had before. Unbelievable anguish gushed from the depths of me, and I'd swear there were two people present at that moment. I could hear the child in me crying separately as if I'd split in two. Maybe it was a momentary psychotic break. I'll never know, but I've never experienced anything like that before or since.

When I relayed all this to the friend who'd suggested I do this, he said, "Perhaps your dad felt unworthy of it, so the praise embarrassed him. Maybe it was too much for him at the time."

That made sense because my dad was never one to seek praise. At the age of twelve, I forgave him almost instantly and continued to love him fiercely, but I believe that ever since that time when he saw himself through my eyes, he didn't see what *I* did. He saw a monster. For that reason, it was *he* who could never forgive *me*. I understand, too, that he never intended to shatter me into a million pieces. He was in a million pieces himself. Even as a child, I saw it, and the pain I'd released while doing this fourth step was largely due to the somewhat repressed empathy that I had for *him*.

They say it's always darkest before the dawn.

While I was working on that fourth step, I hadn't been to my parents' house in months. My mother came to visit David and me, but my father didn't want to see me—that is until my mother put her foot down.

"She is my daughter, and I want her here."

He caved, but I doubt he was planning to talk to me.

Ringing the bell when I arrived, I waited nervously with David at my side. My mother was the first to appear in the doorway, but my dad was not far behind. From the expression on his face, he didn't have a clue as to how to handle my arrival.

I hugged my mom first and then went right up and hugged him as tightly as I could. He reciprocated.

"I love you," I said.

His voice was cracking again. "I love you, too."

Then I said I was sorry, and he said *he* was sorry.

When we sat down to dinner, he toasted me, saying, "Today, we start over again."

From that day onward, we had an adult father/daughter relationship. He stopped seeing the kid I was, and I stopped seeing him as a threat to my very existence.

To this day, people say to me, "I don't know how you could have forgiven him." Maybe they're able to see him more clearly than I ever could, but I honestly don't know how I could *not* have forgiven him.

THERE IS NO BOAT

"If we meet, let's keep sex off the table for now," I told Jace. "That will remove the pressure that anything has to go in that direction. It will be easier."

For him, it was rejection again because he knew we were attracted to each other, and we'd been talking to each other for years. My ground rules also played into his concern that I'd idealized him, that he was merely the target of my fixation, and that I might be disappointed when I saw him.

That prompted me to tell Bridget that I guessed I'd missed the boat for certain things.

"What boat?" she bellowed. "There *is* no boat! Unless you're talking about going on a cruise, and you missed *that* boat!"

I cracked up at that and gave her a tight squeeze.

"Seriously," she said. "It's never too late."

She was right about that, but my priority was to start writing again. I'd always intended to get back to it, but one obstacle after another had deterred me. Now, as I plunged back into it, it wasn't as easy as I remembered. Maintaining focus was the first challenge. Initially, small goals worked best, so I made it a point to write for at least half an hour a day. As I gained momentum, the time I spent writing increased, and before I knew it, it got easier. I had a new energy, and I was up at the crack of dawn, filled with inspiration. The stillness of those hours, with only the birdsong and the moonlight accompanying me as I wrote, was pure bliss.

In addition, I read book after book—thrillers, fantasy, horror, sci-fi, poetry, and even memoirs. I love reading almost as much as I love writing and, since then, I've been going through a book a week.

My back issue became more manageable, as well, since I now enjoyed a flexible work schedule where I was mostly at home. Still, I frequently visited a chiropractor in the building where I worked. My worst problem then was anxiety.

Despite that, it was a fun time.

I bonded with my nephew—Melissa's little one, Tyler. He was adorable with his brown hair, usually in a crew cut, and Missy's big hazel eyes. He'd been sketching and drawing since the age of five, and he was about six when he gazed out the backseat window of his mom's Lexus and said, "I'm just afraid I will run out of things to draw." If you asked him if he could do a certain thing, his response was, "Of course, I can!" He was chock full of energy and confidence.

David and I had a lot of fun with Melissa and Tyler at pumpkin patches, corn mazes, and amusement parks. We attended Halloween, Christmas, and St. Paddy's Day events. We saw movies and went to restaurants for celebratory birthday lunches. One Halloween, Tyler was Paul Stanley of the rock group Kiss for a day, so the rest of us dressed as the other Kiss members. I was Ace Frehley! People around the neighborhood waved at us as if we were the real deal. We laughed so much that day, the same as we did whenever we played board games at my place or whatever else we did. It was the kind of laughter that went silent but didn't stop—hearty, knee-slapping stuff I'd remember later for further amusement.

Once, referring to me, Tyler told his mom, "She thinks everything is cute and funny."

David agreed with that, and Melissa laughed. I often, without realizing it, said things were cute or funny. What can I say? When I had the three of them with me, joy filled my heart, and I was practically walking on air.

As for David, well, you often hear a mother say that her daughter is her best friend. And, over the years, my *son* had become my dearest friend.

We had amazing conversations. We watched sitcoms together—*The Big Bang Theory, Two and a Half Men, Everybody Loves Raymond,* and more. We played video games. Sometimes, he'd sit at my vanity table and flip my makeup mirror around to the four times magnified side, so he could laugh when I looked into it, expecting to see my face normal sized.

I'm incredibly proud of him, and I love him more than anyone and anything. But it was clear to me that I'd begun to heal from my traumas while parenting him. There were my illnesses and disabilities, and he'd been without a father. It concerned me that he might've felt the weight of the world on his shoulders, so I wanted to make sure he knew he wasn't responsible for taking care of me.

"None of this is your fault," he'd say.

Still, whenever I read books or watched something about parenting, I'd ask him a question about something I'd learned. For instance, after I read Jennette McCurdy's book, *I'm Glad My Mom Died,* I asked him, "When you were a kid or a teenager, did you ever sense emotional pain coming from me?" Given what I'd read, I wanted to be sure I'd shielded him from a lot of that, impossible as it might seem.

He said he never sensed that I was in pain then, emotionally or otherwise.

Therapy helped me, as did pulling in information from multiple sources.

I read about PTSD and complex PTSD, wondering if that might explain my hypervigilance and tendency to isolate. Nurturing relationships was still a complicated thing, especially considering the required continuity. Now and then, something prompted me to explore another avenue, but I'd leave no stone unturned when it came to healing because we can't fix what we don't know is broken, right?

SHATTERING TRUTHS

In 2015, I published *Shattering Truths*, a psychological thriller framed around my experience with rape, and I did it to debunk a few assumptions about rape victims.

However, since I'd chosen to fictionalize it, it was bound to have a little less impact. I regret the decision now, and in examining it, I realize how afraid I was of coming clean with the bold-faced truth.

That book began in my head decades ago and went through many alterations and transformations. I was anal about how I wanted to tell that story. It's hard to be flexible when you are that emotionally involved, and, honestly, we usually become emotionally invested in our books, so we are incredibly biased. I needed honest feedback and then to let go of what wasn't working.

In one of the early drafts, I'd decided to start at the beginning of my character's life. By page 455, the main character was still twelve! I can't help but laugh now about how ridiculous that was. I had so much to learn, and the learning continues, as it should. Eventually, *Shattering Truths* began the year of the rape and ended a year later, during the aftermath. I created a more focused story with plenty of dark suspense and gothic horror to raise the narrative stakes.

A major reason I wrote *Shattering Truths* was that I was tired of people saying some victims didn't "act" like a person violated or abused. There is no one appropriate, inevitable way to act. It doesn't matter how others dealt with the same circumstances. The reverberation varies the way individuals do.

For example, following a rape, not all victims are repulsed by the touch of an intimate partner. Some women can go on to another sexual experience or relationship without delay, while others can't do that for a long time. Some of us may verbally acknowledge what happened but still be in emotional denial, not fully processing it for years. We delay our reactions and then spend years working through the trauma from that point on, but it doesn't mean it didn't happen. I'm also certain that some survivors *never* fully process the trauma.

When people ask victims why they didn't come forward before, it's usually in cases where push has come to shove, and it's time to disclose. In my experience, I've found that most people would rather not ever talk about shameful things that happened to them, including rape and other kinds of abuse. Most of us don't want to be victims and often can't admit it or come to terms with it, and it never gets to a point where we're seeking justice or revenge. Many of us have had things happen to us that no one else knows about.

Another myth is that victims of physical and sexual abuse will act scared of the perpetrator. They may, but they may not. Often, they stand up to the perpetrator and fight back. They may also love that person or believe they do. Further, in dysfunctional relationships, people can physically, emotionally, and psychologically hurt each other and still convince themselves it will all work out. I assure you that the addiction to and obsession with one another rages on. They can be making wild, crazy love and laughing together after feeling their partner is a threat and wanting to be free of them.

It's also been said many times, but I'll repeat it: Women don't have to dress provocatively. Sure, I was attractive in my clothes, but that's practically a given when you're young. It doesn't take much to provoke someone; you do it without effort. Rape, more than anything—is a power struggle. It has less to do with being attractive than being vulnerable at the moment, and, for predators, vulnerability alone is appealing.

Even if the targeted person appears overtly sexual, there's a good chance that the person was victimized before. It's a vicious cycle because it invokes feelings of shame and unworthiness, which, in turn, intensifies the hunger for attention, admiration, and validation. A pattern of self-punishing develops, so it's particularly disheartening when women join in the chorus of saying someone may have been asking for it. Rape means there was no consent. Therefore, nobody asks for it, and nobody deserves it.

Some people will say it was inevitable, given the person's lifestyle. There's the question, "Well, what did you expect was going to happen?"

Well, we expect people not to rape us.

When the #MeToo movement, initiated by Tarana Burke, took off in 2017, it filled me with hope. Not long after that, however, an ugly backlash seemed to emerge, which continues to this day, and that terrifies me.

No one's asking for sympathy, but a little empathy can result in people not minimizing or justifying crimes of abuse. Because, no matter the circumstances, there isn't any justification for it. The only person ever guilty in a situation of rape is the rapist.

I never realized that my unconscious or subconscious goal from the beginning was to ultimately find the courage to turn myself inside out and share my journey. We need to do this for each other when we've experienced and survived things others struggle to overcome. For me, it was time.

Before *Shattering Truths*, I'd published a couple of poetry books, *A Dark Rose Blooms* and *Remnants of Severed Chains*—mostly poems I'd written over thirty years. After *Shattering Truths*, I started an online magazine that I kept going for a year or so. During the pandemic, I wrote and published *Awake with the Songbirds*, my third poetry book.

Whether I may have done better or not, every one of these accomplishments is extremely important and even sacred to me because they show that my will to live has prevailed. I should have died many times and often have a sense that I'm living on borrowed time and creating in a race against time. For that reason, I write from my heart with so much love and joy. Of course, I wish I could've done it sooner, but it takes time to be ready, and I'm ready now. I'm also eternally grateful for the opportunity.

UNBEARABLE LOSS

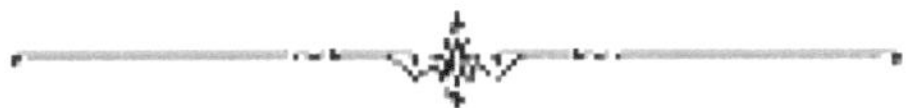

I t's hard to say when it started or what caused it, but I ultimately noticed left/right confusion while under duress. It's more common than people realize. You know your right from your left, but when under pressure, your brain cannot process it. I also noticed that when there's too much stimulation, I won't hear everything a person says, or I have to reread the same page or restart a movie.

I had an MRI, and although they didn't find any obvious neurological issues, I panicked while in the machine. The clicking sounds drove me nuts. I felt claustrophobic and wanted desperately to get out before they finished.

Not long afterward, I experienced another panic attack in my chiropractor's office. No one I've ever met has had a more calming influence on her patients than this chiropractor. She was gentle and Zen, an angelic nurturing type, and I adored her. She connected me to an electrode machine, placing warm heating pads on my back, and the music she played was tranquil and gorgeous. I should've relaxed, but my anxiety took over when she left me alone.

It occurred to me that the last time a wave of anxiety and panic began, Mitch was dying, which led to me being put on Klonopin. Now, my dad wasn't doing well, and my mother had had a quadruple bypass. I wondered if my main trigger was people I love passing—leaving this earth and leaving *me.*

Neither of my parents ever complained much about pain, and I don't recall any time my father did, but now he had pain that would suddenly make it difficult for him to walk or get out of the car. If he was finally acknowledging it, it had to be excruciating.

My worry about my parents led me back to therapy, and the moment my therapist asked me what was going on, I started crying. It was a pretty uncomfortable scene because she sat there observing, nothing more. She wanted to put me on Klonopin, and I was adamant about not going back there. Klonopin was good for many people, but it wasn't good for me with my history.

She said, "I have anxiety patients who are afraid of working out in a gym or at home. They can't tell if they're overdoing it, and it makes them anxious—afraid they'll go into cardiac arrest. When I put them on the medication, they don't think about it and just keep going."

I pictured people doing jumping jacks until they fainted or died but without a care in the world. I didn't take the prescription she offered, but I did take a leave of absence from work. At that time, I couldn't cope and needed a time-out.

My visits to my parents became more and more frequent. My dad loved the old black-and-white movie classics. If you asked, "Who's that?" about any actor of that era, he knew and responded quickly with enthusiasm. He wore a delighted smile watching James Cagney as George M. Cohan in *Yankee Doodle Dandy*. Leading up to the days he got sick, he'd be sitting in his recliner, enjoying one of those old films or something like *Bonanza*. My mom would be in another room, watching soap operas—American soaps and Spanish telenovelas. I'd go back and forth between them, spending time with each of them.

Once, it was my mother and me alone in their living room. Something must have occurred to her, which prompted her to share some of her memories with me.

"The way I grew up, you didn't talk back to your mother and father or your teacher," she said. "If they told you to do something, you'd do it. If you didn't listen, they gave you a beating. I would climb a tree, and when my brother saw me up there, he'd tell me to come down. They didn't ask questions. My brother would take me in the house, make me take off all my clothes, and then beat me with a strap."

"For climbing a tree?" I could hardly believe it since I would never lay a hand on David.

"For climbing a tree," she confirmed. "I got plenty of beatings. My sister saw the marks once when I was staying with her, and she took me to my brother to show him. She told him, 'If I see these marks again, you'll lose those stripes.' Because he was in the Cuban army and had a lot of stripes on his uniform."

I ached for her. "That's awful, Mom."

She shrugged. "That's the way it was."

"If that's the way it was, your sister wouldn't have been so upset," I said.

"No, it was like that, believe me," she insisted. "My brother was good. He was strict, but he was good."

By now, I was teary-eyed. What else had happened to my beautiful mother? I could only imagine.

"Sometimes, I didn't have anything to eat but a piece of bread," she went on. "I was so hungry. And sometimes, my sister took the bread away from me because she was still hungry. We had nothing. We couldn't afford anything. The only toy I had was this little red doll my teacher gave to me."

She began to cry. "This little red doll. I didn't even know what to do with it, what I was supposed to do, so I was throwing it against the tree."

I hugged her then and cried with her—my precious mother.

The extent of how poor her family was in Cuba had never come to light until then, but I was glad she could share some of herself. My father had often shared parts of himself, what he'd endured. Perhaps they'd shared enough with me so that each little piece that snapped appropriately into the puzzle brought me closer to them—these people who became my earthly parents. I continued to love and cherish them.

Shortly after that heart-wrenching talk with my mom, my father was diagnosed with lung cancer and liver disease and hospitalized. My mother was terrified. She couldn't imagine a life without him.

"I'm scared," she told me, looking more fragile than ever.

"It's going to be okay." I doubt my hug did enough to alleviate her fear.

The following day, she had a massive stroke.

Now, they were both in the hospital. Telling my dad that his wife was in the hospital, having suffered a stroke, while he was there fighting for his life was not easy, but he held on to hope. He hoped they'd both survive, but she died within a week.

No one wanted to give my father the heartbreaking news that she had passed, especially while he was so helpless in that hospital bed. He'd always been the brave soldier, and now he was at the mercy of everyone and everything.

He asked about her daily, the mere thought of her lighting up his big beautiful eyes. I was the one who told him she didn't make it.

The light vanished from those eyes immediately. "Oh, she passed away?" He cried, and to see him crying was painful. We cried, too, the bunch of us gathered around his bed that day.

The sun was bold and bright for days after that, and then dark clouds covered the sky. It didn't matter. The whole world gets a little darker for any mother's child when she is no longer a part of their universe.

My father was upset that he couldn't attend her wake. And though I hate wakes and funerals, hers were lovely, with plenty of flowers everywhere. She hated flowers, maintaining that they were for dead people, but I sensed she'd have appreciated them in this generous outpouring of love. Lying in her casket, she was tiny, a little doll, and still so pretty. At one point, Bridget and I huddled together in folding chairs, hugging each other and crying.

After my dad was finally discharged and home for a while, he mostly stayed in bed. He didn't want to watch TV or read anything. It killed me to see him that way. He was a man who'd worked hard all of his life and made sure his family had everything. He loved a woman and stayed faithful to her until the very end. I wanted desperately to comfort him, but no one could. He was so naïve when he came to the U. S.—merely determined to be a good man, citizen, husband, father, and productive member of society. He'd faced harsh disillusion and inexpressible emotional pain.

His physical pain and worsening condition landed him back in the hospital before long. He could barely sit unassisted, but he wanted to go home, and, just like Mitch, he didn't think he would die.

"You mean there's no cure?" he asked with tears in his eyes, referring to the cancer.

My heart bled for him.

He died a week after my mother passed.

His military funeral was one of the most beautiful things I've ever witnessed. My tears fell throughout. Melissa and I were handed the American flag at his burial and thanked for his service. I was so proud of him.

DREAMS

I t was a recurring dream for many years.

I'm in the bleak underground, waiting for a train. There's just enough light from the incandescent lamps to cast a dingy yellow glow. Trains pass, but they look ancient. Still, they are un-defaced by familiar graffiti. Near the passenger doors, the stops each train would make are listed on a flipping board. I don't recognize any of those places.

Rooted to the platform, I ask strangers for directions. None of them have ever heard of this place I want to go to—never heard of Woodside, Queens. Lost and disoriented, I feel deep distress and despair.

In my mind, I recall Manhattan's glittering skyscrapers seen at a distance, beyond the river and the bridge. I remember my train rumbling speedily toward the heart of Queens, passing through the tunnel into the sunlight. Sometimes, I'd catch the sunsets when my train emerged from the tunnels, and I was in awe of the dark navy sky and its sweeping reign over the houses with their golden-lit windows. Or the trail of light orange and the vibrant, darker orange that faded into a pale gray sky.

The strangers around me finally mention places that sound somewhere near where I want to go—still far, but I have some hope I'll get closer. I'll get there eventually. And I'm willing to settle for that.

Oddly, we're outside now, still on the platform, but it's more colorful here. I see trees and recognize the stranger beside me, but he's barely an acquaintance. The train chugs along, but it's too crowded when it arrives. I can't get in, but he does. There's simply no room for me. I don't fit.

Suddenly, another train barrels toward me, its rapid arrival quite unexpected. I hear the beeps and clangs, and I think, "That's the one."

Without hesitation, I scramble on board. I never check where it's headed. We travel farther and farther away from all that's familiar. Soon, I am far from the place I call home and everything and everyone I had ever known. We pass an endless green sea with a boat in the distance. We are somewhere remote. I don't recognize this place.

My dreams are vivid, yes, and colorful, and my recollection of them is thorough.

In another persistent dream I've had since my recovery, and until recently, I ride a motorcycle that I'm so proud to be riding. (I've only ever ridden on the back of one.) As the dream progresses, the motorcycle becomes a bicycle, which I did ride as a kid, and, in the dream, I'm still thrilled because I'm cruising everywhere, including up and down the dark streets of Woodside, my old stomping ground.

I'm experiencing freedom in this dream, and I'm celebrating it, so I'm happy. Except that the bike gets smaller and smaller until I'm on a tricycle that I've obviously outgrown.

There's also a recurrent nightmare where I have to get home from Roosevelt Avenue—that walk home at night from the park I'd dreaded as a kid, as well as the route home after work from the train station when I lived in Woodside. It's light at first in the dream but gets darker and darker until it's completely dark. I'm never a kid in the dream, but, still, the dilemma frustrates me and plays out as an obsession. Whatever way I choose to go, that long, seemingly deserted hill can't be avoided, which in reality is true unless I take the route from the crowded, brightly lit storefront area on 61st Street. Even then, I'd have to go past the place on Woodside Avenue where it's eerily quiet at night.

More recently, I dreamt that I was stranded somewhere and ran into my parents. I asked for a ride home, and they refused for some reason that made no sense. At first, I thought, well, it's beginning to snow now and starting to get dark, but I'll make it. As I walked, it continued to grow darker. The snowfall became heavier, so I tried running. Creepy people tried to lure me into alleys. Somehow, though, I got past those creatures and arrived home.

My son was asleep in his room. I must've gone to sleep, too. In that same dream, I awoke in the dark to find the door locks broken off the door. A sign was on the front door saying, *I hate you. I will destroy you.* It was written in blood. People with cold, angry eyes and a few angels floated around the room. They did nothing to physically harm me, but they were holding my son captive, so I charged in there like a martial arts movie hero, kicking them all. They had an invisible shield I couldn't penetrate, so I went to the door, opened it, and began screaming and begging for help. No one answered.

Now, I can easily interpret what that awful nightmare meant, but David said, "You should never go to sleep. Your dreams are horrifying."

That had me splitting my sides, and he was equally amused.

Transportation is a common theme in these dreams, and I am moving by bike, train, or on foot. I think, symbolically, it has to do with where I'm going—my path or journey, my goal, and whatever happens in getting there. There's the persistent question of whether I'm heading in the right direction, and, according to a book I'd read about dreams, train stations represent transformation. I don't think any of these dreams suggest I am lost, but I am consistently unable to go home, and I don't fit in or belong there.

The destination is always Woodside, although I haven't lived there in decades and will never have to make that walk again from any street. Woodside, with its good, its bad, its horror, and its beauty, will always be special to me, and I get those bittersweet pangs of nostalgia when anyone so much as mentions my hometown of Queens. However, my fear at the time I lived there was possibly intense enough to carve out a permanent space in my subconscious mind. Or, it merely represents a place of origin because I've wondered if pursuing your ultimate goals means you can't go back.

The "threats" in my dreams are all of the obstacles.

Interestingly, I was about to say I hadn't had a "train" dream in a while, but one occurred the other night. In this one, all the subway stops had their names changed. Some were crazy names like Anywhere You Want to Go, while others simply said 50th Road or some other ordinary thing. As usual, I had no idea where any of those stops would leave me on the way to *Woodside*. The platform on this station was perilously narrow, so I had to be careful, even sidestepping rocks while navigating what little room I had.

On a lighter note, I once dreamed I was a cookie, and mobs of people chased me, wanting to eat me. Amused, I told David that I'd had that dream.

"Of course you did," he replied, and we shared a good laugh.

CONTINUAL HEALING

The maintenance is ongoing.

I celebrated twenty-seven years of sobriety in January of 2023, but I still have trouble sometimes pushing that little voice out of my head that tries to discourage me. It tells me: *They hate you.* Or: *They will hate you. Nobody wants to hear what you say, and no one wants you to succeed. If you're here today, gone tomorrow, it doesn't matter. Nobody cares!*

We have to constantly fight that voice and keep going, remembering that some habits are harder to break.

Another example of persistent habits:

For a long time, and, again, even with many years of recovery under my belt, I'd often ask people if they were mad at me.

"You always think I'm mad. I'm not mad," Melissa would answer.

More recently, it was Jace. "You always think I'm going to be mad."

Even my son has had to say more than once, "It has absolutely nothing to do with you."

Someone explained to me recently that this stems from childhood trauma. It's from a time when you walked on eggshells and dreaded the wrath you'd incurred and the price you'd inevitably pay for unleashing it.

It doesn't help that people like us become hypervigilant in gauging reactions and reading between the lines. We learned to note the slightest change in a person's facial expression, and we pay close attention to what their eyes convey—or their smile. We're acutely aware, too, of what they're not saying. For this reason, people become quite transparent, so if what they're telling us doesn't match what we're reading, it's challenging to accept it when they say nothing's wrong. These things were once critical for us to learn because we had to brace ourselves for wrath, humiliation, rejection, disappointment, etc.

Acknowledging this theory isn't to assign blame. Understanding it paves the way for us to correct behavior because we can't go through life micromanaging the reactions and responses of others. We can't push them into reassuring us that everything is okay or will be okay, as we may have wanted our parents to do.

What we can do, however, is protect ourselves and trust that if someone cares enough to foster the relationship, they'll tell us when we've done something wrong. We can learn when to trust our instincts and when to re-examine them, and then we must let the chips fall where they may. I'm not going to lie, though—it's still hard.

Now, here's something I find both interesting and amusing: During the first two decades of my life, I thought I was so important—undoubtedly, while at the same time fearing down deep that I was worthless. However, I learned through social media that so many people I knew in those days don't even remember me! Talk about a well-deserved blow to the old ego, right? It was truly humbling. Untreated issues create such a distorted perception of things. In my mind, I was a legend, I'm sure.

There *was* someone I'd worked with at a publishing company that I reconnected with on Facebook. I was twenty-one when we first met; she was a few years older. I thought she was so beautiful, and she'd been through a rough time. Though I wasn't well acquainted with her back in the day, her attitude fascinated me. So, when I found her on Facebook, I was certain she wouldn't remember who I was.

Her response was, "Of course, I remember you! You were so cool to me! You were gothic before anyone knew what that was! Very smart, discerning, yet sensitive. Withdrawn as you were, you were direct, honest, and extremely talented with your gift of writing."

She said that she and I had exchanged our writings and that I was a good critic, giving her some great guidelines. I do remember sharing our writing. I don't recall much of what I'd said then, but if it helped, I'm glad.

As for her other comments, I was smart in some ways but not others, and I was not at all discerning. Sensitive and direct, yes, but I was only as honest as I could be with myself. As for being "goth," I think she meant "emo." (I'm smiling here.)

In terms of progress, there's little evidence today that I'd ever had body dysmorphic disorder. When I go to lunch or dinner with someone, I never leave the table, or if I do, it's quick. I'm able to be fully present for my companions and able to thoroughly enjoy the conversation. So, there is hope!

I still hate posting photos of myself. They embarrass me. Praise triggers an uncomfortable reminder of needing validation in the past, and of being in bondage to it. It seems I haven't been able to disconnect entirely from that obsession, but I'm working on it.

The good news is we are always healing, as individuals, as friends, as a family, as a nation, and as a planet. As part of that process, we continue to expand our consciousness, and we wake up every day one step closer to who we are meant to be—the best person we can be under our everyday circumstances.

Every one of us will have one challenge or another that we continue to face until we get a handle on it. So, while I cringe at memories of things I said and did years ago, I love that, as we recover, we know better than we did in the past.

A FEW UPDATES

I can't close out this story without a couple of updates.

Remember when I mentioned in the introduction that I lived happily ever after?

Okay, well, someone else's idea of what constitutes a good life or "happily ever after" is not a one-size-fits-all.

You can be someone for whom relationships are too complicated.

You can be going through something in your life, processing trauma you may have denied for too long, or you can be going through physical changes in your body. Either way, you might not have the desires other people expect you to have.

Maybe all you want right now is a friend. Friendship is the best foundation, anyway, for whatever may evolve beyond that.

It boils down to this: Not everyone wants the same thing, and that's okay.

When I reflect on what Mitch wanted for a happily ever after, and what he went through, I still cry for him.

At this point in time, I prefer to write and live primarily in my own little world than to continually bear witness to the world's imbalance and insanity. I once thought I wasn't a people person, but I realize now that I love people. I was just never sure how to deal with them.

These days, however, a sacred innocence in me has returned. The ever-present inner child in me is at peace and full of joy. I can see the world's beauty with the eyes of that child. Even when things get crazy, I sit with this peace. If that peace slips away from me even for a moment, I'll grasp it again and keep it clutched in my fist.

I do still talk to Jace. We e-mail each other every now and then, and we had a phone conversation earlier this year. Talking to him on the phone is an experience I can't describe. It's always as if I'm reconnecting with a soul mate in one form or another. His voice is soothingly familiar, and his laughter just melts me.

We talked a little about my days with Mitch, and I said, "I was so impressed with any bit of knowledge he had that I didn't have. I wanted to be impressed! I wanted to be in awe and in love." I laughed.

"No, I totally get it," Jace said.

"But when I met you—oh, my God, *you* taught me so much," I gushed. "I mean, that was—"

"A whole 'nother level of knowledge," he joked.

We both laughed heartily at that.

"Your insight helped me so much," I said. "But you were right that I had to take you off the pedestal."

"Yes," he said. "I'm just a guy."

"That makes it so much easier for both of us."

"Oh, hell yes!"He laughed again.

"It wasn't fair to either of us," I realized aloud. "It was fun, though—at least for me. I hope it was for you, too, most of the time."

"It still is," he confessed.

"Well, I have taken you off your pedestal."

"Have you?" There was that old apprehension.

"Of course," I replied. "You wanted me to."

"Yes, I did. I don't belong there."

"But, having said that, I am not wrong to say they don't make many guys like you, Jace."

"They don't make many babes like you," he replied.

I felt my cheeks turn pink and my heart was about to burst. I wanted to cry, hug him, and dance around the room. "Anyway," I said, "I still think the world of you."

He responded to that with, "I think the world of you too."

Moving on to my sweet David—he's one of my beta readers for the books I write. He goes through the work with a fine-toothed comb and is quite good at catching little errors.

While reading about a fight between two characters, where the hero kept fighting his outmatched opponent, David said, "The fight was over. He already won, but he (the character) kept going. It's not a good sign when someone doesn't know the fight is over."

He's quick, too, to point out when someone is co-dependent. I'd taught him a lot about that, and he's never been anything but sober in his life. He never had to wear the blinders I'd needed even after many years of sobriety.

David once pointed out how I wrap myself in a cocoon on the sofa even on the warmest nights, even if I have to put on the fan or a/c, and he further pointed out that I sleep with my arms protecting me. The soft blanket was the equivalent of a warm hug, and maybe it was the child in me, but he surmised it was a trauma response—past stuff.

Lastly, I miss my mom and dad. I'll never forget my father's military funeral or that little red doll story my mother told me. Her cashmere coat has remained in my closet for many years, and it still fits. I could never bear to give it away.

THAT ROAD

I saw a meme the other day that said, "Please stop getting into relationships when you need therapy and an exorcism." Okay, the exorcism is a bit extreme, but it is true that we must conquer our demons.

And that's why I plunged fearlessly into that seemingly endless abyss where we face painful truths and endure the grueling healing process. Many people deliberately avoid it or scatter a little bit of dirt to the side and then dart off in another direction, taking cover until they become grounded enough to dig a little deeper. They don't want to uncover the truth because they have an inner sense that it won't serve them well. Indeed, at the moment, it won't, but it definitely will in the long run.

The path I took made me a better human than I once was, and I became increasingly more authentic because I'm no longer trying to fit in where I don't belong (and being treated like an imposter). That is my truth because I once lived a false reality about everything, including who I was.

It's not hard to understand why people cling to illusions and delusions that comfort and protect them. Living in ignorant bliss has its advantages. Fantasy often bests reality, and sentimentality can give us an illusion of innocence in a safe and familiar world. It's so easy to be impatient with people, but we could all use patience from others. We're trying, and we're doing our best. Breaking the cycle of continuous damage to ourselves is a divine process.

We can wear masks for a lifetime, not knowing who we are or what is real. Or we can begin to peel off one layer of untruth at a time as if we're peeling an onion or discarding a myriad of veils. Uncovering and accepting the truth dissipates the shame that drove us to compete with others and try to control them. We learn to love with our whole hearts—not just others but ourselves. We understand how vulnerable we are, so we walk away from people who aim to exploit our vulnerabilities. And we keep getting better at it. That's good because before we understood it, it was easy for others to lead, fool, and enslave us.

At this point, denial has ceased to be our sole comfort and our way to survive. The payoff is no longer worth it. We continue striving to become more and more authentic, and we can do something unrepentant narcissists can't seem to do. We can wake up each day and decide to be the best person we can be because we can *empathize* with others, put ourselves in another person's place, and respect boundaries. We have better life skills to cope. Threats to our serenity may be opportunities to utilize the tools we've acquired and to practice our new skills.

We become more understanding as we become more aware. We learn to examine our actions and motives and not fear what we find. We don't have to be perfect. More important is the desire to recognize and correct hurtful behavior as we move forward.

Love is good, but to be comfortable loving and being loved in return, we must realize we deserve it. We must realize we are worthy. Getting to that place opens another door in the journey of our recovery from past trauma and emotional abuse. Beyond it, more beauty awaits—and more joy.

One final note—

In the earlier days of the COVID pandemic, a talk show host said, "Life is not meant to be spent avoiding death."

That was interesting to me because I'm among those who spent the first half of my life living recklessly and death be damned. The next half was spent fiercely protecting myself. I don't have to live dangerously anymore. I want to savor everything and everyone, stay in the moment, and cherish every second. Maybe now I realize there are so many better options between one extreme and the other. It's always about balance, right?

A few years ago, Melissa said to me, "You're my hero. You're the strongest person I know."

As far as that goes, I just don't want to die. I'm not *afraid* to die. I just don't want to, and that's that. And while I'm alive, I want to feel the best I can feel and be the best person I can be.

That's me—trying not to die.

PART III
TRIBUTES

A LETTER TO MY FATHER

Dearest Dad,

I had a dream about you last night and woke up crying. I couldn't sleep after that. In the dream, you were angry with me and full of hate. You had shut the door on me and left me out in the cold. I kept calling to you with a child's unbearable anguish. You didn't hear.

At some point, I cried, "Help me, Daddy." And, finally, you came. I thought you were going to hurt me with your scarred and violent soul, but you didn't. You hugged me. Well, you didn't just hug me. You gave me the kind of hug I'd wanted from you since childhood, the comfort I always needed, and I didn't want to let go.

I miss your smile and your jokes, Dad—your handsome face, and all of your wisdom, but I have to ask. Does a father realize he is the first man a girl gives her heart to completely? The first man she trusts blindly and with unmitigated devotion? Did *you* realize?

I used to think I was hard to love. Whatever people said—men, especially—I wanted to believe them. Deep down, I didn't. Not a word. And every time a man took something from me that I didn't want him to have, every time a man tried to silence me, belittle me, or make me doubt myself, I punished him, pummeling him with words and crushing him with my goodbye. I could be angry with them—but not with you.

What if things had been different between us, though? Would I have been less vulnerable? Would I have had the confidence to be my authentic self, knowing I was worthy and lovable? Would I have chosen more wisely? Would I have stopped running and hiding, oblivious to my weaknesses and my desperate needs? Would I have respected myself more? Might I have found someone I could love for real? Someone who could have loved me back? Because I didn't let them; I made sure they couldn't.

Well, no matter. That's all changed now. I picked up the shattered pieces of my heart and began to love myself.

It's easy to defeat someone when you have all of the power, when you are on a pedestal from the start and make all of the rules. You can create vulnerabilities and punish the very same, though you don't mean it. You can erase one's humanity because of your denial, your self-loathing, and your shame, though you're not aware of what you are doing. You can damage a person almost beyond repair. And, after the wrecking ball passes, the cleanup of that wreckage rests solely on the tiny shoulders of that same person. Yeah, those shoulders get bigger, but, somehow, it all gets harder and more complicated.

I cleaned up that mess, though. The void lasts forever, and many people can attest to that, but I got those things I needed. It just takes ongoing effort to hold on to them. And by the time I had a child of my own, I knew all too well what a child needs. I was able to give him that, but I couldn't give him *you*. I'm proud of him, and I'd like to think you'd be proud of him, too, but it doesn't matter now.

Look, maybe you didn't give me what I needed, but you gave what you had. You were a hero to many, and I know why they loved you. I know why *I* loved you. Sure, it's easy to love someone when you think they are perfect—when you hold them up on a pedestal and pretend that they are everything you need and always wanted. You fell off that pedestal long ago, Dad, but I loved you so much, flaws and all, and I still do.

That's unconditional love, and though you couldn't give that to me, I still gave it to you. Because guess what? You deserved that, too, from the people who didn't give it to you in the first place.

Yeah, I know why you were the way you were. You could never understand me, but I understood you. Although you couldn't hear me, yours was the loudest voice I'd ever heard in my entire life—a voice that continues to bellow in my ear for a lifetime. It kept me from standing up; it kept me from fighting; and it kept me from winning. I finally did all those things because I couldn't lose any more. I climbed in spite of you, because of you, and *for* you, because you couldn't do it yourself, and I understand that.

When you were angry, devastated, and tortured, I tried to tell you that it would be okay, that I was sorry for you, and that I loved you, but it seemed too much for you to bear at the time. Then, in the end, I forgave you, and you forgave me. It took a lifetime, but we got there.

Sigh. There are many things we never got to do, Dad, and it's too late now. You're gone. But I do have some fond memories of you that I will cherish always.

And here's what I wish.

I wish I could go back in time with you—to those boyhood days when you were punished severely for no good reason. Those days when you were shamed, ridiculed, ignored, and had your feelings invalidated. I would tell you how awesome you are, and all you could be and do with your life. I'd tell you I believe in you, and that you have everything you need to succeed. I would say over and over that I love you to the moon and back, so you would know how worthy you are of that love. And maybe you would have grown up to be what you wanted, and have felt no shame.

Then when it was your turn, you could have done the same. You would have known I was not an extension of you and didn't have to represent you or your ideals. Perhaps you would not have expected such a "go with the flow" conformist-type of kid who didn't make waves but one who sang to a song you couldn't possibly hear. You would not have lost empathy. You wouldn't have cared about how others saw me or what they thought of me. You'd have treasured me for the person I am.

It's hard not to feel that twinge of emotion when I hear the father tributes of others and about how their fathers are their heroes. I honestly wish everyone could beam with that pride and feel safe, content, and protected in that eternal bond.

The aching in my heart is that I want that for everyone. I wish all people who didn't get what they needed as children would give that and get it back in abundance in whatever way they can. And I'm infinitely grateful to every hardworking mom and dad who gets up every day ready and willing to get it all right, including you.

You were not my champion, nor my child's, but you are indeed a hero, Dad. Your sacrifices have never gone unnoticed. They never will.

Rest easy, Dad, and know you will always be in my heart.

SHE HATED FLOWERS

She hated flowers, and I wondered why
That was,
When diamonds less radiant
Diminished her gloom,
And she delighted in the fragrance of her favorite perfume.

She hated that they withered and faded,
I thought;
That their petals broke loose,
And they barely hung on.
She hated that they were thrown away,
With every trace of them gone.

They were delicate and fragile like her,
I'd say;
The kind of thing
She felt so undeserving of.
It's such taxing work for the weary,
Simply to nurture and love.

She clung to her own greenness and vigor,
I thought.
Exquisite as they were,
They brought too much sorrow.
She detested caring for those who
Would not need her tomorrow.

She was too oppressed to provide refuge,
I found.
I heard heartbreaking stories,
Where she had it rough.
She did the best she could, I know,

But it was just never enough.

She is every bit like the flowers,
You know.
Warms your vulnerable heart,
With kindness and grace,
Brings happy tears to your eyes,
And the most joyful smile to your face!

She regales like a queen, and she stuns,
I say.
And I love her,
As I do those flowers she hates!
Some have penetrable walls, you know.
She has padlocked iron gates.

THANK YOU FOR ENOUGH BEAUTY AND JOY

Despite mournful envy and
Dejected wrath,
We bask under blue skies,
Bewitching stars,
And mystical moons,
Loving rumbles of thunder,
Glistening raindrops,
And a hazy peaceful sunrise.

In the face of
Sorrowful greed,
We delight in magnificent mountains,
Bountiful oceans,
Turquoise lagoons,
Beautiful blossoms,
And the green, green grass
Of springtime.

Through raging anger,
Aching sadness,
We treasure radiant sunsets,
Seek marble courtyards,
Ancient architecture,
And splendid arched bridges.
We sing the praises of
Breathtaking falls.

Even crushed
And bewildered,

GRATEFUL TO BE ALIVE

We are captivated by
Exquisite winged creatures,
Tropical forests,
And the critters we nurture.
We embrace the power in our divinity
And the superb magic of everything.

With every threat to the world
We belong to
And embrace,
We are ever grateful
For smiles,
Rapturous affection,
Laughter,
And love.

We're mesmerized by
Otherworldly visions
And plentiful hues.
We revel in books and dreams.
We cherish
The light in ever-curious
Truth seekers,
And in every miracle that strengthens us.

PART IV
PARTING THOUGHTS

SOBER BY THE GRACE OF GOD

One of the most significant concepts of the 12-step program of recovery can be difficult for those whose beliefs don't align with the mainstream vision.

I remember being told in meetings that "EGO" was, essentially, "edging God out." Not mentioning "Him" or crediting "Him" for your success in staying sober would raise many eyebrows.

I was also taught in meetings that A. A. is not a religion. And then I would hear something like, "We can't open the gates of Heaven and let you in, but we can open the gates of Hell and let you out."

When I was a newcomer, all of that confused me.

The program literature clearly states that we surrender to a power greater than ourselves—as we understand that greater power to be. It's important because we're told that our journey to wellness begins only when we surrender to that higher power.

For many people, that is the deity or deities they grew up believing in. And, for some of us, there is our ancestral religion or the polytheistic or pantheistic worship of nature as the divine.

The program was never meant to exclude atheists or agnostics, either. They may see their higher power as their higher consciousness and moral compass. You don't need a religion to have either of those things.

God can even be a celebration of all that is good, and believing all that is good is God. GOD, as many have said, also stands for "good orderly direction."

When we look at it that way, the program's God-related slogans apply, regardless of our vision of the divine.

Sober by the Grace of God.
Let Go and Let God.
Trust God.
If God seems far away, who moved?
But for the Grace of God, there go I.

And because we are advised to pray daily, we are reminded, in the program, that trying to pray is praying, and that prayer can be well wishes, good thoughts, positive energy, and just sending love and light.

Spirituality is, essentially, the ability to get our minds off ourselves and to rely on better judgment, regardless of where that comes from on a day-to-day basis. And just wanting to be a decent human being counts. It counts a lot.

DON'T TAKE YOURSELF TOO SERIOUSLY!

There was a time when the people I dealt with were merely making appearances in the soap opera that was my life, or so I must have believed on some level. I starred in it, directed it, and expected each actor to play their role as I created it. Under these circumstances, less-than-favorable outcomes are magnified and often unendurable. Even petty slights are infuriating and upsetting.

In twelve-step programs, it's called "Rule 62"—Don't Take Yourself So Seriously! Becoming aware of that and then understanding it and accepting it was another thing pivotal to my recovery.

We have to be able to laugh at ourselves! Have you ever noticed that people who take themselves too seriously are the perfect target for internet trolls? I observed one guy on Twitter complaining that trolls wouldn't leave him alone. It was evident from his feed that he'd been sitting around, answering them for quite some time. That is a waste of energy because trolls are devoid of empathy.

Bullies tend to throw stuff out there to see what will stick. They know it when they hit a nerve, and they'll use that to provoke you. The more misery they cause, the happier they are. These are not people you can reason with or convince. If they can't get a rise out of you, it's not fun for them. So, it's best never to "feed a troll"—not so much as a crumb.

We don't have to tolerate bad behavior, but we don't have to live in agony because of other people's behavior and perceptions. And we don't have to be obsessed with damage control. That's a full-time job, with plenty of unpaid overtime. And it's exhausting! Allowing people to infuriate us and rob us of our serenity gives others way too much power over us. Humility saves us from ourselves, keeping us aware that we're human and flawed.

Before I understood Rule 62, I told someone, "It's not that I want to be better than others. It's the opposite; I strive to be acceptable because I feel inadequate."

Inadequate in *my* view because I aimed for perfection. I didn't understand that I wore my inferiority complex inside out. I'd taken it to the superiority complex level, never realizing that those were two sides of the same coin. It never occurred to me that I held myself to a higher standard than others.

The first thing I had to do was take myself down off the pedestal. (Yes, we can put *ourselves* on pedestals, too.) I had to realize that I was not the star of everyone's show. Things are happening to everyone on the planet—not just me.

Before I grasped "Rule 62," I expected fairness, always, no matter what. I had to learn that there's so much about this life that isn't right, and life's been far more unfair to others than to me. It's all relative, and I had to process the fact that while we can fight for justice when appropriate, life ultimately isn't fair, period. Accepting that removed a tremendous burden from my shoulders.

Humility, in my view, is something we continually strive for, not a trait we crown ourselves with because we've risen to sainthood. And none of what I'm saying here means we're not important, or we shouldn't have healthy egos. But if we try not to perceive ourselves as overly important (more so than anyone else, anyway), then we're less biased when it comes to ourselves. We're able to recognize certain things for what they are and not take so much personally—be it constructive criticism, a bit of teasing, or someone being an ass.

It helps me to acknowledge that I'm not this person the whole world is watching and with staggering expectations, hoping I will fail. Also, if we stop looking for adversaries, perceived enemies, and their agendas, for the most part, they somehow cease to exist.

Again, it comes back to balance for me, but when you're able to keep an open mind, discernment about what to take personally and what to blow off becomes more effortless.

As an author, I put my words out there in a world divided on many topics. The varying opinions don't always come from someone with a reasonable frame of reference. Someone may read about a tragic event and say it isn't an accurate portrayal. You can write about something that actually happened or describe exactly how it was, and someone might view it as a misrepresentation because that's not what they experienced. People do have personal biases and triggers. Sometimes, they're turned off by something that has more to do with them than with you. I've noticed fellow writers getting two-star book reviews for reasons unrelated to the book. Internet trolls may say negative things merely because they can. Also, the best writers out there have had plenty of critics.

But not every critic is a troll, which is essential to acknowledge. Some people don't have a vested interest in us and are not biased, and, quite often, they're right on the money.

A bit of lightheartedness and a good sense of humor are critical.

Years ago, I realized I could change my relationship with criticism by changing my perspective. Criticism isn't comfortable, and we don't like feeling uncomfortable, so we tell ourselves we can't handle it. If we take ourselves out of that fear mode, acknowledging that we're not comfortable but can handle it, it's easier to decide how we'll do that. Stressing makes things worse.

In those moments, it also helps to remember we're not alone—others are going through it or have been through it. I tell myself I'm no less capable of handling it than they are, and it only *seems* so much worse because it's happening to me.

Sadly, though, some people fear criticism and rejection so much that they don't pursue their dreams or find true happiness.

As far as I can tell, we must keep listening to learn. On a personal and professional level, there's always room for improvement. I am obsessed with learning more and more about things that knocked me for a loop when I had to deal with them in others or myself. I can't help being grateful for these opportunities and challenges to overcome the obstacles that derailed me.

Falling in love with the process of learning, growing, evolving, and recovering helps us to succeed more and suffer less. It's about wanting to be the best we can be. It's okay to be vulnerable, but only as long as we know we are and how! Then, instead of worrying about how others perceive us, we do what we do from the heart. I tell myself this: I'm another person trying to learn and figure things out here. We are transmundane beings in an astounding old universe. We are vulnerable—not merely to the force of nature and random happenings, but to each other. Life gets better when we accept ourselves as a part of everything rather than the center of everything.

I maintain that until we fully heal from whatever we need to recover from, we remain in bondage to something or another and are prone to obsessions. Disentangling ourselves from that is a painful process, but as I witness people becoming who they were before the pain and unwarranted shame, I have no doubt what awareness can do. It tells me there's hope for everyone.

THE WOUNDS LOVE WON'T HEAL

I once had a habit of making excuses for people.

How many times can we try and try again, hoping things will be different? Sometimes, the people we think are ports in a storm turn out to be the rips in our sail.

The truth is, most of us have precarious relationships with others where we find ourselves setting or accepting boundaries to maintain that connection. Maybe it's an intolerable behavior issue or substantial differences of opinion. There are situations, too, where people grow up with devastating trauma. Family members have different outlooks about what happened, maybe even different experiences. One may still feel the agony of the hurt they or someone else caused in doing what they felt was right. Things said may remind you of the pain they caused you or the pain you caused them.

These situations are loaded for the simple reason that you care about these people. If you didn't, you could easily blow them off and never have anything further to do with them.

And sure, it's painful. You wish things were different. It saddens us that there was so much good, and we cherish the memories to the point of tears. We may wonder, *Can we ever get it back?* If we did, would it ever be the same?

What I've found is, when considering forgiveness in any situation, a critical thing to decipher is, *What really happened?* Sorting out what's true and what's not is more important than appeasing others who need to deal with their own wounds. Their place in the healing process is different from ours. Denial has consequences for both parties, so did we play a part in the conflict? If so, what was it? We can take responsibility only for what we contributed to the falling out.

Maybe the falling out stemmed from an argument, someone else's meddling, or someone's denial. Perhaps it was because of lies and fragile egos, smear campaigns, and the rush to judgment.

Whatever it was, for any kind of resolution, both parties have to come to the table with an open mind. There must be a willingness to walk hand in hand through that minefield together. It's hard because, quite often, the trust isn't there any longer. And you have to be willing to trust someone to do that.

There's a difference, too, between reaching out and setting a trap. We can't be condescending or aim to "win." We have to be genuine and sincere, let go of any bitterness or resentment, and respond only from a place of caring and love. You can have so much love for someone and still have to handle your interaction with them like you're holding a piece of glass.

There are no-fly zones in these situations. Believe me, there was a time I'd have flown my plane right into that restricted zone and not for a moment realize the potential damage I'd cause to the relationship. I'd gotten used to a cycle of being hurt and fighting back. Sometimes, we are blinded by rage, and we keep hurling it at someone, but we don't realize they're bleeding, too.

These days, I think of what I might say in these circumstances and recognize how it could go wrong. Often, I decide I can say nothing. Or I wonder how to rectify a situation or resolve a conflict, and every way I might think to approach it, I see a flashing red light, and it's just *no. Don't. You can't. There's a need to tread gently, take care.*

Plenty of people out there can discern these situations, I'm sure, but many of us had to learn.

No doubt, it's wonderful when the resolution of a conflict results in mutual forgiveness and a starting point for healing the relationship. At the same time, we can't allow people to deny the reality of what we experienced, and we can't accept their spin on it if it has no basis in truth. We don't want to hear the justification for what cannot be justified, or for the other party to minimize the damage. We can't let them guilt or shame us into keeping quiet or making concessions.

Sometimes, however, their message is clear. Maybe it's always been clear, but it takes a while for us to accept. Their words and actions have repeatedly shown us they are not in our corner. They may not be against us, exactly, but they're not for us either. They don't respect us or our boundaries. They're not concerned about our feelings. Nothing's ever truly resolved in a relationship like that, and nothing changes.

We lost this person long ago, and it has already broken our hearts a thousand times. *Is this someone we ever really had or truly knew?* We lost the chance to dysfunction, and not even obligatory love and commitment could save it. It's reached a point where suiting up and showing up simply hurt too much.

It hurts to admit when we've chosen someone or something that isn't right for us, and when we're trying to fit where we don't belong.

And, for various reasons, not everyone is in a position where they can simply walk away. There may not even be a lot they can do to protect themselves or limit interaction. They may not be able to avoid participating in the drama.

Those of us who do walk away will often mourn what we couldn't have. Some holes remain unfilled for us. Some stories will never be heard or told, and some scars won't ever heal. We say goodbye with so much weight and with a burden too hard to hold. It's more than sorrow. It's grief. And you miss what you wanted that to be.

We can feel this profound grief even in walking away from people who weren't that close to us because we feel like they *should* have been. Those ties were supposed to bind but didn't. Instead, they turned out to be so weak that they broke a little more at every difference of opinion, each instance where we stood up for ourselves, or any time people looked at us and didn't see themselves.

I've learned that the pain that follows in walking away is worth getting that toxicity out of your life. Even if the people you're walking away from create a false narrative about you and make you out to be the devil incarnate, it's still worth it. It will hurt less over time, or maybe it will always hurt a little, but you'll be okay. You were brave enough to show up to this shitshow again and again. You tried to fit in. You tried to make it work. If it didn't, well, love and acceptance await you elsewhere. In AA, I heard the slogan: *You can't heal in the same environment that made you sick.* I believe that.

It's important to realize we deserve to be happy. A few cherished loved ones are far better than dozens of people hanging on simply to make life difficult. We can't fix or save everyone. We can't always make things right.

To this day, there are people I'd love to drop a line to and ask how they're doing or just to say, "I miss you." One might ask themselves: *What are safe topics we can discuss? Should we stick to a public forum in responding to one another rather than talking on the phone or by text? Can we support one another in ways that don't involve us in their lives?* I find these things helpful in dealing with others where caution may apply. It's often the difference between reacting and responding. Realize you're communicating with another vulnerable human being who likely has been dealing with their own trauma. They are not bulletproof.

As I'm sure everyone knows, you can love people to the moon and back even when your relationship with them is broken. You may forgive them and want the best for them while moving on without them. I've learned the best thing to do is keep sending them love and light, along with your inner hope for peace and the willingness for them to heal.

I send you love. I wish you well. I wish you peace. Sometimes, that's all we can do.

Most importantly, though: We must forgive ourselves as well. All we wanted was love.

THE NARCISSISTIC ABUSERS WE LOVE

My theory is that malignant narcissism is at the heart of the world's dysfunction. I'm convinced that we're dealing with the chaos of the world's trauma, shame, and pain. It's the gift that keeps on giving—with the worst possible repercussions, and it spreads through the universe like a poison. I believe this suffering, which leads to more suffering, is a cycle we can break with recognition, empathy, and a genuine desire to change.

While I'm certainly not a professional, I've dealt with my share of narcissism throughout my life. Unfortunately, many people have endured far worse than what I've experienced, and some have been damaged beyond repair. Whatever we can do to help others toward the light in the darkness can mean the difference between their giving up and holding on.

Dysfunctional narcissists tend to expect that those in their family and circle of friends appear normal *by their standards*. Every member of their family or circle has to also validate and reinforce whatever they think, say, and do to nurture the notion that their perception is always accurate. That's crucial to them because their deepest fear is, if they are wrong about that, what else are they wrong about? And can they possibly be wrong about everything they believe to be true? They're not ready to examine any of these possibilities.

Sadly, *you're* the problem if you don't toe the line. Therein lies the tragedy. Whether it's family or friends, you must either get on board or take your broken heart someplace else. Celebratory events meant to be about joy and happiness have you walking on eggshells, and they often leave you on the defensive. Bigoted opinions fly, but you'll ruin the mood if you speak up against them. You don't recognize yourself. You just know you don't belong there.

Further, these dysfunctional individuals withhold support, validation, admiration, attention, and approval from those they perceive as threats or competition or anyone who challenges the reality they've constructed. They reject, bully, intimidate, and seek to humiliate these perceived adversaries. You want them to root for you, but they're more likely to sabotage you with discouragement and disinterest.

Quite often, these abusers will demonize someone because they don't have the same power over that person they so expertly wield over others. And, quite frankly, when you are the target of their malice, their heartbreaking actions can crush your spirit and leave you with paralyzing trauma and fear.

Most of us already have an underlying fear that people won't love us for who we are, which, through suffering from narcissistic abuse, gets distorted into the notion that no one will ever love us—period. Underneath it is a chronic sadness that never really subsides, and shame overwhelms us.

Not being loved for who we are is one of the things people fear most in life, a fate worse even than death, and many young people out there are killing themselves for that. They fight to cope with one trauma after another until they reach a breaking point and can't cope anymore, and then they shut down. The message is: *That's enough; I can't do this anymore. I'm done.*

Often, when people feel that desperation, getting beyond thoughts of suicide is only the first hurdle. From there, it's a long haul to reclaim themselves and their capacity to love.

As victims of narcissistic abuse, we may also feel a sense of loyalty to the abusers, and we may wish to protect them. Denial becomes a method of survival for us, too. It doesn't help that narcissistic abusers can be charming. We may find them so lovable and irresistible that we're desperate to be wrong about them.

We often genuinely *love* a narcissistic abuser and hope we can help them. I know that was true for me—and I've been in that situation more than once.

It's wise to remember that people who want to recover will do the work required to repair themselves. People who are not aspiring to change may not be willing or ready to examine themselves, acknowledge their mistakes, take responsibility, and begin the process of learning, growing, and healing. If they are not there yet, and you confront their behavior, they'll likely act as if your question or statement is shocking, offensive, or absurd, and they'll think you're the one with the problem. The moment you put them on the defensive, it becomes even more critical to discredit you to themselves and their circle of family and friends.

It won't matter what you say to them or how kind you are; your words will not move a narcissist who isn't ready to change. You think you can meet them halfway, but if believing you, understanding you, and finding a way to co-exist peacefully with you doesn't work with their agenda, they don't compromise. Even if they care about and respect you, the extent to which they care has to be greater than their need to be perceived in the most flattering light.

The payoff they've gotten from selling their narrative is a lot to give up because they'd have to be willing to risk losing the false alter ego they created to survive. It's easier for them to dehumanize a perceived enemy and rationalize that this person deserves their retaliation, no matter how vicious it is. They can't afford to put themselves in your place and understand your emotional pain or see how they may be the ones who caused it.

I mentioned empathy several times now because that's an essential factor here. Empathy is what sets the recovering victim apart from a hopelessly disordered narcissist because it is empathy that makes us want to do better and play fair. We're eventually willing to relinquish the narcissistic "payoffs" because we care about others. In my experience, I've found that as long as we have empathy for ourselves and others, we can rise above the character defects that burden us and make us a burden to others.

It takes time and requires ongoing self-maintenance, but we are generally more powerful than the obstacles that derail us. In this instance, I'm not talking about chemical imbalances or illnesses beyond anyone's control; I'm talking about things that are beyond our control simply because we didn't understand them at the time.

Longtime endurance of narcissistic abuse leads us to question our judgment and sometimes act to prove that the negative assessment of ourselves is correct. We may be attractive, intelligent, talented, or whatever, yet we fear we are inferior and unworthy of love and success because the people we want to love us—the narcissistic abusers—are incapable of genuine love. And if we are the reminder of their shame, they fear us as much as they fear the true selves they've buried deep.

When we choose to break the cycle, however, we learn to spot trouble from the get-go and avoid it. Even better, narcissistic abusers will tend to keep their distance because they'll realize they're not able to manipulate and control us.

And that's a good thing.

D.K. SANZ

SOME FINAL THOUGHTS ABOUT BIGOTRY

People say, "You can judge a man by how he treats his inferiors." I say no! We don't have inferiors! Some people have more apparent talent or money, better positions, fancier cars, higher functioning brains, or genes that make them appear more attractive, but there is no reason for *anyone*—and I do mean *anyone*— to hang on to an illusion of superiority.

There's a lockstep mentality that passes from generation to generation. Parents teach bigotry, and, to many, their parents can never be wrong. With a subconscious or even conscious fear of not being accepted or not fitting in with their loved ones, these children embrace the ideologies passed on to them and, in doing so, form alliances that continue to reinforce them into adulthood.

In terms of religion, I never want to shut people down for believing or not believing what the various holy books say. I can't dismiss the cherry-pickers seeking to find a safe middle ground. If a person has genuinely "lost their way," they can find it again. I've met good, kindhearted people of just about every faith, so simply believing and practicing a religion isn't the problem. People are entitled to their beliefs so long as they're not committing or otherwise condoning crimes against humanity.

As someone who is fifty percent Latina, I've also experienced racism on a minor scale, and it gave me *some* idea of what it might be like for people who experience hate, discrimination, and oppression on a much larger scale. If you are a member of any group that is oppressed to one degree or another, you are acutely aware of the global and systematic imbalance. As a result, many of us have a pretty good idea of how terrorizing it can be when your rights are denied, or you're not treated with the respect and dignity you deserve.

For me, opposing bigotry is not about being "politically correct." Having empathy for others is simply *correct*. People go to war over bias and entitlement. They discriminate and violently target others based on the same. It becomes a case of "We hate the same faction, so it's clear who the enemy is."

It's not about tolerance, either. There's a lot of destructive and harmful behavior that I can't and won't tolerate. But who am I to merely "tolerate" a person's ethnicity, sexuality, socioeconomic status, or religious philosophy? Those are things to be welcomed, not tolerated. I don't want anyone's rights to be denied any more than I'd want my own rights restricted. There was never a time when that did not feel inhumane to me.

Detractors are fond of saying that people who defend the rights of others who are denied whatever privilege they enjoy have a "savior complex." When I first heard that, I allowed myself to ponder it for a bit, given that I've been speaking out against bigotry since I was twelve. It was instinctive then, and it's instinctive now because I never wanted to live in a world where bigotry was normal. It never made a difference to me if people on either side were happy or unhappy about my stance.

It always made sense to me that you cannot know a person just because you're aware of their race, ethnicity, religion, or sexuality. No group is perfect. You need to get to know individuals because we are all different.

For many people, when someone who is not like them hurts them, they postulate that it reflects on that group's culture. They won't consider their own people who've done the same thing or worse. Without having genuine relationships with the people from whatever culture they shun, their impression is based on limited experience. They go by stereotypes or by what they've read in the news or learned from TV.

I've experienced unprovoked attacks from people who did not look like me, but *I've also been attacked by my "own" people,* and although my worst experiences of sexual trauma were at the hands of white, Italian Catholic males, I've always known that not every white, Catholic Italian guy is that way. That same benefit of the doubt should be extended to people who belong to different groups.

Among the things I'd been taught, what truly stuck with me in life was the whole "love one another" thing. Yes, I really liked that part. Isn't it a fundamental theme in all religions? No one is perfect, but if we can do better, we should. Life's hard enough, and it helps if we cheer each other on along the way.

If we must keep influencing our children with our thoughts, let those thoughts be reminders that we are *all* divine, and divinity surrounds us, and in that way, we have much more power than we realize. We have that power for a reason. We don't see everything yet, and we don't know everything, but we are creating the future—the world we want to live in, and the world we will leave our children. We can keep evolving toward a much higher consciousness and create the idyllic world we envision.

I read something recently that said we should treat everyone as sacred until they begin to believe they are. That is the ideal way to live, isn't it? It might solve many problems in our world, individually and collectively. I'd love to commit myself to that, to remind myself of that always.

So, whoever you are, you are beautiful! You are a divine creation and the very essence of love. Don't let anyone take that away from you!

HAVE YOU SURVIVED YOUR LONG DARK NIGHT?

You see through shadows and fog. So much obscured. It's a murky reality where confusion reigns—crisis after crisis, unending drama, and boundless pain. You bury the fear that would deplete your strength. It's become harder to function and wearisome to hope. You sink into despair. Light peeks in at the top of the hole, but every move toward it overwhelms you.

You thought the cavalry would have arrived by now, riding up on rugged horses, but there is no cavalry.

You think you can't do this. You want to die.

Think about it.

If you can't do this anymore. All of the stuff you don't want to do, and you can't do the other stuff, either—the beautiful, incredible, and amazing stuff. Those things that make you smile, laugh, ooh, and ahh—and all of the blessed wonders that fill your heart with joy will be gone along with the pain.

People say the best thing you can do when you're feeling hopeless and powerless is to take the focus off yourself and help others. Bring smiles to people's faces with a random act of kindness. It works.

But if you're feeling too weak right now, not quite ready to save yourself, hang in there. We're human, and we don't always have to be strong. The world feels cruel and cold right now, and the suffering around us hurts. The suffering of the world is too much, yes. We're all so vulnerable, but you're not alone. We're here with you.

We call upon the earth's angels to construct the symbolic pyramid that surrounds you, protects you, and guides you. We send you the healing light of unconditional love. You'll be surprised at what a difference a day makes!

If you're not too defeated, maybe that sink-or-swim moment has arrived. Perhaps this is where you surrender. You'll know when the time is right. You're going down the rabbit hole to dig in and dig out, regain your clarity and calm, and restore your peace and joy.

And then the long, dark night comes.

You approach it as what you've become, the persona that provided the armor you wore, and the persona you constructed to protect you in the darkest of times. It was a godsend that's slowly become a fire-breathing monster, diabolical and dangerous. You don't need that anymore. You don't want it.

But it's turbulent in this period of darkness. You feel disoriented and bewildered. There is so much to grieve.

You may be broken now, and things look rather bleak. I know. You may not believe me when I say you can heal because your heart is breaking in a way it never has. It's like every broken heart you've ever had has come together to magnify the brokenness. It seems everything has fallen apart, but soon it will all come together again, I promise you—the way it was supposed to be. Deep down, we have the answers. When we are ready, we'll align our will with the will of our highest power of love and light.

I'm here with you.

So many memories come to mind—the child you were, the adult you've become—so much anguish for what happened all those years ago. You never wanted to let anyone down, I know. You feel everything so intensely. Just don't tell me that you don't deserve better. You do. Don't tell me you're a failure. You're not. We learn from every mistake. That's not failing; it's growing. You are a beautiful, empathetic being of love and light. And don't say hope will damn you. It won't always, I promise.

It's okay to acknowledge regrets and feel every wound that keeps hurting and the sadness of the torment that has yet to subside. Yes, it's agony. You will cry harder than you ever thought you could. Every version of you that's existed cries with you. Especially that child in you who's waited so long for your comfort. That small child who was thrilled by the universe in every waking moment? That innocent child is still there and wants you to fight for both of you.

You care so much about everyone. Care about yourself, too! You help everyone, my dear. Help yourself. The child is fragile and wailing. It's the ghost that's haunted you for many years, but those childhood ghosts don't unnerve you now. Your sobs are theirs, as are your tears. This child is releasing your pain. Hug that child.

Every version of who you've been will need that comfort and compassion. Don't be afraid to wrap all of your former selves in a blanket of love and show them they are worthy of that! They were just trying to survive. *You* were just trying to survive. After years of taking hit after hit and getting back up, maybe you learned how to compartmentalize, stay calm, and protect your energy, as I did.

It's hard to fight the urge to share more words of wisdom, some of which you may not be ready for, but I can plant a seed. I'm here, and don't you apologize—not to me. It's not too much for me, ever. I'll never regret a moment with you. Just breathe. Take deep breaths as often as you need. You have to trust a little. I got you, my friend, and you're going to be all right. I love you so much!

And when the light of day shines on you after this long night, you'll find you are a warrior and a conqueror, too—one who will conquer one thing after another in life.

You slay your demons so that the fierce dragon you desperately needed can transform into the beautiful paladin that champions your survival. And here you are now, a weightless dragonfly with mesmerizing beauty!

They say home is where you wake up and try again. Well, you're home now.

GRATITUDE

By luck, I have always had plenty of food and water. I have not had to experience the extreme oppression that is prevalent in other parts of the world. I have warmth. I have more clothing than I will ever need. As if that is not enough, I have much more.

I am grateful that the passion in my heart lives on; that I can wake up every day and do what I love. I am grateful for the privilege of sharing what I love with the world.

I am thankful for people I can cherish, people who need me and believe in me, and people I can also believe.

I am grateful for all of our heroes, warriors, and survivors.

I wish everyone could have what he or she needs, feel safe, and have the same rights. Therefore, I am grateful for people who spread peace, help others, help animals, help the planet, and stand up for justice.

I am grateful for everyone I have ever known, and what they taught me.

I am grateful for forgiveness that brings peace and second chances.

I am grateful for solutions.

I am grateful for freedom.

I am grateful for change.

I am grateful for truth.

I give thanks for everyday pleasures—writers and books, music, art, dancing.

I am grateful for the sun, the clouds, and all of the beauty that surrounds me.

I am grateful for home.

I am grateful for this moment.

I am grateful for imperfection, silliness, and madness.

I am grateful for fantasy and imagination.

I am grateful for kindness, for hugs, and for all of the love and light in the universe.

I am grateful because there is something beautiful in everyone.

I am grateful to be alive and to have this day.

I am grateful for fond memories of childhood that overshadow the painful ones.

I am grateful for many years of sobriety, for increasing clarity, and for having been ready to heal.

I am grateful for all I have been able to resolve internally, for the darkest moments, and for rising from every fall.

I am grateful for the realization that my ego distorted my perception.

I am grateful for learning from my mistakes and for being able to work through the tough stuff.

I am grateful that I am not bitter.

I am grateful for not giving up and for hanging in there until it was okay.

I am grateful for laughter.

I am grateful for all of the learning and evolving.

I am grateful for the beaten dragons.

I am grateful for finding my truth and my voice.

I am grateful for letting go of unworthiness, for self-respect, and for learning to stand up for myself.

I am grateful for learning to love myself as I am, for letting myself become kinder, for learning to love deeply, and to be able to be there for others.

I am grateful for learning how to be strong, how to share joy, and for having learned to trust my instincts and myself.

I am grateful for defying limitations and for not shrinking to please others.

I am grateful for the desire to grow and how it is finally exceeding my desire to hold on, for the strength and courage to let go of the things that weighed me down.

I am grateful for the surviving child in me, for my strong wings, for the doors opening for me, and for the ones that closed behind me after teaching me what I needed to learn.

I am grateful for the shedding of masks and my embracing of authenticity.

I am grateful for the ability to see people and things as they are, including me.

I am grateful for being able to see things from another's point of view.

I am grateful for the ability to feel empathy and witness the empathy of others.

I am grateful for the amazing struggle that is life.

I am grateful for the ability to keep learning, for all of the opportunities to be better and do better, and for all of these reasons to smile.

I am grateful because I have everything I need.

Lastly, I am thankful to those who care about my journey and who care about what I have to say. Thank you for reading and listening to me.

D.K. SANZ

To those who are struggling, I walked through the fire to get here, and I am still walking. Don't you give up!
~DKS

ABOUT THE AUTHOR

D. K. Sanz is the author of *Shattering Truths*, a novel published under the name Kyrian Lyndon. She has published three poetry collections, *A Dark Rose Blooms*, *Remnants of Severed Chains*, and Awake with the Songbirds, as well as several articles for *Rebelle Society* and *The Voice of Literature* e-zines, all under the Kyrian Lyndon name.

D. K. loves psychological thrillers, horror fiction, nineteenth-century British literature, parallel universe fiction, and dark romanticism. She enjoys music, art, history, fitness, video games, and cooking.

You can visit her blog at http://www. kyrianlyndon.com